SOCIETY IN CRISIS
Our Capacity for Adaptation and Reorientation

SOCIETY IN CRISIS
Our Capacity for Adaptation and Reorientation

EDITED BY
KURT ALMQVIST, MATTIAS HESSÉRUS
AND IAIN MARTIN

BOKFÖRLAGET STOLPE   AXEL AND MARGARET AX:SON JOHNSON FOUNDATION FOR PUBLIC BENEFIT

CONTENTS

MEDICINE AND MORALITY

SOCIETY AND LEADERSHIP IN CRISIS

INTRODUCTION

The Engelsberg Seminar is normally held on the site of the former Engelsberg Ironworks, now a conference centre and UNESCO World Heritage Site, in Sweden's Västmanland county. Like many other events, the 2020 seminar had to be cancelled due to the global coronavirus pandemic. To compensate for the lack of an in-person event, the Axel and Margaret Ax:son Johnson Foundation for Public Benefit launched an online communications platform called *Engelsberg Ideas*.

The essays in this year's Engelsberg anthology, which is entitled *Society in Crisis*, were initially published on that platform for an international audience in the summer and autumn of 2020. The aim of this volume is to provide a perspective on the pandemic in which we currently live and to highlight and analyse other crises that have affected the world in the past as well as the present.

The global order that arose after the fall of the Berlin Wall in 1989 and the breakup of the Soviet Empire in 1991 appears rather fragile today. China is challenging the United States in the geopolitical arena as it increases its global influence with its Belt and Road Initiative. Hong Kong's relative autonomy has been suppressed, and now China is also threatening Taiwan with its military might. During President Trump's term of office, uncertainty increased around America's role as guarantor of world peace and the global order, while the future of NATO came into question. Challenges to liberalism and the capitalist market economy are presented today from many sides.

Populist parties on the left as well as the right have seized upon widespread dissatisfaction. In many cases, the impacts of migration have contributed to the rise of these parties. In this era of mass migration, when perhaps 70 million people or more have left their homes because of war or economic conditions, it is difficult to see an end either to the waves of migrants or to the factors that fuel grievances in the countries where those migrants are present. In the event of a worst-case global warming scenario coinciding with accelerating population growth, as some scientists fear might happen, even greater waves of migration could occur, with major consequences for contemporary civilisations and societies.

The British historian Arnold Toynbee (1889–1975) believed that civilisations develop via their ability to find solutions to the challenges they face. This development requires what Toynbee calls 'creative minorities'. However, these minorities eventually stagnate and degenerate into 'dominant minorities' which turn inwards and lose their ability to solve the everyday problems of the wider population. But when crisis strikes, human creativity is awakened. Social crises are solved by individuals.

Ösmo, Sweden, 1 January 2021

Kurt Almqvist
President, The Axel and Margaret Ax:son Johnson Foundation for Public Benefit

GLOBAL POLITICS

A socially distanced protest against government
policies during the coronavirus lockdown in
Tel Aviv, April 2020.

THIS CRISIS HAS THE CAPACITY TO BE APOCALYPTIC

Peter Frankopan

One of the greatest challenges that emerged from the Covid-19 crisis was the difficulty of decision making. 'There is no historical model,' said the German chancellor Angela Merkel at the end of April 2020, when talking about the problems of trying to tackle not only the virus, but the precarious economic situation facing a largely shut-down world. China's leader Xi Jinping, who was speaking on the same day, was more optimistic about the lessons that could be learned from the past. The Chinese people, he said on a visit to Xi'an, had 'grown and matured by learning from the experiences of difficulties and deprivations'. The pandemic had a silver lining, he remarked, noting: 'Great advances in history have come after great catastrophes.'

He may well be right. The pandemic has led to many transformations already – from the way we communicate with each other, cope with lockdowns, and queue when (and if) we shop. The world is changing in front of our eyes.

Office life may never be the same again, with Barclays chief executive Jes Staley pondering whether 'putting 7,000 people in a building may be a thing of the past'. After many false dawns, education may now move decisively to online learning. Fashions may change enduringly, with face masks becoming as common in Britain as they are in some parts of Asia even after the crisis has passed; Chanel, Burberry and Louis Vuitton have moved quickly into helping design masks and gowns for healthcare workers – presaging the fact that more stylish versions could become a staple on fashion show runways and the new 'must have' item in new collections.

But one of the most striking trends that has emerged during the pandemic is the pressure that freedoms are being put under all around the world. In some cases, this has led to extensive repressive measures. The pandemic saw newspapers shut down in the Middle East, social media controls enhanced in Turkey, and fines and even hefty prison sentences threatened in China and Russia as well as in several other countries for the sharing of gossip, rumours and fake news about the coronavirus.

In Kazakhstan, sweeping new powers gave the president, Kassym-Jomart Tokayev, the ability to intervene in everything from legislation on health to public procurement, from currency regulation to the implementation of international obligations. In Hungary President Orbán claimed the authority to rule by decree with no time limit imposed, leading to howls of protest by some leading European politicians like Norbert Röttgen, tipped as a future German chancellor, demanding censure by the European Union.

More than 80 countries declared a state of emergency as a result of the virus, according to the Centre for Civil and Political Rights. In some cases this resulted in impassioned debate about the erosion of civil liberties, for example in Israel, where the government approved a controversial measure in March to digitally track those who had tested positive for coronavirus.

In Britain, meanwhile, the 329-page 'Coronavirus Bill' was passed in a single day – suspending the requirement for local authorities to meet the eligible needs of the disabled and vulnerable people, among others, and authorising the cancellation or rearrangement of elections and the closure of ports and borders. Police releasing drone footage of walkers in the Peak District, officers reprimanding people for using their own front garden, or Thames Valley police issuing appeals for local residents to inform on each other if they suspect they are 'gathering and then dispersing back into our communities' during the lockdown show that the relationship between citizens and the authorities has changed dramatically in a matter of a few weeks. The new mantra of our pandemic and post-pandemic world is best expressed by Thailand's prime minister, Prayut Chan-o-cha, a general who himself took power in a coup in 2014, when stating: 'Right now it's health over liberty.'

There are, of course, pockets of resistance, such as in the US, where armed militias gathered on the steps of some state assemblies to demand an end to lockdown. Ironically, they were encouraged by President Trump who issued a series of tweets effectively urging civil disobedience. 'Liberate Michigan!' he tweeted, 'Liberate Minnesota! Liberate Virginia!' But even in the complicated and contradictory United States of 2020, things have not been straightforward, with Trump asserting that his powers are not so much presidential as dictatorial. 'When somebody's the

Thai Prime Minister Prayut Chan-o-cha,
March 2020, Bangkok.

president of the United States, the authority is total, and that's the way it's got to be,' he said in a press briefing in mid-April – a few weeks after he had boasted that 'I have the right to do a lot of things that people don't even know about', before a bilateral meeting with Irish prime minister, Leo Varadkar.

The push away from democratic norms to autocratic measures is framed by the justification that the crisis is so severe as to require emergency measures that usually reflect a war footing. So it is no surprise that so many leaders around the world have referred to the coronavirus as a 'war', nor that wartime parallels are the ones we turn to in order to make sense of the situation; it is no coincidence either that the death toll from the Vietnam War was used to give context to mortality figures in the US, or that casualty numbers at the height of the Blitz in the 28 days to 4 October 1940 were set against those arising from Covid-19 in the four weeks to mid-April.

The sheer scale and extent of the problems that the pandemic has brought individual countries and the global economy more generally go some way to justifying the search for such dramatic analogies: employment figures released in May showed that almost 40 million Americans lost their jobs in just eight weeks. When taking account of those aged 18–65 who are students, homemakers, sick or retired – who make up around a third of the workforce in the US – this meant that over half of the working age population of the richest country on earth were heading into the summer not earning a wage.

Many economists have looked to the Great Depression that followed the Wall Street Crash to draw comparisons about the loss of jobs and the collapse of GDP. But while the impact of the crash of 1929 did have global significance, its effects were much more limited. In the world of today, supply chains span not just multiple countries but multiple continents.

A report released by the International Labour Organisation (ILO) put matters in stark terms: about 50% of the entire global workforce are in 'immediate danger' of having their livelihoods destroyed. Richer countries that are supporting jobs through furlough schemes may not have the resources to do so indefinitely; but no safety net at all exists for the majority of those with jobs in other parts of the world. As ILO director-general Guy Ryder put it: 'No income means no food, no security and no future.'

The consequences have the capacity to be apocalyptic. The World Food Programme (WFP) warned that we could be facing 'multiple famines of biblical proportions' in the near future, with the impact most acute in the poorest parts of the world where food insecurity was an issue long before the authorities in Wuhan first identified a new emerging infectious disease. We are facing a 'perfect storm', said David Beasley, executive director of the WFP. Economic pressures, a fall in foreign exchange earnings in the developing world, export restrictions and collapsing food supply networks alongside a devastating series of locust storms in East Africa and South Asia may result in death tolls that dwarf those of the Covid-19 crisis. It is possible, said Beasley, that '300,000 people could starve to death every single day over a three-month period.'

It all looks so unfamiliar to a world where, just less than two weeks before the UK was locked down (belatedly, as it turned out), the chancellor, Rishi Sunak, delivered a budget that talked of economic growth and an increase in public spending. At that time, discussion was centred on a controversial new third runway at Heathrow rather than about bailouts to secure the future of airlines and whether even the biggest carriers would survive the year. The lack of engagement with the reality of what was happening was best captured, as usual, by President Trump, who interrupted his health and human services secretary, Alex Azar, who had finally managed to secure a slot to brief the president on coronavirus, only to ask what he thought was a more pertinent question, namely when a ban on flavoured vapes would be lifted.

Instead, in the first half of 2020, we found ourselves walking into a time that would be profoundly difficult, where inequalities would sharpen and, as Angela Merkel warned, democracy itself would be challenged. The timing could not have been worse. Even before the current crisis, democracy was in trouble. As a study by the Cambridge Centre for the Future of Democracy has found, not only was public confidence in democracy already at the lowest point on record in the United States, as well as in many countries in Western Europe, Latin America and Africa at the end of 2019, but that dissatisfaction was particularly pronounced in high-income countries. The equation now becomes more complicated. As well as keeping the dissatisfied happy, governments will need to protect the disenfranchised during the long road back to the living standards we had come to expect and which will now decline, at least in the short term.

This is particularly important because disease and pandemic aggravate inequalities. Covid-19 has already done just that, in multiple ways.

First there is the disproportionate impact that the virus has had on those from minority backgrounds in the UK, and on African-American backgrounds in the US, where mortality rates were significantly higher than in the white population. The most deprived boroughs in London were those hit worst by the pandemic. Educational inequalities widened, with schools in deprived areas struggling to teach as efficiently as those in other parts of the country for a variety of factors, including availability of computers and access to high-speed internet. The digital divide had already had a major impact across society as a whole, with recent research showing that those with access to higher levels of income and good broadband services were less likely to break lockdown and thus less likely to put their lives – and those of others – at risk. Mental health impacts were unevenly distributed too, with evidence published recently suggesting that those who lived alone faced greater problems than those living with a partner, while those with young children at home faced different challenges and difficulties than those with elder offspring, or those with none.

The correlation of disease with inequality is not just an important one: it is one that helps us better understand the world around us. Throughout history, infectious diseases have been the leading killers of the poor; even in modern times, before coronavirus, they were responsible for the deaths of around two thirds of those living in sub-Saharan Africa. Parts of the world affected by extreme poverty are disproportionately those where infectious diseases thrive.

In turn, areas that suffer from a high disease burden are typically caught in a poverty trap, where economic productivity is low and generating resources to improve the situation becomes impossible. Disease therefore not only has a close link to long-term poverty but also to illiberal, autocratic politics. Elites are usually reluctant and unwilling to share the benefits of rising wealth, and often have to be forced to do so. The European experience over the last three centuries, although chequered, has been instructive: widening of participation in the political process has been accompanied by the development of institutions, laws and protections to distribute rights more broadly.

It is no coincidence, then, that the most rapid social progress (albeit imperfect, given how recent religious, gender, sexual and other equalities are in reality) correlates closely not so much with climate and geography as with the lack of prevalence of infectious disease. Britain's last experience with plague, for example, was in the 1660s – which was not the case, for example, in Russia and the Ottoman empires. Likewise, malaria, typhoid, cholera and yellow fever had much less impact on cooler northern Europe than on the south of the continent, and certainly much less than in many parts of Africa, Asia and the Americas where they thrive, meaning not only a different economic and demographic experience to other parts of the world but a different political trajectory too – not only more democratic, but more tolerant, more open and less fearful of strangers and of travel.

As is becoming increasingly clear, more worrying than the medical emergency caused by Covid-19 is the disease's long-term economic and social after-effects. It will take time before international travel resumes and returns to the way it was before the outbreak spread from China. That in turn affects how young people who would have gained experiences back-packing, or those who had yearned to see the Silk Roads for themselves, will view the world around them. We will hear fewer languages, have fewer opportunities and be exposed to fewer ideas as a result.

And pandemics bring long-term consequences too. Rumours spread widely during the 1340s, as the Black Death took hold, that the disease was the result of a conspiracy by the Jews to kill off Christian populations by poisoning wells and importing poisons from abroad. In many towns and cities, Jews were persecuted and murdered in large numbers. Astonishingly, attacks on Jews in Germany in the 1920s and 1930s were six times more likely to happen in towns and cities that had seen pogroms during the late Middle Ages. Deportations of Jews to camps from 1933–44 was statistically far higher from these places than from other towns too – suggesting that long-term memories are not just forged but maintained across centuries: xenophobia, the fear of strangers and suspicion of outsiders are all by-products of large-scale outbreaks of disease.

A key question in the short term will be related to the elites whose position is strengthened after the current pandemic. Unlike after the Black Death where vast mortality numbers among the workforce meant a fall in the supply of labour and thus a rise in wages, Covid-19 will not do the same – as there will be no similar massive reduction in labour. In fact, the opposite will be the case, with a surplus exacerbated by the digital revolution, the rise of robotics and AI – which provide competition for human labour and new opportunities in many industries that favour those at the top of the income pyramid and are detrimental to the majority of workers, taxpayers and citizens. Rather than providing a possible springboard, as has been the case in the past, the timing of this pandemic may serve as a stone around the neck of social mobility.

In contrast, it is not hard to see how the pandemic may herald a new era of feudalism, where more and more assets are concentrated in the hands of the few. Last year, Oxfam estimated that the net worth of just 26 individuals exceeded that of half the world's entire population – and the rise in fortunes will now extend this imbalance further, creating the same processes that have held back social, economic and political development in places with long and recurring experiences of disease.

This is shown in a Forbes report of May 2020: despite unprecedented state borrowing, extraordinary pressures on jobs and growing concern about the implications of a very major economic contraction, the wealth of America's 600 billionaires had risen by more than $400bn since the start of the pandemic. That provides considerable food for thought – or should do – for governments in developed countries where democracy and social mobility have long been cornerstones of progress and enlightenment.

These now risk being put under considerable pressure even if the pandemic of 2020 quickly becomes a thing of the past – something that is not lost on other political systems, not least China's, which presents a different model that is at least in part based on defining itself against the way that the West behaves, does business and treats its citizens.

Just over 200 years ago, Immanuel Kant wrote an essay entitled 'What is Enlightenment?' in which he sought to argue why granting citizens more rights and freedoms benefited the state, as well as the population at large. The answer, he argued, was that we must 'dare to be wise'. This seems to be a very fitting motto as we ponder what lies ahead of us today; and I suspect that states that are fortunate to be ruled by leaders who are both wise and brave will emerge better off in the short and the long term.

Turkish President Recep Tayyip Erdogan, Iranian
President Hassan Rouhani and Russian President
Vladimir Putin attend the fourth trilateral summit on
Syria in Russia, February 2019.

GEOPOLITICS OF A PANDEMIC

Helen Thompson

The geopolitical world has become decidedly dangerous over the past decade, and the pandemic has advanced a coming reckoning with those dangers. There are three primary stories to understand, all of which predate the Covid-19 crisis but will be shaped in outcome by its fallout. The first concerns China's integration into the world economy and its geopolitical ascendancy in East Asia. The second is the decline of American power and the ascendancy of Russian power in the Middle East, and the third is the return of the United States as an energy power. These stories overlap, especially around energy. Together, they have left Europe as a continent and the EU exposed to a succession of external and internal shocks.

China's deep integration into the world economy through export-led growth supported by World Trade Organisation membership, western investment in China, and complex manufacturing supply chains was supposed to make the world more secure. Viewed optimistically in the 1990s, it allowed China to become much more prosperous without becoming more geopolitically powerful. A China tied to western export markets, capital, and technological knowledge and lacking the naval power to challenge the United States' ability to maintain open seas for trade, according to this logic, should have been militarily weak and have no interest in trade or technological warfare. In this peaceful inter-dependency, Hong Kong served as a portal. It integrated Communist-party run China into the capital side of the American-led world economy whilst providing a safeguard that allowed China to maintain financial restrictions and western investors to put their trust in common law. When China also began in the early 2000s to act as a creditor to the United States, a mutual US-China dependency indeed appeared to materialise, even if it was, as Lawrence Summers – Bill Clinton's former Treasury secretary – characterised it, perhaps best described as 'a balance of financial terror'.

But there were always reasons to be rather more pessimistic about how far this international economic environment could ever have served as a source of geopolitical stability. From China's point of view, export-led growth required an active exchange rate policy, large-scale dollar reserves, and local-currency losses. In the US, allowing more Chinese imports and offshoring production sacrificed many manufacturing jobs whilst hugely benefiting corporate executives. Although it was politically easier for the corporations to lobby to defend the China policy than it was for workers to attack it, this political imbalance suite could only be sustained for so long. Indeed, China's exchange rate policy soon created a direct target for the discontent. As early as 2005, China was forced to show just enough flexibility over the yuan to keep the protectionist pressures in the US Congress at bay, even as it could not act to change the trade outcomes without inviting an internal crisis.

The 2008 crash transformed the US-China economic relationship in ways that have been geopolitically disruptive ever since. China's Pacific-oriented growth model proved too vulnerable for comfort in Beijing. The Chinese leadership turned towards Eurasia for investment and opportunities and then, in the Belt and Road Initiative, committed to creating a transport infrastructure to support them. This move created the conditions for a sharp divergence between American and European interests around China. Yet China's response to 2008 also deepened its American dependency on the financial side. Corporate China's sizeable dollar borrowing left China acutely susceptible to the Federal Reserve's monetary tightening when it began in 2014. China's efforts to make the yuan an international currency to achieve more monetary and financial autonomy have largely failed, and China has more reason to fear externally-driven financial instability than it did a decade ago.

Beyond the political conflicts generated by trade and finance, China's economic rise always had to become its own source of severe geopolitical tension. Once China could spend more freely on a navy, it would have taken a serious act of self-restraint for China's leaders to accept American dominance in the eastern Pacific as a permanent reality. Indeed, the fact that enough of the American corporate and political class were tied together, through lobbying and campaign donations, in reaping benefit from the American end of the China relationship constituted a reason why China could take geopolitical risks in pursuing regional hegemony.

Chinese Navy destroyer Yinchuan (175) prepares
for departure from Hong Kong, 2017.

An economically-rising China also had to throw the international energy order into disarray. Chinese oil demand greatly contributed to the surge in oil prices between 2003 and mid-2008, and this oil price shock, allied to the growing importance of natural gas, created the external conditions in which Putin could restore Russian power.

By 2016 there was little room left for illusion in Washington about peaceful interdependence. Either the United States had to accommodate a regionally more assertive China for the sake of China's services to world economic growth – which after 2008 were substantial – or it had to begin to decouple economically, in the reasonable hope that, in the short term anyway, China as the state with the trade surplus and the foreign-currency dependency had the more to lose. Trump's pursuit of the second option was made easier by the American military establishment's growing awareness of the security stakes inherent in technological competition. Long before the Covid-19 crisis hit, there was a broad domestic political consensus behind Trump on this issue. With it, the old story that international political stability requires only aggregated economic well-being across borders was shattered.

As geopolitics reasserted itself, Hong Kong also became increasingly politically unstable in ways that made it a less sustainable conduit. From 2014, the Umbrella Movement showed how many younger Hong Kong citizens were unwilling either to sacrifice Hong Kong's governance to the 'one country, two systems' principle, or accept the material inequalities generated by a large and highly-internationalised financial sector. By the beginning of this year, six months of often violent protests had pushed the Hong Kong economy into recession and the credit rating agencies had downgraded Hong Kong's debt. Through last year Trump and European leaders, aware of the commercial stakes, were pretty cautious in responding to the new rebellion. But without some measure of constitutional stability in Hong Kong, there can be no means of separating out Hong Kong's economic and geopolitical positions, and China cannot remain financially connected to the West.

In the Middle East, there is little left of American military power beyond the Persian Gulf, and Russia has become the pivotal power in most of the region's conflicts. Coming on top of the Iraq debacle, the American-British-French intervention in Libya destabilised the north-African country, and American policy in Syria collapsed into incoherence. American impotence in the face of the ISIS carve-up of Syria and Iraq then allowed the Russian military into the region. This ensured Bashar al-Assad's survival, and strengthened Iran and Hezbollah. As American power dissipated, the US's simultaneous military dependence on Turkey and the Kurdish People's Protection Units was cruelly exposed last year for the untenable position it always was.

Meanwhile, Obama's attempts to deal with the Iran nuclear question independently of the broader regional conflicts was condemned to failure once Russia acted to guarantee Iran and Hezbollah's military presence in Syria. In terminating the Iran nuclear deal, Trump again divided NATO over the Middle East. The dollar's banking pre-eminence ensures that European companies have largely complied with the return to sanctions. Yet there are too many European commercial and energy interests tied to Iran for the major European governments easily to give up on the idea of rapprochement with Iran.

Under Trump, the US has effectively retreated to the western side of the Persian Gulf. This takes American policy back to what it was prior to the first Iraq war, when it relied on deterrence and the threat of retaliation to police the region rather than regime change or policing no-fly zones. As Trump demonstrated over General Soleimani's assassination, the US can use its aerial power to hurt Iran. But the absence of ground troops elsewhere leaves considerable opportunities for Russia and Turkey. Russia has no interest in challenging American naval power in the Gulf. Nonetheless, as an energy power, it divides the US from its European allies over what happens in the Strait of Hormuz by offering Germany, in particular, an alternative oil supply to one that must come through those waters.

The United States' return as an energy power is the past decade's third defining geopolitical feature. A world in which there are three large energy producers – the US, Saudi Arabia, and Russia – would necessarily be different than one in which there was two. But America's new-found productive capacity in oil and gas has been more disruptive than simply establishing an additional producer rivalry.

Prior to the shale revolution, the American reliance on Saudi Arabia, both for supply and to help keep the Strait of Hormuz open, became from the 1970s Washington's most important bilateral relationship. This dependency, and the Saudi willingness to funnel serious money into the US, ensured that Saudi interests were well protected in Washington. Now

French President Emmanuel Macron welcomes
Lebanese Prime Minister Saad Hariri in Paris,
November 2017.

Saudi Arabia has been cast adrift from that Atlantic anchor. The lure of American energy independence encouraged Obama towards a more confrontational approach with Riyadh. With China now the world's premier market for oil exporters, Saudi Arabia had to compete with Russia for pre-eminence eastwards. American shale output, meanwhile, risked an oil glut that would drive prices a long way down. In late November 2014, the Saudis began a price war for market share. But, when they discovered they could bankrupt neither American shale producers nor the Russian government, they had to upend OPEC to accommodate an alliance with Russia to push prices back up to tolerable levels. Moreover, they had to do so after the Russians had already militarily moved into Syria, ensuring more distrust in Washington.

The ensuing internal tumult in Saudi Arabia produced the callow leadership of Mohammed bin Salman (MBS), a purge of the Saudi royal family, and Saudi military intervention in Yemen. MBS has made Saudi Arabia a chaotic power, exemplified by the Saudi government forcing Lebanon's prime minister, Saad Hariri, to resign whilst on a visit to the Saudi capital in late 2017 but then being unable to stop President Macron intervening to restore Hariri to the premiership. Since then Lebanon's politics has descended deeper into crisis with large-scale protests forcing Hariri to resign again last autumn, this time for good.

Nonetheless, there are clear limits to renewed American energy power. American energy independence is unachievable when shale oil and conventional crude oil are not substitutable for refining purposes, prices in good part depend on the security of overall supply, and shale output will fall off from the end of the decade. Saudi Arabia still sits on the world's largest easily available oil reserves and can quickly adjust its production. Consequently, as the Saudis thrash around for a strategic way out of their difficulties, their capacity for disruption has in reality been amplified not diminished.

The Covid-19 crisis has accentuated all the geopolitical fault lines exposed over the past decade. The US-China economic decoupling will accelerate. All US-China trade and supply chains will be judged a potential security risk, not just those that involve high-tech manufacturing. Indeed, the whole de facto geopolitical infrastructure that made the West's economic relationship with China functional is now collapsing. Hong Kong has already become a zero-sum political game. On 22 May, the Chinese government decided to impose national security legislation on Hong Kong after protesters returned to the street. In bypassing the Hong Kong legislature, it effectively terminated the governance arrangements for Hong Kong agreed in the 1984 Joint Declaration. Whilst the Trump administration had previously largely left Hong Kong out of its otherwise more confrontational approach towards China, it now threatens to revoke Hong Kong's trading status. Only China's substantial dollar debt, and its need to maintain the indirect credit line the Federal Reserve has effectively provided over recent months, may now act as a constraint on both an economic cold war and a likely disastrous endgame in Hong Kong and possibly Taiwan too.

The instability in the Middle East and the turbulence caused by America's energy resurgence have proven just as susceptible to Covid-19 havoc. Once the potential size of the economic shock materialised, the Saudi-Russian oil axis fell apart. MBS dramatically increased Saudi production and let oil prices crash, effectively declaring a second war for market share against both the US and Russia. The Trump administration forced him to back down, apparently by threatening to withdraw military support from the kingdom. But the US's ability sustainably to discipline Saudi Arabia is at the mercy of Iran's behaviour.

Here, the oil crash has intensified the crisis in the Persian Gulf. For Iran, a further plunge in oil revenues when its economy was already hurting under renewed American sanctions is a disaster. Rather than letting up on his 'maximum pressure' policy towards Iran to allow the country to deal with its humanitarian emergency, Trump has doubled down on it over the past few months, tightening sanctions and initiating a shoot-and-destroy policy on any Iranian vessels that harass American ships in the Gulf. But he is still unable to persuade European governments to back such a confrontational policy, and presumptive Democratic presidential nominee Joe Biden is singing from a different hymn sheet.

Elsewhere in the Middle East, Covid-19 has again exacerbated existing perils. In Lebanon, the government defaulted on its debt in March, causing the Lebanese currency to slide into freefall. The central bank's decrees make it near impossible for anyone to access dollars in an economy that is dependent on the American currency. Ignoring the lockdown, the protests have resumed, as what was already an economic crisis becomes, with so many people struggling to buy food, a catastrophe.

For Europe, the deteriorating geopolitical environment over the past decade proved disruptive, divisive, and very difficult for either the EU or individual European states to influence. Now the Covid-19 emergency is amplifying the hazards. As the US and China accelerate their decoupling, the EU and Britain are too weak, in the medium term, to walk a path independently of that chosen in Washington, even while the German desire to resist dismantling manufacturing supply chains is already evident. For the EU, how to manage this separation will quickly run into the divisions that have prevented any coherent China policy emerging from the point after the 2008 crash when Chinese investment in EU states began to swell. The fate of Italy – as the largest EU member state to have joined the Belt and Road Initiative, as well as the Eurozone state most at risk of losing access to international capital markets to finance the now necessary substantial increase in borrowing – is pivotal. In proposing new fiscal transfers to Italy, albeit time-limited and outside any new fiscal institutions for the Eurozone, the German government is clearly aware of the high risks attached to letting Italy flounder under this new economic crisis. But this is unlikely to extend to allowing Italy to pursue an independent policy on Chinese investment inside the EU or port infrastructure, when Berlin will need some political space where it can be seen as getting tougher with China to try to protect German companies that manufacture in, and export to, China.

For the EU a qualitatively different China strategy ultimately requires a different Russia strategy. At a grand *realpolitik* level, Emmanuel Macron was correct when, on these grounds, he pressed for a European reset with Moscow last autumn. But Merkel was also right in chastising the French president for his geopolitical freelancing, since his version of this reset appears indifferent to how this can be accomplished with meaningful guarantees for the security of eastern European states and without a change of attitude in Moscow. In wrestling with this problem, Germany too is stuck. German governments cannot lecture France that it must accept the centrality of the German-Polish relationship to the post-Cold War EU, and still treat German energy dependency on Russia as a purely commercial relationship without geopolitical repercussions.

The dangers coming from the Middle East will also now grow. European states must expect renewed migration problems as the crisis in Lebanon deepens, and the Syrian government retakes Idlib. Geography dictates that Europe receives the human fallout of what happens in the

Middle East. But the EU has no more capacity to exercise serious geo-political influence in the region than it did when the Arab Spring began back in 2011, a problem compounded by Brexit and the rupture with Washington over Iran. The question for the EU is whether it can acquire the necessary internal political capacity and realism to make serious geo-political choices in a world ever more fraught with danger – and where it has become so vulnerable to external shock.

Turkish President Recep Tayyip Erdogan takes
part in a prayer program at the Hagia Sophia
Mosque reopening in July 2020.

NEW TURKEY'S OLD POLITICS

Tim Marshall

In July, Turkey's President Recep Tayyip Erdogan decreed that the Hagia Sophia museum in Istanbul would be converted back into a mosque. Built as a Byzantine church in 537, it was turned into a mosque in 1453 under the rule of the Ottomans. But in 1934 Kemal Ataturk – the first president of the secular Turkish Republic and the man who turned Turkey towards the West – saw the soft power benefits for the Republic in making it a museum, in celebration of a shared history. It was a message to the West: 'The door is open to all.'

Erdogan's Turkish and English language Twitter accounts were a paean to inclusivity – the mosque would be 'wide open to all...Hagia Sophia, the shared heritage of humanity, will continue to embrace all'. However, the Arabic language version of the website of the Office of the Presidency carried a different tone – the move 'heralds the liberation of the Al-Aqsa Mosque' which sits above the Western Wall in Jerusalem. The president's decision was 'the best response to the loathsome attacks on our values and symbols in every Islamic region... With the help of Allah the Almighty, we will continue traveling on this blessed path, without stopping, without weariness or fatigue, with determination, sacrifice and persistence, until we reach our hoped-for destination.'

In a speech to mark the occasion, Erdogan namechecked key battles in Ottoman and Turkish history: 'The resurrection of the Hagia Sophia represents our memory full of heydays in our history from Badr to Manzikert, from Nicopolis to Gallipoli.'

Erdogan was elected as the mayor of Istanbul in 1994, representing the Islamist Welfare Party. In 1998, he served four months in jail for reciting a poem which included the lines: 'The mosques are our barracks, the domes our helmets, the minarets our bayonets, and the faithful our solders...' On release, he helped create the Justice and Development Party (AKP) out of the remnants of the Welfare Party and quickly rose to power. Erdogan's worldview is set squarely against the secular legacy of Ataturk.

His party's vision is rooted in political Islam – a kind of Turkish brand of the Muslim Brotherhood. Its ideologues are lukewarm about NATO and frustrated about their lack of influence in the dominions of the former Ottoman Empire.

In geopolitical terms, Erdogan's 'New Turkey', as it is sometimes called, is underpinned by two related concepts: 'Blue Homeland' and 'Strategic Depth'. Both of these seek to right the perceived wrongs of the past. In the multipolar post-Cold War world, Erdogan sees a jungle full of competitors in which Turkey is a lion seeking to re-establish itself as king.

Turkey's Unique Strategic Depth

A guide to Erdogan's thinking can be found in the career and words of the former leader of the AKP, Professor Ahmet Davutoglu, who served as his Foreign Minister from 2009 to 2014 and then as Prime Minister from 2014 to 2016. His 2001 book, *Strategic Depth*, is the structure upon which the foreign policy of Erdogan's 'New Turkey' is built. His proposals for expanding Turkey's strategic depth are based on a 'dynamic interpretation of geography' to give Turkey a more active foreign policy.

Davutoglu argues that Turkey possesses a unique psychological and physical 'strategic depth' due to its history and geographic position. It commands the Bosphorus Strait and the Dardanelles, and thus controls access into the Mediterranean from the Black Sea and vice versa. The core of the country is at its western extremity, around the Sea of Marmara, which means the core has almost a thousand miles of territory guarding it from potential threats to the east. Protecting the core from the west, north, and south requires pushing as far up the northern shore of the Sea of Marmara as possible, and having a strong navy in the Black Sea and the Aegean.

Turkey has land borders with eight countries – Greece, Bulgaria, Georgia, Armenia, Azerbaijan, Iran, Iraq, and Syria – and, as the land bridge between Europe and Asia, it is at the centre of a geopolitical crossroads. Therefore, argues Davutoglu, it must exercise its power in 360 degrees to shape the world around it, while drawing on its historical memory of the glorious past of the Ottomans. This vision represented quite a break from being a mere outpost of the NATO alliance, which throughout the early 2000s chimed with a public narrative that Turkey desired 'zero problems with neighbours'.

Ahmet Davutoglu in 2015 when he was Prime
Minister of Turkey.

Faced with an increasingly aggressive US after 9/11, Ankara maintained cordial relations with the White House for the first decade of the century, whilst simultaneously increasing its influence in the Balkans and the Middle East using trade and diplomacy. It made attempts to help reconcile Bosnia and Serbia, brokered Israeli/Syrian talks, and even reached out to traditionally hostile Armenia. However, in almost all cases it made little concrete progress. And by the second decade, the Americans had been burned by their experience in Iraq and Afghanistan, and the Middle East had become seriously destabilised.

In this context, the ideologues of the AKP understood that growing geopolitical turmoil in Turkey's sphere of influence made the status quo of a passive neighbourhood policy increasingly less compatible with a deep 'neo-Ottoman' conviction that Turkey's destiny is to emerge as a global superpower just as the West goes into decline.

Turkey went on the front foot. It developed into NATO's second most powerful military force. Turkey has become self-sufficient in weapons and has enjoyed success in building a defence industry capable of selling arms on the world market. Its big-ticket project is the TF-X, intended as a state-of-the-art fighter jet to replace the F-16 by 2030. It might have got off the ground earlier but Turkey's purchase of the S-400 missile defence system from Russia was met with pushback from the Americans. The Trump administration persuaded Rolls Royce and BAE not to co-operate on the construction of the aircraft's engines. Nonetheless, Turkey does now build its own tanks, armoured vehicles, infantry landing craft, drones, frigates, and this year launched a light aircraft carrier capable of carrying helicopter gunships and armed drones.

In diplomatic terms, Turkey's shift to a more active neighbourhood policy has alienated many of the Middle East's important actors. Its relations with Israel soured after 20 years of co-operation. The Islamists and nationalists (Davutoglu among them) argued that close relations with Israel were alienating the state from its people and their Islamic heritage. The two countries had till then enjoyed a partnership based on concerns about the Arab states and Iran. But the AKP's political base doesn't include many favourable to Israel. Following 2008, Israel-Gaza relations began to cool.

Turkey viewed the Arab uprisings from 2010–11 as an opportunity to extend influence back into the former Ottoman Empire, but consistently backed the wrong horse. President Erdogan has always had close ties with the Muslim Brotherhood, a transnational Sunni Islamist movement which, at least in principle, seeks to create a Sharia-led global caliphate. As such it is loathed by most of the Arab governments as they know they are in its sights. When the Brotherhood won the 2012 Egyptian elections, following the overthrow of Mubarak, Erdogan was delighted. He hoped to build a strategic relationship with new Islamist governments in Egypt, Libya, and Tunisia – with Turkey as senior partner.

However, the following year the Brotherhood government fell to a military coup led by Egypt's current President, Abdel Fattah el-Sisi. This was roundly condemned by Erdogan, setting him against the new Egyptian leader, who views Turkey as a regional threat supportive of Islamist terrorism. Egypt, which has traditionally seen itself as the leading Arab power, is uninterested in 'neo-Ottomans' gaining influence. Erdogan and Sisi are nationalists with romantic views of their country's roles, which, because they are similar, are resolutely opposed.

This dynamic was apparent in Syria too as Turkey saw opportunities to expand eastwards. After Islamist organisations hijacked much of the mostly Sunni uprising against President Assad, Ankara was quick to offer support in a bid to oust him. Cairo on the other hand began to normalise relations with Assad almost as soon as Sisi took power. When Turkish forces invaded northern Syria, the moves played into the Egyptian narrative that the Arabs faced a threat from 'neo-Ottomans'. Ankara also ran up against Russian interests as Moscow backed Assad in order to keep its Syrian port on the Mediterranean and blocked Turkish aspirations.

So Turkey was on the front foot, but it kept getting knocked back. Even a ceasefire with the Kurdish PKK broke down, resulting in renewed fighting in Anatolia. By 2020, for a variety of reasons, it had fallen out with Syria, Egypt, Saudi Arabia, the UAE, Kuwait, Israel, Iran, Russia, Armenia, Greece, Cyprus, France, the EU and NATO. The EU, which had kept Ankara on a string with its teasing offer of EU membership, accuses it of using the refugee crisis as a foreign policy tool.

Erdogan appears to have decided that his country must go it alone. The 2016 failed coup attempt against him by small groups of the military only reinforced this view. Despite a lack of evidence, Erdogan hinted at what many of his supporters openly said – that the coup was a vast conspiracy backed by a foreign power, the Americans.

Returning to the Blue Homeland

Davutoglu's strategic recommendations influenced Turkey's incursions into Syria, but they have had mixed success and he was side-lined by Erdogan and retired to academia (for now). But a new ideologue has emerged with serious influence on strategic thinking. Former Rear Admiral Cem Gurdeniz has popularised the concept of '*Mavi Vatan*' – the 'Blue Homeland' – and made public a more aggressive stance now prevalent in Turkish military circles. Gurdeniz helped come up with the term in 2006 and, once he left the navy, a series of TV appearances and articles pushed the idea onto the public radar.

It overlaps with Davutoglu's conviction that in order for Turkey to survive in a world seeking to crush the country, it must push outwards. As a naval man Gurdeniz concentrates on the waterways, insisting that Turkey must dominate the three seas around it – the Black Sea, the Aegean and the eastern Mediterranean. Behind this appears to be a long-term strategy to tear up the Treaty of Lausanne (1923) in which the Ottoman Empire lost territory. Supporters of *Mavi Vatan* are also sceptical of their country's membership of NATO and believe it to be an American plot (helped by Greece) to prevent Turkey from rising to its rightful place in the world.

There are broader aspects to Blue Homeland, covering naval policy as far afield as the Indian Ocean, but in popular parlance it has come to mean Ankara's policy in the eastern Mediterranean, specifically vis-à-vis Greece. The discovery of underwater gas fields has exacerbated long-running tensions, and Gurdeniz has seized upon these natural resources to push the Blue Homeland concept. At a minimum, he argues, the eastern coast of Crete should be Turkish, and the Aegean should not be allowed to be a 'Greek lake'. His influence can be found in the title of the Turkish Naval War College's journal, *Mavi Vatan*, and a huge naval exercise undertaken last year also carried the same operational name.

Among numerous provocative statements, this is one of the most telling: 'In the absence of military strength Greece instead relies upon the United States and Europe to act on its behalf…They should know their place.' Erdogan is only slightly less measured. He too has criticised the Lausanne treaty for leaving Turkey too small in territory and has stated that 'Turkey cannot disregard its kinsmen in Western Thrace [in north-eastern Greece], Cyprus, Crimea, and anywhere else.'

When it comes to Crimea, formerly an Ottoman territory, Ankara is not in a position to do very much. It has only a modest fleet in the Black

Blue Homeland 2019. Turkish battleships pass
the Bosphorus during Turkey's largest naval
exercise which took place on all three seas
surrounding the country.

Sea whereas Russia has spent the years since it annexed Crimea in 2014 building up a major force. It is Greece which is most anxious about the Blue Homeland idea and President Erdogan's rhetoric fuels those fears. State TV likes to show maps depicting 'Turkey's National Pact', a 1920 document identifying which parts of the defeated Ottoman Empire the new Turkish Republic would fight for. They include many of the Greek Aegean islands and part of the Greek mainland. Erdogan has appeared in an official photograph of a 2019 visit to Istanbul's National Defence University standing in front of a map showing half of the Aegean belonging to Turkey.

The huge reserves of natural gas in the eastern Mediterranean have complicated what was already a potential source of conflict between Greece and Turkey. Cyprus, of which Greece sees itself as a protector, sits in the middle of a geostrategic highway – the main sea lanes of the eastern Mediterranean, and the discovered gas fields.

As a sovereign state Cyprus has drilling rights around its coastline under the United Nations Convention for the Law of the Sea (UNCLOS). Turkey is not a signatory to UNCLOS but does recognise the 'Turkish Republic of Northern Cyprus' which it set up after invading Cyprus in 1974. It is the only country in the world to do so, but on that basis, and because it claims that the waters around the island's northern coast are on Turkey's continental shelf, Ankara says it has the legal right to operate there.

In 2019 its drilling ships showed up, escorted by a warship. Cyprus appealed to the EU which said Turkey's actions were 'illegal'. In the summer of 2020 a Turkish research ship arrived off the coast of Crete along with three navy ships, prompting Athens to state it was 'ready to respond' if drilling took place. The French quickly sent ships and fighter jets to conduct 'joint exercises' with the Greek military, and with deliberate timing the UAE announced Greece had allowed it to base four fighter jets in Crete. It was becoming crowded down there.

The potential for escalation has been illustrated several times, and has sometimes emerged in surprising quarters. In February, when Turkish frigates sailed close to the Cypriot gas fields, France dispatched its aircraft carrier, the Charles De Gaulle, to shadow the naval forces of its NATO ally. In June the French alleged that during a confrontation with the Turkish navy off Libya the Turks locked their weapons systems onto a French frigate.

Turkey came to an astonishing agreement with Libya late last year, which 'created' an Exclusive Economic Zone (EEZ) stretching in a corridor across the Mediterranean, from Turkey's coast down to the northern tip of Libya cutting through part of the Greek EEZ. The agreement was made with the Libyan government which is why Turkey has intervened militarily in Libya's civil war – if the Tripoli government falls, so does the agreement.

Turkey is increasingly more isolated, and less trusted. It believes it has a trump card as the main guardian of NATO's southern flank. It is indeed a strong card, but NATO has others, even if it would prefer not to play them. Building up NATO facilities in Greece and Romania would partially offset the loss of Turkey. Ankara knows its neighbourhood is a tough one; in the past decade there have been conflicts in four of the countries it borders – Armenia, Azerbaijan, Iraq, and Syria – while Iran remains a competitor as does Russia.

Twenty years of being aggressive have not resulted in significant Turkish gains. Erdogan can double down and keep playing the Islamist nationalist card as he enters difficult domestic political waters, but he needs some victories, or he needs to bring Turkey in from the cold. Achieving either will be a struggle. If he plays nice, he risks his support base seeing him as weak, especially after recent comments in which he said of Greece: 'They're either going to understand the language of politics and diplomacy, or in the field with painful experiences.' In a tough neighbourhood you need friends – and the twin strategies of Strategic Depth and Blue Homeland have left him with none.

Dancers perform during a gala show to celebrate
the 90th anniversary of the founding of the
Communist Party of China (CPC), Beijing, 2011.

CHINA – THE GREAT UNCOUPLING

Jonathan Fenby

As China entered its eighth decade of Communist Party rule in late 2019, the message from the apex of power in Beijing was plain – to realise the concept of a great nation with an exceptional global role. If the world was 'in the midst of change on a scale not seen for over a hundred years', as the country's leader, Xi Jinping, put it, this presented an opportunity to realise the 'China Dream' of progress and greatness. It would be a challenge but, evoking Mao Zedong and the Long March, he portrayed the test ahead as a nation-strengthening process leading to victory.

'Achieving a great dream takes a great struggle,' Xi told a meeting of senior cadres in the autumn of 2019. 'These struggles are not short-term but long-term; they...will not be small: economic, political, cultural, social; building an ecological civilisation, national defence and building the army...foreign relations work, party building and others.' That vision, drawing on history through the legacy of the Chinese empire but firmly rooted in a twenty-first century ideology of power, is now the essential guiding policy for the last major state on earth still ruled by a Communist Party and so forms a key element in the evolution of global relations as the world struggles with the crisis unleashed by the Covid-19 pandemic.

'Socialism with Chinese Characteristics'

Nobody can say they had not been warned about the course the leadership of the People's Republic (PRC) intends to follow, or its determination to carve out a specific course for itself in the twenty-first century. In a speech to a closed Party meeting soon after taking the country's top office eight years ago, Xi talked of working for 'the eventual demise of capitalism and ultimate victory of socialism'. A Central Committee document drawn up in 2013 called for 'intense ideological struggle' to achieve 'the great rejuvenation' of the Chinese people with the rejection of Western principles such as constitutional democracy, universal values, neo-liberalism, promotion of civil society and freedom of the press.

At the Communist Party's five-yearly congress four years later, Xi set out the PRC's ambitions to become 'a global leader in terms of composite national strength and international influence' by the mid-2030s. The PRC would move to the centre of the world stage while 'Socialism with Chinese characteristics' blazed a new trail. At home, the leadership reversed Deng Xiaoping's moves towards separation of powers between Party and government to the benefit of the first while, abroad, it decided that the time had come to abandon his advice that the People's Republic should 'hide its brilliance and bide its time' as it drew on the rest of the world to build up its strength.

Yet, as imperial dynasties discovered in the past, long-term visions often run up against more immediate road blocks. In China's case, significant short-term challenges were plain to see at the turn of the decade. Spectacular as its emergence from Mao-era backwardness and isolation had been, the image of an all-conquering nation on its inevitable path to ruling the world did not stand up to close examination. That might not fit the 'China Dream' narrative propounded by the leadership, but it was one which would present Xi and his colleagues with a choice of direction when the 2020 crisis unfolded.

Superpower Overreach

The economy, the explosive expansion of which had been at the core of the regime's evolution since the post-Mao reforms launched by Deng in the late 1970s, was slowing down even before the pandemic hit. As growth declined, concern rose about legacies from the era of turbo-charged expansion such as the debt mountain built by the huge expansion of credit. Despite the pledge to create 'a moderately prosperous society' shared by the population at large, wealth distribution has been highly unequal, with gaping disparities between the mass of the rural population and the urban middle class. The People's Republic risked being stuck in the middle-income trap as development stalled, vested interests sheltered under the political apparatus and consumption was stunted by the need for high savings given the lack of a fully-fledged welfare system. The pace of economic reform had decelerated markedly. The private sector, which created the bulk of growth and jobs, had been relegated to the back seat as the reach of the 'Party State' expanded.

Despite its advance in such key areas as big data and 5G communications, mainland China lagged in some vital sectors for modernisation, notably advanced semi-conductors. Its population was ageing fast. Although the government was paying increased attention to the environment, the legacy of pollution from the years of heedless industrial growth remained a major problem. Repression of dissent had been stepped up and the mass forced 're-education' of the Muslim Uyghur population aroused international criticism.

Under Donald Trump's presidency, the most important global relationship – with the United States – had moved decisively from the 'constructive engagement' of the past four decades to one of 'strategic rivalry' as China was depicted as the symbol of the downsides of globalisation. Nor was it only the White House that took a critical view of the People's Republic; Democrats joined in the chorus and though American companies might still value the mainland market, opinion surveys showed only a quarter of Americans regarding China favourably. From trade and tariffs, the confrontation had spilled over into the technology China needed to build up its advanced industries and modernise its armed forces, with the giant Huawei company a prime target.

In Hong Kong, protests, directed at Beijing as much as at the local government, continued unabated through the second half of 2019 after pro-democracy candidates swept the board on district councils and were poised to do well in polls for the local legislature the following autumn. In Taiwan, the autonomist DPP president was on her way to re-election with a heavy majority in early 2020. The US was conducting freedom of navigation exercises in Asian waters claimed by China and strengthening its presence in the Indo-Pacific region, notably with India. South-East Asia countries resented China's expansion in the South China Sea. The global Belt and Road Initiative (BRI) of Chinese aid was running into problems in some key countries, with some recipient governments backing out of projects and chafing under the debts incurred with Chinese banks.

Then, as the year ended, came the virus outbreak in Wuhan. This raised fresh questions about the ruling system as the authorities proved slow to react effectively. Governments in developed nations took a fresh look at China, both politically and economically, once the virus spread towards them. Donald Trump blamed the PRC for the spread of 'the plague' and attacking China became a major ploy for the November presidential elections.

As the scale of the challenge represented by the pandemic became clear, and the Chinese economy was crippled by the draconian lockdown deemed necessary to win the 'People's War', a different leadership in Beijing might have been induced to relax on some other fronts, if only to gain breathing space. Apart from the health challenge, the economic out-look was dire given the way the outbreak depressed both domestic and external demand while raising the danger of mass unemployment, social instability and the loss of the Party's main practical claim to rule.

Prudence might, therefore, have prompted a more emollient global attitude from Beijing as a report from the State Security Ministry showed anti-China sentiment abroad at a 30-year high. If reviving 'constructive engagement' with Washington seemed impossible, then at least the PRC might seek to nurture partnerships with governments which felt they had been left adrift by the Trump administration's go-it-alone approach and looked to China as a helpful partner in times of global stress.

But that was not to be. It did not fit the concept of supremacy that had become baked into the political machine which ran the PRC. Instead, the pandemic proved to be a watershed flowing directly from the new, tougher vision of China's objectives and how to pursue them, accelerating the drive to show the superiority of the PRC model of governance and tighten the leadership's grip on power.

Xi was up-front about the opportunity that the 'People's War' against the disease offered – to show 'the significant advantages of the leader-ship of the Communist Party and the socialist system with Chinese characteristics', as he put it in a tele-conference with 170,000 Party cad-res in January. After initial slowness to act and cover-ups, the general secretary assumed the role of commander-in-chief. Blame for any short-comings was loaded on to the local government in Hubei prov-ince who were replaced by envoys from the central apparatus. The Party, alone, could be the source of national safety and salvation. Messaging that deviated from the approved version was repressed. Independent bloggers were silenced. The 'Chernobyl Moment' of pop-ular alienation from the regime forecast by foreign commentators was choked off under cover of the massive lockdown while attention shifted to reviving the economy and clamping down on any threat of a second wave of the pandemic.

An empty street in Wuhan during lockdown,
March 2020.

Foreign criticism of the initial failure to limit the spread of the disease and of the way it then spread outside China prompted a defiant response even as Beijing stepped up its supply of medical equipment abroad, some of it on a commercial basis and some as aid, some of it gratefully received and some found to be sub-standard. As relations with the West sharpened and the Republicans adopted anti-China messaging as a prime theme for the presidential election, Beijing heightened its rhetoric, seeking to divert attention from the origin of the disease and initial shortcomings to the less impressive record of foreign governments in controlling the pandemic once it spread across the world.

A Foreign Ministry spokesman suggested the virus might have been imported by a US team competing in a military sports competition in Wuhan. Foreign food imports and travellers from abroad were blamed. 'Wolf Warrior' diplomats at Chinese embassies attacked their host governments. Australia was subjected to sanctions on grain exports to China when it called for an independent investigation into the origin of the virus. With a pledge of $2 billion to fight the virus, China set itself up as the champion of the World Health Organisation as the US prepared to leave the global body, accusing it of having been taken over by the PRC. Official media homed in on the fast-escalating death toll in the United States and contrasted this with the numbers in China; when protest welled up in American cities after the killing of George Floyd in the early summer, anti-US Party and State propagandists had a field day.

The Chinese leadership, meanwhile, did not let the pandemic slow down its pursuit of plans in other directions. Indeed, the crisis offered useful cover for action while other countries were preoccupied in fighting their own outbreaks. So, the spring and summer of 2020 saw a flurry of activity that took little or no account of the reactions it provoked, and cemented the tougher policy approach which had been brewing in Beijing through the previous decade.

Relations with the United States plunged further with Beijing giving no ground in response to criticism of its handling of 'the China plague' from President Trump and Secretary of State Pompeo. Purchases of American farm products, energy and industrial goods under the Phase One trade agreement signed in January ran well below the agreed levels as the PRC ramped up buying from Brazil as an alternative (and cheaper) supplier. Apparently unwilling to make the final break with the PRC, Trump still pointed to 'the great deal' he had made on behalf of American farmers. He remained vague on what threatened sanctions over Hong Kong would entail while the Commerce Department relaxed some of its prohibitions on Huawei. Observing the rift between the Trump administration and US allies in Europe and Asia, China showed every sign of going its own way regardless of pressure from Washington, counting on domestic economic and electoral pressure in the United States to hold the president back from the brink, whatever his rhetorical outbursts.

A New Era in US-China Relations

US-China relations have thus entered a new phase in which Beijing is ready to move towards disengagement and reduced dependence on the power across the Pacific – if not complete decoupling. This may have come sooner and been more radical than the PRC leaders had expected thanks to the virus and Trump's re-election tactics. But, while the president's tariff war followed by musing about the prospect for unravelling the whole relationship with the PRC kept the spotlight on him, China was also resetting its course to reflect its own priorities and the buttressing of its system that was the leadership's first concern as the Communist Party matched its domestic concentration of authority with external power projection.

At its annual plenary session (delayed by the virus till late May), the rubber-stamp legislature, the National People's Congress (NPC) drew up national security legislation for Hong Kong designed to bring the former British colony to heel and choke off the pro-democracy movement by riding rough-shod over the 'one country, two systems' formula adopted at the 1997 handover from Britain. Ignoring promises of 'a high degree of autonomy' for the territory until 2047, the move unabashedly asserted the primacy of the 'one country' to do as it wished, reinforced by the presence of mainland security agents and suggestions of special courts. This could only strengthen concern about the extension of mainland Chinese norms to the city and the impact on the rule of law there, not to mention raising doubts about its future as an international financial centre if it became 'just another Chinese city'.

China stepped up maritime pressure on Malaysia, Vietnam and Indonesia in the latest round of its expansion in the South China Sea, as well as giving reefs and atolls Chinese names. Planes and warships undertook patrols menacingly close to Taiwan, in some cases intruding on its

Following pages: President Xi Jinping speaks at the military parade marking the 70th anniversary of the founding of the People's Republic of China, 2019.

air space, while Beijing's language about reunification grew tougher – with a senior People's Liberation Army (PLA) general reviving talk of mounting a military attack on the island if there was no other way of heading off independence. In the Himalayas, the PLA conducted exercises on the disputed border with India and fought frontier clashes that left dozens of soldiers on each side dead.

The budget for the PLA was boosted by 6.6%, and Xi, who is also chair of the Central Military Commission, told the military to 'think about worst-case scenarios, scale up training and battle preparedness'. Spending on instruments of power projection such as the navy and the missile force was increased while Xi paid constant attention to ensuring the PLA's loyalty to the regime.

Continuing the Leninist concentration of Communist Party power that has been a hallmark of Xi Jinping's premiership, a new top-level security group was established under Politburo control. Central control was increased in the name of fighting the virus. Journalists from major US news organisations were expelled. Chinese bloggers who raised questions about the handling of the virus were detained along with several more prominent critics of the leadership. On his 67th birthday, on 15 June 2020, the Party journal, *Seeking Truth*, added to the cult built up around the leader by declaring that his teachings – known as 'Xi Jinping Thought on Socialism with Chinese Characteristics for a New Era' – were 'Marxism for the twenty-first Century'.

China Sets its Own Course
It is now half a century since Richard Nixon opined (in a *Foreign Affairs* article before he won the presidency) that, 'We simply cannot afford to leave China forever outside the family of nations…the world cannot be safe until China changes.' His successors, Republican and Democrat, along with many other Western leaders, generally based their China policy on the belief that, as the People's Republic became richer and more globally connected, it would become 'more like us'. Given the Communist Party's focus on power and self-preservation, and China's long history of regarding itself as an exceptional nation poised between heaven and earth, this was always a mistaken belief. But it is only now being recognised as a mirage, fostered by mutual overlapping interests that have been overtaken by political and ideological drivers.

Beijing's present policy path means that it is quite ready for conflict – open or tactical – with the nations whose co-operation Deng saw as necessary to the PRC's positive evolution. China does not want to exclude itself from international affairs; on the contrary it wants to foster a world where Chinese standards replace those of the post-1945 US-led system. Above all, the leadership does not accept the need to be part of a family of nations led by the United States, as was the case during its economic rise that depended heavily on globalisation and opening up to international forces. A China-centric world, increasingly free of overlapping interests with foreign powers, is the aim, and this is seen in Beijing as attainable so long as the PRC sticks to its guns, defends its red lines of national sovereignty and plays on divisions among states which formerly marched in step with the US.

After four decades of growth, the economy remains key to the regime's health, but the leadership believes it does not need to play second fiddle to any other power and can assert what it sees as China's time for global greatness. This may lead it to overestimate its own strength – the PRC remains shot through with flaws while the prevailing disarray among the democracies may not persist. But the world is shifting even as it fragments, and China is set on its course, whatever the outcome.

German speed skater Anni Friesinger skates a
victory lap with her country's flag after setting a
world record at the Salt Lake City Winter
Olympics, 2002.

A WORLD OF NATIONS AND STATES
IS HERE TO STAY

Donald Sassoon

The nineteenth century may have been the age of nationalism but the twentieth was the age of nation states, and the era of nationalism is very far from coming to an end. In 1900 there were just over 50 formally sovereign states (without counting statelets), 19 of which were in Europe. In 1960 there were over 100 such states. And there are double that number today.

How and why have states proliferated during the last 150 years? The debate over whether the state is growing or shrinking rages on, fuelled by the difficulty in defining the state. The new states were formed either by secession – breaking away violently or peacefully from a wider unit (eg former British colonies, Norway from Denmark, Slovenia from Yugoslavia) – or by unification imposed from above, as was the case with Italy and Germany in the second half of the nineteenth century. Secession is much more common, absorption is rare.

Each new state, however small, maintains all the paraphernalia of sovereignty largely established in the nineteenth century: passports, borders, armies, uniformed police, currencies, national anthems, national days, and central banks – later even airlines, national football teams, and entrants in the Eurovision Song Contest or the Miss World competition.

Though some European states have adopted a single currency and abolished border controls, all of them celebrate a 'national' culture, have at least one or more national television channels that give priority to national news, and impart their national history in schools where children are taught to be proud of their country, even though most would agree that there is no personal merit in being born in any one particular place. They are given a somewhat embellished account of the birth and development of their nation.

The litany is fairly similar – a literary genre – poised between lachrymose, self-pitying victimhood and vainglorious accounts of heroic deeds. 'We', it says, have been around for centuries, or even more (1066 in Britain;

966 in Poland; since Romulus and Remus in Italy; since Plato and Aristotle in Greece). We have written glorious pages of history and they would have been even more glorious had it not been for the dastardly acts of our oppressors. Eventually we achieved our freedom, our independence, our happiness, and we, who are unlike everyone else (for we are Croats and not Slovenians, Italians and not Austrians, French and not Germans, Ukrainians and not Russians, etc.), can finally be like everyone else: members and possessors of a country, a nation, defenders of a remarkable literature, a major culture, a beautiful language, and a unique landscape.

We tend to think that a state is defined by its borders, but the borders and boundaries of most of today's sovereign states are a relatively recent creation. This is as true in Europe as it is across the globe. An Italian state, in any shape or form, has only existed since 1861, but Venice and its region were not incorporated into Italy until 1866 and its capital, Rome, only in 1870; the current borders with Austria have been extant only since 1919. Although an island, the present boundaries of Great Britain are even more recent. In 1707 England and Scotland united, and Ireland became part of the United Kingdom in 1801, but the boundaries changed again in 1922 when the Irish Free State came into being, ahead of the establishment of the Republic of Ireland in 1949.

History has dealt with borders and populations in a cavalier way and determined that a place could be part of a state for reasons that had nothing at all to do with national feelings – a relatively simple task since in most cases such feelings did not exist. Had Immanuel Kant been born in 1946 in Kaliningrad rather than in 1724 in Königsberg (as it then was), he might have been a Russian philosopher rather than a German one. Had Arthur Schopenhauer been born in Polish Gdansk in 1946 rather than in German Danzig – as it was when he was born there in 1788 – he would have been Polish. The inhabitants of Corsica are now French, whether they like it or not (and some still don't), only because France acquired it in 1770. Had this not happened, Napoleon (born in 1769) would not have made history. The people of Nice are French today because it was handed over by Piedmont to the French in 1860. Had that not happened, its inhabitants would have felt as Italian as those of Genoa and would have supported Italy's national football team and not that of France. The city of St Louis in Senegal is an older French city than Lille, since St Louis became French in 1659 while Lille was annexed to France by Louis XIV

*Emperor Napoleon I in Coronation Robes, 2 December
1804*, François Gérard (workshop of), 1805–1815.
Rijksmuseum, Amsterdam.

in 1668. Lorraine became French only because Louis XV married Maria Leszczyńska, the daughter of the Duke of Lorraine. Yet for much of the twentieth century the children of Lorraine were taught in French schools that they were descendants of '*nos ancêtres les Gaulois*' ('our ancestors the Gauls'). Even this belief that the Gauls were the ancestors of the modern French came about only in the nineteenth century.

French boundaries may have been unstable but they look as solid as rock when compared to those of Poland. The Polish state celebrated its 'thousand-year history' in 1966. Yet its borders have expanded and shrunk constantly. In 1634 'Poland' was very large (it included Lithuania as well as bits of Moldavia and Prussia). Then Poland began to shrink and, after the Second World War, it 'shifted' to the West as it acquired former 'German' territory and lost some to the Soviet Union on its eastern flank.

Thus each nation state builds its own special 'national' history, however chequered. Montenegro (or, in Slavonic, *Crna Gora*, 'Black Mountain'; Montenegro is the Venetian name) is one of the 'newest' European states, but it had been sovereign before the First World War (though its tiny borders changed over time), having successfully resisted complete subordination to Ottoman rule. It was amalgamated into Yugoslavia in 1919, and regained its independence in 2006 when it seceded from what was left of Yugoslavia (ie from Serbia). It acquired its own constitution, but not its own currency, having decided to use the euro even though it was not actually in the European Union. It had a diplomatic corps and its own armed forces but not its own language since everyone speaks Serbo-Croat. Local nationalists nevertheless insisted that their version of Serbian should be called Montenegrin, an assertion of identity that older states such as Belgium, Switzerland, and the USA have refrained from: no one speaks Belgian, Swiss or American, but Montenegrins, apparently, speak Montenegrin. The country also has a new national anthem, '*Oj, svijetla majska zoro*' ('Oh, Bright Dawn of May'), based on a nineteenth-century folk tune with words that have been changed to fit the prevailing politics. Montenegro has fewer than 700,000 inhabitants – fewer than Birmingham in England or Tucson in Arizona, but more than at least 20 other sovereign states (including EU members such as Malta and Luxembourg). Formally speaking, Montenegro is as 'sovereign' as the United States, but in practice sovereignty is limited by the power of other countries. Its inhabitants can affirm their pride in their country, but this is not much different from the inhabitants of Cornwall or Lombardy being proud to be Cornish or Lombard, even though neither has ever been a sovereign state.

Our new brave globalised world is thus also a world of 'them and us', of states, large and small (mainly small), trying to make their presence manifest, taking offence, being proud, and defending, sometimes hypocritically, the sanctity of their borders against secessionist claims by even smaller 'nations' simmering within and aspiring to get out. This is the situation Georgia faces with the recalcitrant inhabitants of South Ossetia and Abkhazia who do not feel they share the same ancestry as those Georgian nationalists who, in a remarkable flight of imagination, trace theirs to the Hittites in 1600 BC. Ukrainian nationalism stands on similarly shaky foundations: Ukrainian nationalist historians, such as the popular Yurii Kanyhin, strongly endorsed by the first president of Ukraine (and former communist), Leonid Kravchuk (1991–94), even claimed that Ukrainians are mentioned in the Bible and are descended from Noah. On obtaining its independence, even Uzbekistan, a former Soviet republic, rewrote its history books making Timur (Tamerlane in the West), once regarded as a cruel tyrant, the founding hero of the country. His equestrian statue now graces the spot where Karl Marx's statue once stood.

The idea of a nation is constructed out of a mish-mash of myth, legend, history, and wishful thinking. The inhabitants of those self-governing units that prevailed before 1800 were seldom self-conscious members of a nation, but were held together by a sovereign, or a religion or a language, or by force of arms or the self-interest of the local elites, or because it was in the interest of foreign powers to let them survive. Central Europe, in particular, was a complex conglomeration of such states and statelets.

Within the boundaries of what today we call Italy, there were at the time of the French Revolution almost 20 such self-governing units. By 1870 all these states and statelets had been amalgamated into a single state: Italy, a state with a history it claimed to be ancient and a language, Italian, only a minority of its inhabitants could speak or spoke habitually. This state joined a system of European states that turned out to be generally stable on its western flank but unstable on the eastern one (the main exceptions to the rule of western stability after 1880 were the birth of the Republic of Ireland in 1949 and the formalisation of Norwegian and Icelandic independence).

Italy divided into its states with their
subdivisions, 1786.

The extraordinary proliferation of states between 1880 and 2020 is almost entirely due to the collapse of the three great empires of the nineteenth century as a consequence of the First World War: the vast Ottoman Empire, the Tsarist Empire, and the Austro-Hungarian Empire.

In the course of the nineteenth century the Ottoman Empire 'lost' Albania, Macedonia, Greece, Crete and Cyprus, Wallachia and Moldavia, Bulgaria, and most of present-day Serbia, as well as Bosnia and Herzegovina. Further 'Balkanisation' occurred after 1918 with the fall of the Austro-Hungarian Empire, but was limited by the creation of Yugoslavia in 1945. Finally, the disintegration of Yugoslavia in the 1990s led to further multiplication of states.

While the Ottoman Empire continued to shrink, the Tsarist Empire, whose formal birth had occurred in 1721, survived thanks to the Soviet Union (though it lost Poland and Finland as well as the Baltic states reoccupied during the Second World War). The fall of communism, however, brought about an entirely new situation. Countries whose claims to nationhood had been more linguistic and cultural than political had to rapidly develop a brand of nationalism relevant to their newly acquired statehood, won without a significant struggle of national liberation. Russia, much reduced in size, appeared to belong exclusively to Russians. Yet, far from being mono-ethnic, the new Russian Federation is home to a considerable variety of ethnic groups, and, as in the Tsarist Empire, numerous languages (24 are officially recognised).

The Austrian Empire, after its defeat by Germany in 1866, reconstituted itself by sharing the task of governing what was an increasingly complex multi-national state with Hungary. The Austro-Hungarian Empire was born in 1867, to the dismay of the Croat and Slovakian minorities: within every majority there is always a minority that, once its minority status is enshrined formally, will struggle to get out.

Of the 20 states that existed in Europe in 1880, only nine had existed in the eighteenth century and only seven of these survived into the twenty-first century. But continuity had hardly been the norm even in apparently long-lasting states.

Even in northern Europe the situation was far from static. Denmark 'lost' Norway in 1814 (to the Swedish Crown) and the provinces of Schleswig and Holstein to Prussia in 1864. Iceland obtained autonomy from Denmark in 1874 but became independent only in 1944. Two new major states were created in the course of the nineteenth century: Italy in

1861 and Germany in 1871. Belgium and Greece had been created in 1830, though Greece in the 1830s was far smaller than it is now and much of its present-day territory still lay in the Ottoman Empire.

There were, of course, plenty of 'nations' in nineteenth-century Europe without a sovereign state and many still exist, such as the Welsh, the Flemish, the Catalonian, the Breton, the Corsican, and the Basque. Thus, contrary to the terminology that contrasts the Old World – Europe – to the New (the Americas), many of the states that existed in Europe in 1880 were no older than those of North or Latin America. This fragmentation is not new. Since time immemorial, no single state or conqueror has been able to unify Europe or even to build a large and stable empire such as China, which survived for at least 2,000 years, or the Mughal in India for at least 200 years.

European fragmentation, already pronounced in the nineteenth century, reached new heights in early twenty-first century Europe. By 2020 there were, in Europe, 42 states if we include Turkey (but not statelets such as Andorra, Monaco and San Marino) and all the former Russian republics east of Turkey (thus excluding Armenia, Georgia, and Azerbaijan, which, however, are members of the Council of Europe – adding them would simply strengthen the point about fragmentation). The increase in European states since 1980 – when there were 'only' 30 – was entirely due to the end of communism, as the Soviet Union and Yugoslavia broke up and the Czech Republic and Slovakia separated. There was only one merger: the DDR was (re-)united with the Federal Republic of Germany. No-one expects any new mergers, while further secessions or separation (Belgium, Scotland, Catalonia) are possible.

Most of the nearly 200 states that are members of the United Nations today have a recent history. State formation coincides with the recent history of globalised capitalism. The economic imperative of the state managing the economy was the key mechanism that favoured the growth of states. Capitalism is often seen as trying to straddle the world, but this is an abstract notion. In reality each variety of capitalism must be nurtured by a state and shaped according to local conditions. There is no single path. Strong states have helped the development of capitalism. Weak states have faced problems industrialising. States that are not effective states, states that became states recently – or that have been subjected by other states – fare worst of all. Our globalised world thus remains a world system of states which call themselves 'nations' (after all we talk of the United Nations – the term United States having already been taken). Nationalists celebrated and continue to celebrate the transformation of the nation into a sovereign state, the idea being that the state embodied the people, something quite different from the states of old, embodied in a sovereign. Friedrich Nietzsche saw this clearly in the 1880s when, in *Thus Spoke Zarathrustra*, he exclaimed:

> The state? What is that? Well then! Now open your ears, for now I shall speak to you of the death of peoples. The state is the coldest of all cold monsters. Coldly it lies, too; and this lie creeps from its mouth: 'I, the state, am the people.'

This 'coldest of all cold monsters', straddling the world, is far from disappearing in spite of all the talk of globalisation and internationalism. Today the forces of nationalism are stronger than those of cosmopolitanism, although it is after all a very ancient idea. Diogenes, asked where he came from, is reported, by a Greek biographer writing in the first half of the third century, to have said: 'I am a citizen of the world' (*kosmopolitês*). And yet politics is still overwhelmingly a national politics. Citizens may not trust politicians but they trust their own more than those of other countries. They expect their governments to protect their own interests above those of peoples who come from outside, those who have the 'wrong' nationality. People still live in their nation as if they were in a village, their hearts fluttering at the sight of their own flag.

A young climate protester in Turin, 2020.

MEET THE ZOOMER GENERATION

Matthew Goodwin

To understand people, Napoleon once said, you have to know what was happening in the world when they were 20 years old. For today's early twenty-somethings – known as 'zoomers', so-named as the first generation that, born between the mid-1990s and the late 2000s, has never known anything other than a world with the internet – the world is a highly unstable, volatile and threatening place. Take my university students who graduate this summer as an example. They have already lived through not one but two financial crises, considerable political turbulence and now, in their most formative years, a major global pandemic.

Amid the extreme turbulence of 2020 it has become almost a cliché to quote Lenin's observation that there are decades where nothing happens and weeks when decades happen. The sheer chaos and volatility also recall the more amusing observation that when future historians claim to be experts in the year 2020, they will have to state which quarter of this year they have specialised in. Both quotes come to mind when thinking through the long list of formative experiences that zoomers have witnessed in an incredibly short period of time – the Great Recession, a sovereign debt crisis in Europe, austerity, Islamist and far-right terrorism, a refugee crisis, a discussion about Greece possibly leaving the European Union and then the United Kingdom actually doing it, the shock of Donald Trump's victory, the rise of populists in many democracies, the sharp decline of more moderate social democratic parties but also the emergence of a more radical Green and radical left politics that is reflected in Greta Thunberg, Jeremy Corbyn and Alexandria Ocasio-Cortez. This is a generation raised on polarisation, fragmentation and challenges.

Zoomers might be the first generation to have lived their entire lives online, and the most racially and ethnically diverse generation in history, but they will also be defined more than most by coming of age and trying to get ahead in a post-pandemic world. As we know from psychology, seismic 'shocks' like pandemics tend to produce feelings of uncertainty and fear, stoke perceptions of threat and alter the calculations that people make about risks and rewards. Attempting to enter the labour market during moments of crisis leaves deep scars.

There are three salient effects that we should be aware of: life-cycle effects that concern differences between people based on their point in the life cycle (eg becoming more conservative as we age); period effects that follow a specific event that impacts on entire populations at the same time (eg the effects of living through the Second World War); and cohort effects, which take place when these shocks have different effects on different generations (eg a particular crisis having a particularly strong impact on a particular generation because of where it is in the life-cycle). It is, for many reasons, too early to know exactly how this crisis will impact on zoomers but that should not stop us from offering a few hypotheses about how it might produce some of these period and cohort effects (one basic problem is a lack of reliable, longitudinal data, and so much of what I say below is drawn from a range of cross-sectional surveys, secondary data and reports).

I have argued that Covid-19 looks set to have four major effects on geopolitics, all of which will also impact on zoomers. First, the crisis is already fundamentally and perhaps permanently transforming the relationship between the citizen and the state. Some argue that while the Wall Street Crash of 1929 represented the failure of financial markets and paved the way for the return of the state, via the New Deal in America and welfare states in Europe, it was then the end of the postwar boom and a period of stagnation in the 1970s that represented the exhaustion of the state and paved the way for the return of the markets, via Thatcherism and Reaganism. Fast-forward to the post-2008 Great Recession and it was time for the markets to overreach and open the door to the state which, combined with the current crisis, now looks set to become much bigger and far more interventionist.

Zoomers in particular have watched the state intervene on not one but two occasions in little more than a decade – propping up financial markets after the Great Recession and then propping up entire societies amid the Great Lockdown. For these reasons, this is a generation that is instinctively sceptical of the argument that markets can 'go it alone' and can be relied upon to work for the common good. After all, this is a generation that really has no memory of the pre-2008 era. All it has known is market failure and economic crises. Zoomers are also coming of age at a time when their leaders and governments are fairly relaxed about a new era of mega debt.

Even before governments became bigger and more interventionist, zoomers were already predisposed to hold pro-government views. In 2018, for example, 70% of zoomers said that 'government should do more to solve problems' while 29% felt 'government is doing too many things that are better left to businesses and individuals'. Compare these views to boomers (split evenly 49% versus 49%) and the even older silent generation (split 39% for government and 60% for individual responsibility). Clearly, these views might evolve over time but so far there is scant evidence that zoomers would relate to Ronald Reagan's argument that 'government is not the solution to our problem – government is the problem'.

Second, there are good reasons to expect this crisis and the surrounding environment to have a profound impact on the values that will drive zoomers in the future. As scholars like Ronald Inglehart have demonstrated, it was the economic security and rapid expansion of higher education in the postwar decades that had a strong impact on the earlier Baby Boomer generation – driving a 'silent revolution' that led to the rise in more lifestyle-oriented and expressive liberal values. Unlike the earlier 'greatest generation', which had come of age amid economic depression and global war, baby boomers did not need to worry about the 'basic needs' of physical and economic security and so were free to move up Abraham Maslow's 'hierarchy of needs', to pursue things like social status, esteem and recognition.

This also had negative effects. As scholars such as Christopher Lasch and Michael Lind argued, the liberal revolution also paved the way for a new global 'meritocratic' elite that was more narcissistic, increasingly global in outlook, and less attached to nation and place. It became increasingly detached, isolated in homogenous networks, and appeared to show little interest in the virtues of community, responsibility and obligation to fellow citizens. Alongside the wider 'liberal drift' in values, this more insular elite provoked a strong backlash. Starting in the 1980s and 1990s, a 'silent counter-revolution' took place as an alliance of blue-collar workers and affluent social conservatives rallied together around a new wave of conservative and national populist movements, from Brexit and Boris Johnson to Sebastian Kurz in Austria and Donald Trump in the

United States. These were quite distinct movements and should not be lumped together but all shared a general desire to uphold the nation state.

Zoomers, however, are moving in a very different direction and look set to deliver a revolution of their own in the years ahead.

Recent research on their values and priorities suggests that across a range of social and identity issues they do not simply look like the more liberal millennials but are, in fact, even more liberal. They are incredibly progressive and pro-government, view rapidly rising rates of racial and ethnic diversity as a good thing and, in America, are less likely to view their country as superior to other nations. They are also notably harder on Trump than millennials – only 22% approve – although they are also less likely to turn out to vote than their older relatives.

This liberal outlook flows from several characteristics that have made zoomers rather unique. They are more likely to have been born and raised by degree-holding, liberal baby boomer and Gen Xer parents. Recently, the Pew Research Center found that whereas nearly half of zoomers were living with parents who held at least a bachelor's degree, only around one in three millennials could say the same. Meanwhile, zoomers have lived through a series of formative experiences that have likely cemented their progressive outlook – the backlash against Trump, the rise of an even more adversarial campus culture, the increased salience of climate change as an issue and, more recently, the protests over George Floyd's death. It seems likely that these formative experiences are encouraging the adoption of a more 'woke' brand of identity liberalism, much in the same way that the civil rights campaign, the sexual revolution and protests against Vietnam proved highly influential for the boomers.

This looks set to open the door to what John Gray has called 'hyper-liberalism'. Focused far more heavily on identity than economics, and less interested in traditional drivers like social class, hyper-liberalism is characterised by a more radical individualism, a strong interest in tackling both present and past 'social injustices', a willingness to repudiate aspects of national culture and tradition that do not conform to this outlook and, more generally, advocates ideas that flow through 'critical race theory' – ideas like 'white privilege', 'intersectionality', 'toxic masculinity' and 'patriarchy'. Many of these, as we have seen in recent months, have moved from the margins to the mainstream and it has often been zoomers who have been their most passionate advocates. The image of a zoomer

Protesters in Portland, Oregon, walk past a mural
with George Floyd's last words, July 2020.

graduate in New York criticising a member of the police for lacking the same level of education is highly symbolic.

It is important not to exaggerate the pace of change, however. For one thing, several reports on zoomers suggest they are more financially risk-averse than other generations. New data in the United Kingdom also suggests that zoomers are a little more conservative than the slightly older millennials (though they still accept many of the central pillars of the liberal drift). For example, one recent study found that zoomers are diverging from millennials by appearing just as right-wing as today's 40-year-olds. This too should be kept in perspective, not least because the Conservative Party in Britain recently only attracted 21% of 18 to 24-year-olds. But such findings do provide reasons to be cautious about the claim that all zoomers are drunk on 'woke' politics. Indeed, even before the crisis a major report by Ipsos-MORI concluded that, contrary to the clichés, zoomers are 'better behaved, more trusting, socially-minded and less materialistic'. They were notably more trusting of others than millennials, more likely to be active in their community, more likely to say they would avoid buying products for political reasons and less likely to feel that things they own say a lot about how well they are doing in life (a finding reflected in work in Brazil, where zoomers were also less oriented around the 'self' than millennials).

It should also be remembered that whereas zoomers are on track to be the most highly-educated generation, they are also on track to be the least experienced; only one in five were working in paid employment in their teenage years in 2018, compared to more than one in four millennials and more than four in ten Gen Xers at the same point in their lives. Zoomers might have higher levels of education but this is not necessarily matched by strong life experiences. Their passionate promotion of more obscure political ideas that circulate on campus might not always resonate with their counterparts who have avoided university, or members of older generations who view such theories as a threat to their established traditions, institutions and ways of life.

Nonetheless, zoomers do look set to not only sustain but accelerate the 'liberal drift'. Ideas that were once pushed by the older baby boomers and which divided society, such as same-sex marriage, enjoy widespread support among zoomers – 84% say this is a good thing or 'doesn't make a difference'. Only 15% oppose it (versus 32% of boomers). Similarly, more than one in three zoomers (in the United States) say they personally know someone who is referred to using gender-neutral pronouns (versus one-in-ten boomers). Meanwhile, when asked whether forms that ask about a person's gender should include options other than 'man' and 'woman', nearly 60% of zoomers say they should – leaving them ten points ahead of millennials, 19 points ahead of Gen Xers, 22 points ahead of boomers and 27 points ahead of the silent generation. Another factor that might come to separate zoomers from their older counterparts is the growing politicisation of business, with corporates today – from Nike to Ben and Jerry's and Uber – being far more willing to take the (liberal) side in the identity wars. As the liberal conservative writer Andrew Sullivan observed: 'We are all on campus now.'

While zoomers might press the case for more radical social change, it also looks likely, in my view at least, that they will simultaneously demand more radical economic change, too. Covid-19, as we know from a string of reports, is leaving those already left behind even further behind. It has hit low-skilled service-sector workers hard and that includes many zoomers. Three months ago, America's Pew Research Center pointed out that half of the oldest zoomers had either lost a job themselves or knew somebody in their own household who had – which was a significantly higher proportion than for millennials, Gen Xers and boomers. Zoomers thus find themselves in a strange position – on the one hand, they are on track to be the most well-educated generation in history but, on the other, they are entering the labour market in the middle of one of the most challenging periods in history.

Unlike millennials, who entered the labour market amid the 'double crisis' of the Great Recession, which was both economic and political, zoomers are now trying to enter the labour market amid a 'triple crisis', which cuts across health, economics and politics. Recent research suggests that it will cast a long shadow. Rather than being a 'great leveller', pandemics tend to lead to a statistically significant increase in the Gini coefficient – a key measure of inequality. Five years after a pandemic hits, working-class and less well-educated citizens are still likely to suffer disproportionately. Recent studies find that more than half of Americans under the age of 45 have lost their jobs, been put on furlough or had their hours reduced.

Furthermore, we know that people entering the labour market during a period of crisis tend to suffer throughout their lives – they tend to remain on lower earnings trajectories for decades to come. Lots of research in countries like the UK makes clear how millennials and zoomers were already lagging behind where older generations were at the same point in the life-cycle – they were more likely to suffer low wage growth, leaving them with similar earnings to cohorts born 15 years earlier, are more likely than their predecessors to work part-time, to work in low-pay jobs, to be less likely to move jobs and so less likely to achieve pay rises, to have lower rates of home ownership, harder commutes, spend more of their incomes on housing and, at least for millennials, to live on disposable incomes no higher than they were for Gen-Xers at the same age.

This appears especially salient in southern Europe where zoomers are coming of age in more impoverished and indebted economies. They have had very different experiences from their counterparts further north. Even before the crisis, millennials and zoomers were grappling with unemployment rates of around 6% in Germany and the Netherlands but 29% in Italy, 31% in Spain and 36% in Greece. Such figures no doubt contributed to *The Economist*'s description of these voters as the 'pyrrhic victors' of globalisation – generations that played by the rules, did what they were supposed to do but today 'have singularly failed to reap the expected benefits'. Thus, one recent study found that younger voters in debtor states are notably more sceptical of the EU than their counterparts in creditor states, while other political scientists show how sharp, sudden crises are often followed by a significant decline in political trust and confidence in democracy, and increased pessimism.

Much of this will heap further pressure on an already fraying intergenerational contract. The slightly older millennials, who recently overtook boomers to become the largest generation in America, according to the 2019 census, were also the first generation on record to say, overall, that they would rather have grown up when their parents were children. Millennials were hit hard by the Great Recession, got back on their feet during the recovery and are now getting hit again by the Great Lockdown. But the far more strained intergenerational contract – anchored in the idea that each generation should expect to be a little more secure and prosperous than the last – looks set to continue under zoomers. This could easily translate into stronger demands for economic reform and redistribution.

It is telling, for example, that the vast majority of zoomers flocked to Jeremy Corbyn in the United Kingdom and are clearly supportive of a more radical economic settlement. But it could also just as easily translate into apathy or alternative modes of participation. Zoomers may conclude that on a whole array of issues – climate change, intergenerational unfairness, economic and racial equality, student debt and more – the established politicians have simply failed. This is also a generation that has grown up looking to voices and figures outside of conventional party politics – to vloggers, YouTubers and social media entrepreneurs that steer clear of legacy media channels but are highly active in alternative forms.

One of the key lessons of the crisis that was sparked more than a decade ago, the Great Recession, is that political churn tends to lie downstream from economic chaos. Had we tried to guess the political effects of the Great Recession amid the collapse of Lehman Brothers then I doubt that we would have been accurate. It was only years later that we were finally able to stand back and make sense of what our future historians will most likely brand the decade of volatility. Similarly, we will have to wait years until we can fully make sense of the effects of the current crisis on zoomers. This period of turbulence, uncertainty and risk could push them to hunker down and seek shelter in apathy. Or, instead, we may be on the cusp of another major liberal revolution as a backlash to the revolts of Brexit, Trump and national populism. If that revolution comes, it looks likely to be driven not just by demands for more radical economic change – long the cry of revolutionaries – but for even more radical cultural and social change, too.

PHILOSOPHIES OF CRISIS

Le jeune malade, Ary Scheffer, 1826.
Rijksmuseum, Amsterdam.

ANCIENT LESSONS FOR MODERN CRISIS

Lawrence Freedman

Life is short, the art long, opportunity fleeting, experiment treacherous, judgment difficult
FIRST APHORISM OF HIPPOCRATES

The first treatise on 'epidemics' is attributed to Hippocrates, the Greek physician who lived 25 centuries ago, invariably described as the 'father of modern medicine'. He gave the word its medical meaning as a disease 'which circulates or propagates in a country'. Historians of medicine have debated whether his description of the 'Cough of Perinthus' is the first of an outbreak of influenza, or was really about diphtheria. It was most likely a reference to a collection of diseases notable for their winter onset and their dynamic quality. Thucydides had already provided his own vivid account of the 'Plague of Athens', that took the life of his hero Pericles and almost his own, killing 25% of Athenians, and coming in waves, returning twice after making its first devastating appearance. Although Thucydides claimed that physicians were helpless in the face of the plague, some accounts credit Hippocrates with curing it by lighting fires to fumigate the air.

Hippocrates also introduced the idea of a 'crisis'. This was central to his theory of how diseases progressed. At some point, often unexpectedly, a decisive moment would come in a patient's battle with a disease. Once this moment passed the result of the battle would be known. The patient would either be dead or recovering. The concept remained influential in the centuries following Hippocrates. Crises continued to be identified by doctors as inflection points that were apt to arrive suddenly with little warning. A common example would be when the sort of fever associated with pneumonia rose to dangerously high levels and then either abated or consumed its victim. There was a natural drama to such moments which is why they often appealed to novelists. Vivid descriptions of attempts to soothe and calm delirious and distressed heroines were mainstays of nineteenth-century fiction, appealing to sentiment and also serving as a metaphor for the thin line separating salvation from disaster. In *Sense and*

Sensibility, Marianne Dashwood recovers; in *Little Women*, Beth March sadly does not.

By this time 'crisis' had migrated into general use, describing any situation in which a decisive change, for better or worse, was imminent. Instead of high fever, the non-medical symptoms were chronic insecurity, compounded by the pressures of time. Irresistible forces hurtled towards immovable objects. A future that had recently been viewed with confidence was now clouded with uncertainty and full of danger. Economic crises came to be associated with financial panics, with runs on banks, or sudden losses of business confidence leading to stock markets crashing. For students of international relations, the continual possibility that independent states, wary of each other and jealous of their interests, might collide made crises a natural way to depict those tense confrontations which could end with either a lurch into war or a reversion to peace.

By definition, a crisis was not a hopeless condition. Salvation was possible. Some unexpected development could swing the situation back to safety. An ingenious plan might be devised to retrieve the situation. During the Cold War, when war was likely to lead to a nuclear catastrophe, it was realised that it was both necessary and possible to prepare for crises in advance so that not too much was left to chance. Crisis management was raised to the level of a vital strategic art, requiring a pragmatic combination of resolve and flexibility. Crises tested a leader's character in a way now associated with President John Kennedy during the 1962 Cuban Missile Crisis. This episode more than any other forged our image of a true crisis, with stressed governments, emergency meetings, exceptional measures, regular news bulletins, anxious waits, and time running out as the decisive moment approaches. It was also a crisis that ended without calamity. So long as it does not break in the wrong direction, a crisis can therefore be a time for creativity and determined, innovative action. At times of crisis we do not expect governments just to 'wait and see'. We expect action. We are uncomfortable with the idea that some situations are beyond our control.

The great Covid-19 pandemic appears as a crisis in both the medical and non-medical senses. It is about a disease which hits individuals almost along Hippocratic lines, with the critical day coming after about a week, when the patient's condition either deteriorates or improves. Boris Johnson conveyed this meaning when he recalled the moment when he was in intensive care at St Thomas's Hospital with Covid-19 and 'it could

Soviet cargo ship, the Fizik Kurchatov, carrying
missiles, leaves Cuba en route for Russia during
the Cuban missile crisis, 1962.

have gone either way'. The pandemic's own dynamic is a function of the numerous individual cases, with permutations of symptoms, infectivity, resistance and severity. The coronavirus can lurk around for days and weeks before suddenly growing quickly and getting a grip on a population. In just over two months it moved from being observed in the Chinese city of Wuhan to almost overwhelming the health care systems of Europe and North America. Each separate health crisis became a political crisis, as governments scrambled around to find ways to suppress the virus's inexorable, exponential growth, desperate to prevent the situation getting away from them.

All this required an aggravated form of crisis decision-making. All decision-making is conducted by fallible human beings working in flawed organisations with inadequate information. Crises are extreme cases, when these fallibilities, flaws and inadequacies are more on display than usual. Walter Bagehot, in his *The English Constitution* of 1867, spoke of how a 'great crisis' required the 'pilot of the calm' being replaced by 'the pilot of the storm'. More 'daemonic' qualities would be needed of a sort that could be harmful in normal times – 'the imperious will, the rapid energy, the eager nature'. With a crisis the time pressures are intense, with incessant demands for quick decisions that have to be made on the basis of patchy evidence, still subject to interpretation, and cursory evaluations of alternative options. The decisions have to be made in a media spotlight, propelled forward by occasional injections of panic, and taken despite fatigue. Yet the decisions must also be presented with a show of calmness approaching sanguinity so as not to spread alarm. Almost inevitably they end up focusing on symptoms more than causes, short-term impact more than long-term consequences.

And yet, even with all the stresses and strains, crisis decision-making can also be liberating. The imperatives of the moment drive the process. Policies that were previously unthinkable become unavoidable. No one dares restrict vital spending. Bureaucracies are galvanised into action. So long as the public appreciates the gravity of the situation, and something potentially effective is being done, it will be tolerant and supportive. Even though aware of past mistakes – and if there had been none, surely there would now be no crisis – the public also wants to see the situation brought under control and a return to relative tranquillity. And in this respect Covid-19 provides a spectacular example of crisis decision-making: barely three months after the first symptomatic cases were identified, a collection of governments, varying in so many respects, many normally cautious and risk-averse, effectively shut down their societies and economies.

All crises end with a reckoning as the costs are counted and the bills reach the Treasury. In this case the costs cannot be set so much against any tangible gains but instead against the even greater losses averted. More seriously they are still being accumulated. Although in May, governments began to take the first tentative steps to ease the stringent restrictions imposed in March, caution and risk aversion is now back in play. They might look forward to a day when the great pandemic could be officially declared over, when the coronavirus will have run its contagious course, when vaccinated people will gather and greet, travel and work, when economies will move back into a high gear, and investors find sufficient optimism to start placing bets on new ventures. But they are not there yet.

The trauma of the first half of 2020 will leave an indelible mark, but it is only the first of a number of stages. We cannot be sure what will come next. In some countries the virus may be down but it is certainly not out. The virus's reproduction rate may have been successfully suppressed to below 1, permitting experiments with normality, but it would be something of a stretch to describe the situation as being under control. Treatments are still being explored. Only mass immunisation will provide a sure relief, and that may well not arrive until 2021. It could all come back again.

Hippocrates distinguished between perfect and imperfect crises. With a 'perfect' crisis the sick person would either die or recover completely. It was known to be perfect when the symptoms of recovery were favourable, clear, secure and trustworthy. With an 'imperfect' crisis the recovery was incomplete and there was the possibility of the disease recurring in the future. Hippocrates linked this question of perfection and imperfection to his concept of a critical day, a fixed time after an illness was contracted. A crisis on this day was likely to be perfect. On other days it would be imperfect. Even if the patient emerged in an improved condition there was the possibility of a relapse into an even more dangerous condition. In this respect, the great pandemic of 2020 is an imperfect crisis.

One of the most famous descriptions of an imperfect crisis in international relations is E H Carr's *The Twenty Years' Crisis*, published in 1939.

Carr's book was about the interplay between utopianism, which required that the world be made to fit to an imagined ideal, and realism, which took the world as it was and made the best of it. Carr blamed utopianism's refusal to come to terms with questions of power and interest for another war starting some two decades after the previous one ended. Instead of resolving the question of war, the effort set in motion in 1919 to create a harmonious world without war had led to one crisis after another. To help make his point, Carr quoted a 1938 comment from former British foreign secretary Anthony Eden: 'It is utterly futile to imagine that we are involved in a European crisis which may pass as it has come. We are involved in a crisis of humanity all the world over. We are living in one of those great periods of history which are awe inspiring in their responsibilities and in their consequences. Stupendous forces are loose, hurricane forces.'

In an imperfect crisis the period up to the first critical point results in an unsatisfactory, indecisive outcome and may not lead to recovery, at least not until another critical moment is reached and possibly not even then. Carr described his book as an attempt to 'navigate…relatively uncharted waters' and this is what we need to do with the pandemic. This goes beyond the observation that it is not yet over, so it should be viewed as a 'marathon and not a sprint'. It requires a different sort of mental picture of where we are and what might be coming.

The first picture was of single curves. These curves represented for individual countries the numbers of daily cases, hospital admissions and fatalities rising and falling. Peaks were reached, usually quite quickly, and then there was a decline, usually more slowly. Governments described the key aim as one of 'flattening the curve' to prevent their health services being overwhelmed. Because some curves were flatter than others this encouraged a natural search for explanations as to why this might be so. In the UK, which had one of the more mountainous curves, there developed a standard form of comparison, common on social media, noting that in other countries, with curves more like gentle hills, particular interventions were made (say effective testing and contact tracing, early lockdown, or screening and quarantining). The implication was that if only the UK had adopted this intervention in a timely fashion then its curve would look a lot flatter. On Twitter, correlation is king and causation languishes in exile.

It is not, however, the case that absent any interventions all countries would have had the same experience so that all curves would have looked the same. The coronavirus did not affect all countries in the same way. It was capricious. It hit Brazil but not Venezuela, devastated Tehran but largely left Baghdad alone. A number of factors influenced these curves from the start. A young population certainly helped. So did geographical isolation, between countries and within them. Fewer travellers meant less transmission. Luck also made a difference. Thus one part of the explanation for the dire numbers in the UK, in addition to policy errors and inadequate testing, was the dominant role of London, the largest city in Western Europe, deeply connected to the rest of the world, through a range of networks. Cities tend to high population densities, constant mobility, with areas of relative deprivation, all of which make them susceptible to high rates of infection. Another was the misfortune in having people taking their half-term breaks in Spain and Italy at just the wrong time, seeding infections across the country. A number of possible explanations might be advanced for Germany's relative success in keeping down the death toll: Berlin is half the size of those other cities, but it was also closed down before the others. There was an extensive testing programme, but the virus also appeared to have entered Germany through a younger demographic.

When it comes to South Korea the best explanation of its ability to get an early grip on what looked like a dangerous outbreak was the fact that not only was it linked to a religious cult, but an early realisation that it was both possible to quarantine this group and isolate it from the capital Seoul.

The curve left us fixated on a single peak. But we have an alternative metaphor with waves, inherently dynamic and with one always followed by another. The epidemiological models with which we entered this crisis show waves. Not just a single wave, rising to its crest and then subsiding, but a series, and with the awkward possibility that the more the first wave has been suppressed the bigger the waves to come. The models assumed that any given population would be equally susceptible to the coronavirus, taking account of the much more severe impact on the elderly. In this respect if, whether by good luck or good management, infections were kept down in the first wave then the population would be left more vulnerable to a second wave simply because there would be less immunity. It was the case, for example, with the Spanish Flu that the second and third waves were worse than the first. The experts in virology and public health keep on warning that if we do not stay alert and maintain a

1 Clemenceau, Wilson and Lloyd George Leav-
Palace of Versailles After Signing Peace Treaty.

Georges Clemenceau, Woodrow Wilson and
David Lloyd George leaving the Palace of
Versailles after signing the peace treaty, 1919.

degree of social distancing then later in the year, perhaps this time mingled with seasonal flu, the coronavirus will come back with even greater force.

There were therefore natural worries as restrictions were eased that the first wave was not yet over and that too quick a return to 'normality' would simply invite further outbreaks, undoing whatever good might have been achieved with the early stringency. Governments were criticised for failing to alert their people until it was almost too late about the consequences of the onward transmission of the coronavirus from China to their countries. They must now alert people to the possibility of it making a depressing return and dampening down optimism that the worst is behind us and that the position from now on will only improve.

Governments surprised themselves with what they asked of their people, and how well they complied. But can they be sure of the same response if they have to ask again? Just as the first wave appeared in a variety of forms, this is also likely to be the case with the second. How individual countries will fare will depend on permutations of the (possibly changing) properties of the virus, demography and geography, luck and policy. Sweden, for example, while requiring some social distancing, chose to endure a tougher first wave than their neighbours in the belief that mass infection would confer future immunity. For the moment the first wave has proved to be tougher than expected without there yet being grounds for confidence that a sufficiently large proportion of the population has become immune to limit future transmission. It is certainly not yet a 'herd'. A number of American states decided that the economic costs of lockdown were too great and that those that might die as a result of a looser regime are collateral damage, and possibly not greater in number than those for whom a severe economic recession may yet prove fatal. A number of those states are now showing significant numbers of new cases.

Some, for example New Zealand, that not only locked down early but also benefit from their isolation, expect that their advantage will enable them to react quickly to any early infections and so keep them down. It may be that those populations coming out of a bad experience will be more vigilant in the future and stay wary of crowds and close contacts. Those that got off comparatively lightly may be more relaxed and ready to take risks. And then of course the optimists hope that a vaccine can be developed quickly. So instead of the neat, regular sine wave of the models, Covid-19's future appearances might involve steep gradients, sharp spikes, occasional bumps, slight perturbations or nothing at all. This is why this is an imperfect crisis. A peak was reached and recovery began but it was less than complete and the disease has not been eliminated and may return with greater ferocity although possibly less. But it is also an imperfect crisis for another reason. The health crisis has triggered an economic crisis that will be longer lasting and even more deadly and disruptive in its effects. This will have its own dynamic that countries will address in distinctive ways, although they will benefit from international cooperation. The health and economic crises will continue to influence each other.

The economic crisis has made itself felt through its own curves, with debts and unemployment moving sharply up as economic growth and investment move sharply down. These are not so much curves as steep cliffs, and despite early talk of bouncing back in a 'v-shape', until there is confidence in a sustainable health recovery there is likely to be only a modest economic recovery. If more severe outbreaks of Covid-19 cases are on the way then countries already heavily indebted may find it diffi-cult to operate at the same level of resources. Or take the dog that has yet to bark in this crisis or is only starting to be heard. Most pandemics find their way to the developing world where they cause the greatest carnage. It is not the case that the countries of the southern hemisphere have escaped completely – Latin America is emerging as a major centre of the epidemic – but most have yet to be hit to the extent that would have been predicted from past experiences. This may well be the result of their youthful populations. One of the most important questions for the rest of the year is how much this continues to be the case. But developing coun-tries are already suffering economically, both from their own precaution-ary lockdowns and the recession enveloping the developing world. Will their populations be so well placed to withstand the coronavirus in the future if it has been weakened by poverty and food shortages? Moreover economic shocks are generally bad for health. Whatever the virus gets up to, those people who are poorer, hungrier and stressed will become vul-nerable to a range of ailments.

And then there is going to be a third crisis, a consequence of the insta-bility caused by the health and economic crises. Within and between countries there are the symptoms of political crisis. Governments see their performance scrutinised and will be challenged over poor decisions. Electorates may veer away from relief and resilience to a more explosive mix of anxiety and anger. Within the EU solidarity will be tested. Relations between China and the US, already poor, have been aggravated. If governments start falling and conflicts are aggravated then we are in for an even worse time. At the same time political crises should also be amenable to leadership and innovative thinking. The political crisis has yet to reach its fever point, and how that is resolved will be the most critical for the future. So long as it is survived then it should be possible to do a better job on the health and economic crises. With imperfect crises there is no prospect of early salvation. But nor do we need to consign ourselves to fate as if it has all become too much.

Yu the Great, Southern Song dynasty (1127–1279), Ma Lin.
Collection of the National Palace Museum, Taipei.

LEARNING FROM ASIAN PHILOSOPHIES
OF REBIRTH

Jessica Frazier

I
n the spring of 1931, central China emerged from a two-year drought and a particularly harsh winter into a season of unrelenting rain. High on the Tibetan plateau, the ice and snow began to melt and flow inexorably over drought-hardened earth towards the Yangtze valley below – one of the world's most densely populated regions. Multiple cyclones hit during the summer months. By August the vast heartlands of China were scoured clean by floods unlike any on record. Cholera outbreaks followed, decimating the homeless starving population. This was one of history's most deadly disasters – approximately 500,000 people were killed in the flood itself, and something like three million more by its after-effects.

From the earthquakes and tsunamis of Japan, to the epidemics that ravage India regularly, Asia is particularly prone to natural crisis. Indeed, the sense that we live in a volatile cosmos informs the history of the world. Add in the influence of rebellions, revolutions, and regime change, and we find that every culture's literature has a template for dealing with crisis. Europe's narrative trope of the 'hero' is often that of a well-armed monster-hunter whose main purpose is to conquer brief eruptions of chaos. Theseus and Heracles, Arthur's knights and Marvel's superheroes kill monsters, fight invaders, and then their quest is done. Crisis is dealt with by renewing the system as quickly as possible. In Asian literatures we tend to see narratives about what it means for a society to be transformed by crisis. Stories tell of technologically-adept Chinese emperors, animist spirit-negotiators, and yogic deep-dives into destruction itself. Instead of simply asking how we can return to 'normal', these philosophies ask: when crisis threatens, how can we survive, transform our societies, and improve them?

Chinese Floods: the science-emperor restores order

Drainage from the world's highest mountain range, the Himalayas, into the world's largest ocean, the Pacific, leads to vast amounts of water moving across a huge area. Northern China and Mongolia's deserts nearby mean that the rivers are regularly silted up by fine sediments. The Yangtze, the Yellow River, Haui and others are a permanent threat of disaster in China's history. One scholar estimated that more than 1,500 floods of the Yellow River have taken place since the middle of the first millennium BC. Sabotaging dams, reservoirs and canals became a major mode of Chinese warfare, and today the Yangtze's Three Gorges Dam remains not only China's, but the world's largest hydro-electric power station.

The 'hydraulic empire' theorists of the twentieth century hypothesise that water – the control of, access to, and protection from – was the basis from which humanity's first great civilisations emerged. In his 1957 book, *Oriental Despotism*, Karl August Wittfogel drew on the communist intellectual Ji Chaoding's history of irrigation to argue that just as the Nile produced Egypt, the Indus produced India, and the Tigris-Euphrates gave rise to Mesopotamia, so China was rooted in 'hydraulic power' which dealt with flooding. The five ancient 'Classics' give some support to this thesis. In the *Sh j ng* or 'Classic of History', one of the founding stories of Chinese culture tells of the devastating Gun Yu flood that, according to myth, lasted two generations. At the beginning of the great flood the Emperor Yao, appointer of the seasons, laments:

> See! The Floods assail the heavens! …destructive in their overflow are the waters of the inundation. In their vast extent they embrace the hills and overtop the great heights, threatening the heavens with their floods, so that the lower people groan and murmur: Is there a capable man to whom I can assign the correction of this calamity?

The 'capable man' turned out to be a humble engineer called Gun Yu. He became famous in myth as the man who 'tamed the waters,' not through some feat of supernatural power but as a work of co-operative technological planning. Over 13 years travelling the country, Gun Yu introduced an innovative project of digging.

Hydrological technology today remains one of the most important features of Chinese landscape; it ensures that the whole vast landmass is habitable as a single safe region capable of civilisation. Thus Yu the great, the wise filial inheritor of a civil project to which he devoted his life, became the model for heroes who conquer crisis through the (unglamorous but realistic) powers of intelligence and hard work. Confucius said of him, 'I can find no flaw in the character of Yu…He lived in a low, mean house, but expended all his strength on the ditches and water channels. I can find nothing like a flaw in Yu.'

Yu is the epitome of governance in the classical Chinese worldview, where the good leader is portrayed as a variant of the Taoist sage. Like the character of Cook Ding in *The Zhuangzi* who could butcher an ox as smoothly as if it was butter, because he was so utterly aware of every aspect of the organism, the good leader learns the system through dedicated study and makes exactly the right, prudent adjustments. In response, the people are supposed to follow his orders, as the *Tao Te Ching* (49) makes clear: 'The people all keep their eyes and ears directed to him, and he deals with them all as his children.'

But the people's obedience was not intended to be carried out in blind trust. Corrupt leadership was heavily censured in the Taoist literature and humble conduct exalted: 'The sage should work without claim to ownership or reward, putting his own person last, personal and private goals…When the work is done, and one's name is becoming distinguished, to withdraw into obscurity is the way of Heaven.' Thus China's history of crisis points to a fragile bond of trust that plays under the surface between the people and their government. Their science-emperor leads his people in resolving crisis with deft efficiency, and in doing so gives the people new tools gained from solving the problem, so Yu's heroic taming of the flood directly contributed to irrigation and a new phase of agricultural civilisation. The leader, who acts without ulterior motives, must also win the confidence of his people and in doing so he helps society fulfil its very essence as a collective agency.

Spirit Lessons: tsunamis and earthquakes of coastal Asia
On the white crescent beaches of Southern Thailand, on the morning of 26 December 2004, fishermen and dawn bathers did not know that a vast pulse of water was at that moment travelling towards them at hundreds of miles per hour. It had been pushed upward by a 'megathrust' from the Indian Ocean's seabed in one of the world's largest earthquakes – smaller

quakes were triggered as far as Alaska. Travelling as an undetected low swell of water in its deep-water form, it destroyed the nearby Indonesian area of Banda Aceh, then one arm sped west to Sri Lanka while the north-east arc of the tsunami deflected around the tip of Sumatra and slowed into the shallow, sparkling waters of the Andaman Ocean. Slower but higher, these tsunami waves crashed into the communities of Khao Lak, Koh Jum, Koh Phi Phi, Phang Nga: whole villages – homes, families, schools and their students – floated out to sea.

A 'divine passions' conception of nature thrives in many Pacific cultures and on the South-East Asian coasts and archipelagos. Demons and deities, storm gods, Balinese volcanic gods, Thai angry sea goddesses and cave spirits are all associated with crises that come from the earth: volcanoes, earthquakes and tsunamis. Indonesia's pearl necklace of islands – the world's largest archipelago – is the product of a fault line that has produced innumerable volcanoes and a near-constant subtle patter of earthquakes. Seasonal monsoons and typhoons pose a significant threat.

The animist cultures of coastal Asia understand these disasters as invisible forces. They are the effect of living in a busy, tempestuous community of spirits. A tsunami is Laboon to the Moken tribe of the Andaman coast, a cleansing weapon of the ancestors sent to punish and eradicate misdeeds. On one beach tsunamis are prevented by offering fertility symbols to Phra Nang, the Sea Goddess. She is a volatile neighbour, but since she cannot be evicted one must make amends when she is angry. The gods are rarely evil, but they are devastatingly destructive and wholly immune to resistance. Animist conceptions of crisis can seem cruel because they acknowledge that it emanates from forces beyond our control. But they are also eminently passionate, interactive, and oddly humane in that they are generally seen as the result of some injury that we ourselves have done to a spirit or god. The response should be the same as when a friend or family member expresses anger. We need to assess our behaviour, reflect on what we have done to upset them, apologise and declare our intention to change things…then alter our behaviour accordingly.

So in 2005 when the communities of the Andaman coast survived the tsunami, yes, they built new tsunami warning systems, escape routes, and some homes on higher ground. But away from the news-cameras, many felt that the right way to protect the community was to apologise to the sea by way of fishing the ocean waters less exhaustively and moderating the

Phra Nang cave shrine, Krabi, Thailand 2012.

polluting effects of mass tourism. Communal debates still exist between those who ignore these concerns, and those who respect them. Balinese Hindu society interpreted the Bali bombings of 2002 as a manifestation of the wrath of the gods, and the aftermath included reflection on how to heal the land of its commercialisation and restore endangered cultural traditions. One outcome was new powers of local governance.

Animist communities can teach people to assess their actions and cultivate greater flexibility in our behaviour. Rather than merely restoring order, the cultural goal is to remain sensitive to possible causes of crisis and be nimble in behaviour. This too is the essence of a society (which we too often conflate with 'tradition') – to adapt to environmental change, remaining self-reflective, dynamic, able to mobilise and to continually envisage new ways to distribute sources of shared flourishing.

Indian Dharma-Kings and Queens

At the confluence of the Ganges and Yamuna rivers in 1899, pilgrims at the vast religious gathering of the Kumbh Mela began to fall ill. They were experiencing the first effects of cholera. On long-distance buses and trains, they took it home with them to villages across India. The pandemic would eventually kill 800,000 in that country alone, and stretch from Russia to America over the next 20 years. Throughout that time, smallpox remained such a consistent presence that it had its own goddess, Shitala. Polio was also 'hyperendemic' with many hundreds of children becoming paralysed daily. India housed more than 50% of all leprosy cases; these diseases have continued to rage throughout most of the twentieth century. Polio has diminished through powerful vaccination efforts in the last decades, but new viruses have arrived. In May 2018 the first patient suffering from Nipah, a virus with 40–75% fatality and no vaccine, was admitted to Kozhikode Hospital in Kerala. And in March 2020 India began one of the largest lockdowns in world history to combat the growing spread of Covid-19. The unique form of social crisis that is disease is woven through the fabric of history, but India is particularly familiar with it.

The Indian subcontinent is too diverse a place to be classified under any single pattern of cultural influence: some faced the coronavirus with fast action grounded in good scientific predictions. In Mumbai, *Coronasur*, the 'Corona-demon', was burned on a pyre. On TV, celebrity pundits recommended Ayurvedic treatments and immune-friendly yoga, and in some neighbourhoods the police danced their handwashing demonstrations to enthuse the public. So too, some areas fractured in their behaviour along lines between Muslims, migrants, and those northern Indians who have what are seen as 'Chinese' features.

If one were to look to Indian classical literature, one might see at least two templates for dealing with crisis: kings and yogis. Many epics and fables celebrate the dharma-king, a philosophically-minded monarch like the *Upanishads*' scholarly King Janaka, or the *Mahabharata*'s reluctant King Yudhisthira or the *Ramayana*'s forest-dwelling King Rama. This kind of king is often poised between a pronounced sensitivity to the social order of dharma, and a yearning for pure knowledge. He tastes the life of scholarly quietism, but must sacrifice it in order to serve the public; nevertheless this reflective disposition lends an enduring depth to his solutions.

It is possible that this ideal arose as a Hindu response to the model established by the Buddhist emperor Ashoka the Great, who ruled much of India in the third century BC and healed the military crisis he himself had created by posting edicts about the moral order of dharma across the country – the Ashokan Pillars. His example was followed by the renaissance monarch Akbar the Great. To some extent, India's 1960s philosopher-president Sarvepalli Radhakrishnan was seen in this light, and it is the image promoted today by Narendra Modi's public relations team.

A recent real-life exemplar is the public servant now celebrated as the 'coronavirus-slayer', K K Shailaja. This former science school-teacher, turned minister of health and social welfare for India's democratic communist state of Kerala, was already a celebrity for having 'slain' the Nipah virus through rapid response and smart science just a year before. Her story became a film named simply *Virus*, and it was as optimistic and inspiring as Steven Soderberg's movie *Contagion* was hopeless and horrifying. As Covid-19 threatened, she acted fast, minimising the pandemic's impact. Forceful as the goddess after whom her film avatar Sridevi is named, Shailaja acted as the ultimate dharma-queen by channelling the will of the community into an act of *lokasamgraha* or 'holding the world together'.

Gandhi during a prayer meeting in New Delhi,
January 1948.

Beyond Repair: yoga, death, and strategic shutdown
As trains crossed India full of the bodies of Muslims, Hindus, and Sikhs
killed in one of history's most intense bouts of ethnic violence in 1948,
Gandhi undertook his final fast. He had completed many in the past with
surprising success: by creating a radical shutdown in his body, he had –
by a kind of sympathetic magic – pulled Indian society into a reflective
shutdown of its own. It had opened up negotiation for immediate changes
in politics that had seemed impossible amidst the ongoing storms of daily
life. His last fast was advertised as an effort undertaken for all of India but
it was designed primarily to persuade Hindus to restore safety to Muslims
being murdered in his own community. It was for this defence of minorities in the face of social crisis that he was assassinated as he came out of
the period of fasting.

But Gandhi's example has been inspirational, and public personal
sacrifice has become a leitmotif of Asian twentieth century political history. It hit the headlines once again in the 1963 photograph of the self-
immolating Buddhist monk, Thich Quang Duc, immersed in flames at a
Vietnamese crossroads.

Duc was protesting against persecution of Vietnamese Buddhists by
the Catholic elite who were in power and remained the largest landown-
ers in Vietnam. Government forces had recently fired into crowds of
peaceful protesters. On 10 June, Duc invited US correspondents to a
crossroads, at which he then arrived in a procession with 350 monks and
nuns. He refused the offer of a younger monk to take his place and then,
seating himself in a lotus position, he asked for a five-gallon can of petrol
to be poured over him. He calmly lit a match, and let it fall onto his own
head. The image of this motionless burning man captured by a member
of the Associated Press let the West know that it was dealing with a cultural world whose attitude to disaster was profoundly different to its own.
Rather than uphold his own life at all costs, Duc was willing to mine the
depths of crisis to the point of utter personal breakdown, as a powerful
resource for change. In a letter he explained his actions: 'Before closing
my eyes and moving towards the vision of the Buddha, I respectfully
plead to President Ngo Dinh Diem to take a mind of compassion towards
the people of the nation and implement religious equality to maintain the
strength of the homeland eternally.'

The self-immolations of other monks followed and continue occasionally to this day. And the ideology of a street shut-down, that reflects hope

that the problematic systems of society as a whole can be similarly shut down, has become an important aspect of Asia's protest culture. We see it in the 'Saffron Revolution' led by monks in Burma, in the crowds of Thai families sitting in the streets with placards saying 'Shut Down Bangkok, Restart Thailand', or in the famous film of a single man standing still on Tiananmen Square halting a line of tanks. As the CBS report on the 1989 Tiananmen incident put it, 'For three minutes in the middle of the day, an army was stopped by a man who stood still...what moves a man to just stand still?'

Thich Quang Duc's experience of Vietnamese Mahayana and Cambodian Theravada Buddhist retreats meant he had extensive training in Yyogic techniques, just as Gandhi knew principles of yoga from his extensive study of the *Bhagavad Gita*. This meant that both were aware of the special place it holds in Hindu and Buddhist soteriology. At the historical root of the classical Indian religions was a period of urbanisation from approximately 500 BC when the cosmopolitan close-quarters of the cities made society acutely aware of the way that suffering punctuates life. The Buddha gave up his own secure position as heir to a northern throne, at the sight of an elderly person, a diseased person, and a corpse. Recognising an ongoing existential crisis embedded at the heart of human life, he joined the movement of ascetic yogis that was growing across northern India, and eventually started a new sector of society – the monastic institutions that would continue to provide a counterpoint to socio-political power across the whole of Asia.

Classical yogic philosophy describes a technique for personal shutdown and is designed to arrest established patterns in the mind and body. Far from being a form of fitness, classical yoga is more a practice of strategic death. Yoga, says the second sutra, is *citta vrtti nirodha*: 'the stilling of the movements of consciousness'. It depicts the mind as a moving flow-tank filled with currents of desire and fear. This movement has its own momentum (which Schopenhauer interpreted as the 'will', and Freud the 'id'), and it takes control of the whole mind. Meanwhile it obscures its own workings so that we are alienated from the truth of our situation, and consciousness becomes blinded with its own fears and objects of desire. Put into collective, modern terms, this means that society sees only its fears (of redundancy, migrants, or infections, perhaps) and its desires (for the next beer, holiday, Amazon package or Netflix series). Rarely are we able to interrupt the patterns of life enough to look calmly below at the causes of those emotions, nor above to gain an overview and map out a plan. Instead the momentum pushes us on into the systemic dysfunctions that cause the crisis, so that we never pause to take stock and change the situation.

The only solution, the text implies, is to strategically 'lockdown' ourselves, undergoing the death of desires and fears – and even of parts of our existing identity – in order to steer in a radically new direction. While yogic meditation was designed for individuals, it is rare that a whole society collectively, and completely, pauses. Self-immolation, hunger-striking, and sitting, kneeling or lying in public places are all localised forms of social shutdown that invite reflection and reform through their silence. 2020 was history's first real example of shutdown on a global scale. The unique conditions of the pandemic necessitated an almost 'yogic' stilling of society, an isolation of its citizens, and a staunching of their habits of consumption.

Commentators remain divided over whether the themes of continuity or rebirth are more appropriate to our situation. All of these stories offer instruction in the lessons of crisis: they are lessons about knowledge-based leadership and the establishment of new lasting structures that will avoid a cycle of recurrence. They teach us about developing greater communal sensitivity to the environmental conditions that generate natural crisis. And they warn us that we may have to destroy some of the old ways to let something genuinely new and better be born. No person or society should have to feel at the mercy of the same old monsters, time and time again. Crisis can be the stone on which civilisation moves upward, and then out of their reach.

HISTORIE FIORÉNTINE
DI NICCOLO MACHIAVEL,
LI CITTADINO, ET SE,
GRETARIO FIO(
RENTINO.

AL SANTISS. ET BEATISS. PA,
DRE. S. N. CLEMENTE SET(
TIMO PONTEFICE
MASS.

M. D. XXXII.

MACHIAVELLI AND THE BENEFITS
OF CIVIL STRIFE

Alexander Lee

When most of us think of Renaissance Florence, our minds probably turn to Michelangelo's *David* or Brunelleschi's dome. But for Niccolò Machiavelli (1469–1527), what distinguished his city was its history of civil discord. Almost from the moment it had begun to govern its own affairs, he argued in the *Istorie fiorentine*, it had been beset by never-ending strife. First, the nobles had fought amongst themselves; then the nobles had fought the *popolo* (the 'middle classes'); and finally, the *popolo* had fought the *plebe* (the 'common people'). Though often catalysed by tax hikes, foreign threats, or famine, these struggles invariably revolved around the question of political participation – and almost always turned violent. In 1378, during the Ciompi Revolt, disenfranchised cloth-workers burned palaces and lynched a public official; while in 1513, Machiavelli himself was imprisoned after being implicated in a conspiracy against the Medici regime.

Admittedly, Machiavelli was not the first to draw attention to Florence's fractiousness. It had been a common complaint since at least the thirteenth century. In *Li Libres dou Tresor*, Brunetto Latini (1220–94) observed that the Florentines were 'always…in discord'. A few decades later, the chronicler Dino Compagni (c.1255–1324) noted that, while his fellow citizens were 'bold in arms' and 'proud', they were also 'contentious'. And in the *Divina Commedia* ('Divine Comedy'), Dante Alighieri (c.1265–1321) shed bitter tears over the fate of his '*città partita*' ('divided city').

What set Machiavelli apart was his attitude towards civil discord. In contrast to virtually everyone else, he did not think that it was necessarily a bad thing. To be sure, it could be dangerous – especially for those who got caught up in the violence. But from a purely political point of view, it could actually be positive. Indeed, if the history of ancient Rome taught anything, he argued in the *Discorsi sopra la prima deca di Tito Livio* ('Discourses on Livy'), it was that civil strife was essential to a city's liberty.

For many of Machiavelli's contemporaries, such a claim was manifestly absurd. As Francesco Guicciardini (1483–1540) argued, the conflicts by which Rome had been rocked were far too destabilising to have been productive of anything, let alone liberty. If the Romans had stayed free for such a long time, he suggested, it must have been in spite of their disunity, not because of it.

Guicciardini had a good point. For centuries past, liberty had carried two subtly different meanings. On the one hand, it could be understood simply as self-government and the freedom from external domination. But on the other hand, it could also mean the freedom to live on an equal footing with one's fellow citizens, under the protection of just laws. Though each of these carried its own implications, the former could not exist without the latter. After all, people only willingly participate in the political process or fight to defend their city if they can be sure of enjoying the same rights and of sharing in public goods to the same degree.

Of course, this wouldn't just happen on its own. Inspired by their reading of Cicero, most Renaissance philosophers recognised that it required citizens to subordinate their private interests to the pursuit of equity and the common good. This, in turn, depended on the cultivation of certain Stoic/Christian virtues – such as prudence, mercy, and temperance. But its implication was that liberty and social harmony were inextricably intertwined. A people at peace were, by definition, free. But if a society fractured, its liberty would be lost – either to an unjust tyrant, who ruled in his own interests, or to a foreign aggressor.

There was method in Machiavelli's madness, however. Curiously enough, he actually agreed with most of what his critics said. He was happy to accept that liberty was in some way related to equity and the common good; and that both were dependent on virtue. Where he differed was with regard to the meaning of virtue itself. Having spent much of his adult life in public life, he had come to believe that traditional conceptions of virtue were out of step with the harsh realities of politics – and that a more 'muscular' definition was required.

In the *Discorsi*, Machiavelli explained that *virtù* should be understood as the willingness to do whatever is necessary to uphold the liberty of your city – irrespective of 'moral' considerations. For the 'virtuous' man, the public good must be put first, ahead not only of private interest, but also of any notions of good and evil. 'When it is absolutely a

Allegory of Good Government, Wisdom and Justice,
Ambrogio Lorenzetti, 1337–1343.
Palazzo Pubblico, Siena.

question of the safety of one's *patria*,' Machiavelli claimed, 'there must be no consideration of just or unjust, merciful or cruel, praiseworthy or disgraceful; instead, setting aside every scruple, one must follow to the utmost any plan that will save her life and keep her liberty.'

The only problem was that people weren't always particularly 'virtuous'. In Machiavelli's experience, they were craven, self-serving fools, who would sooner sell their own grandmother than pass up a chance to enrich themselves. Indeed, the wealthier and safer a society was, the more egotistical and greedy the citizenry grew, the more divided society was, and the more inevitable conflict became.

This was particularly evident in the early history of Rome. In the decades after its foundation, Machiavelli recalled, the city had been ruled by kings. The first of these had been bold, upright men who had given it just laws, strong religious beliefs, and a firm grounding in *virtù*. But as time passed, the more liberty was taken for granted and the more prosperity corrupted the social whole. Disparities of wealth opened up, and a bitter enmity arose between nobles and plebs. As Machiavelli pointed out, their goals were irreconcilably opposed. While the plebs wanted to not be oppressed, the nobles were determined to grind them underfoot at any cost.

For a while, royal authority sufficed to keep the nobles in check. But as the kings succumbed to luxury, they too were corrupted. Growing steadily more overbearing and tyrannical, they aroused such hatred that, eventually, the nobility overthrew the monarchy. In its stead, a republic was founded. As Machiavelli explained, this was designed to avoid the old tensions breaking loose. Combining monarchical, aristocratic, and popular elements, it was structured so that each element would theoretically keep the others in check. But no sooner had the kings been expelled than the nobles once again began to vent their hatred against the people. A bitter conflict erupted – and before long, the disorder had become so severe that the survival of the republic itself was in doubt.

To avert disaster, it was decided to establish the 'tribunes of the plebs' (493 BC). Able to veto any legislation that might be harmful to the people, the tribunes were intended to act as a restraint on the abuses of the nobles. It was, however, a very imperfect solution. Almost immediately, the people began agitating for still more powers, and the nobles looked for any opportunity to clip the tribunes' wings. Though 'the dissentions…rarely caused exile and even more rarely resulted in bloodshed', the 'quarrels and the noise that resulted' were nevertheless so unceasing that, for more than 300 years, social conflict was the defining characteristic of civic life.

It looked chaotic. And in theory, it should have destroyed Rome's liberty. But paradoxically, it did the opposite. Rather than weakening the Roman state, all that disunity actually compensated for its moral decline. It was obvious, when you thought about it. What people like Guicciardini forgot was that, while the nobles and the plebs may have battled it out for centuries, neither of them had emerged victorious. It was as if they were stuck in a never-ending tug-of-war. Fearful of what might happen if they lost, but unable to beat their opponents, neither could afford to relax their grip for a moment. And in doing so, they not only held each other in check – but inadvertently made everyone stronger, too.

Self-interest, in other words, compensated for a lack of virtue. Under constant threat from the nobles, the plebs always had to be on the lookout for any attack on their rights – thus ensuring that equity and the common good were respected. At the same time, the rumbling conflict had also obliged the plebs to take up arms. Since this allowed them to play a more active role in military decision-making, they were able to counteract the nobles' instinctive aversion to risk and open the doors to territorial expansion – thereby securing the city against foreign aggression. As long as social tensions existed, therefore, Rome's liberty was guaranteed.

Unfortunately, things didn't always pan out as they were meant to. As Machiavelli had noted, conflict only had a positive effect if the delicate balance between the nobles and the people was maintained. Provided they were more or less evenly matched, all would be well; but were one to succeed in defeating the other, liberty would collapse and tyranny would invariably follow.

Of course, there were plenty of things you could do to prevent this from happening. The Romans had given the tribunes the power to prosecute anyone who threatened liberty; and, in times of crisis, had even appointed a dictator to restore order. But none of these measures really worked – least of all in the long term. Whatever steps you took to restore equilibrium to the body politic, you would essentially be gambling on someone putting equity and the common good above private or sectional interests. But as Machiavelli had already pointed out, this whole situation had come about precisely because the population lacked the *virtù* this required. If the scales suddenly tipped in one side's favour, he argued, you could

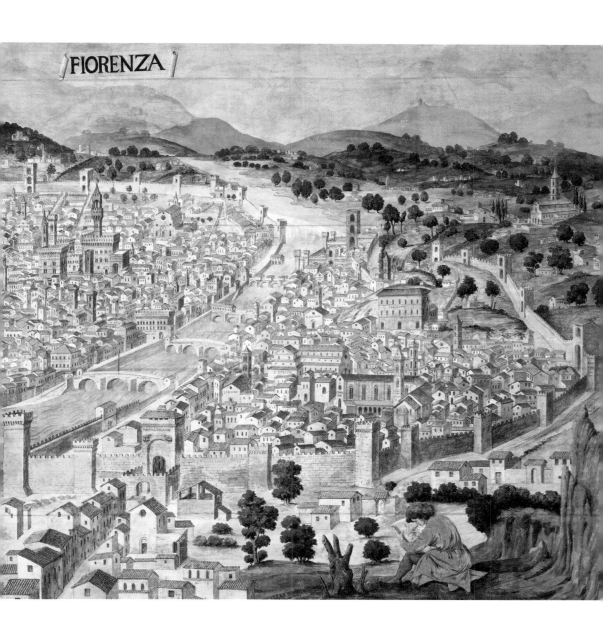

Copy of the map known as the *Carta della Catena*, Florence around 1470.

hardly expect to reset the balance using something that wasn't there.

Once the rot had set in, what usually happened was that a despotic figure would seize control. Sometimes, the very person the plebs looked to for salvation would end up using his office to take power. On other occasions, a resurgent nobility might splinter into factions. Since these generally strove to subvert the organs of state for their own benefit, the frightened plebs would try to align themselves with one or the other – only to find that, in doing so, they had inadvertently handed an unscrupulous leader the reins of government.

This, of course, was the fate which had ultimately befallen Rome. After centuries of tense liberty, an attempt to reform the agrarian laws in 133 BC resulted in a bitter factional struggle, which led to a series of destructive civil wars. In the ensuing chaos, Julius Caesar emerged as the leader of the 'popular party' – and eventually used the plebs' support to transform himself into 'Rome's first tyrant'.

Machiavelli saw that Florence could easily go the same way. It had already come close. Back in the early fifteenth century, Cosimo de Medici (1389–1464) had become the city's de facto ruler simply by 'befriending the people'. To be sure, he hadn't been all that bad. As Machiavelli later admitted in the *Istorie fiorentine*, he far surpassed his contemporaries 'in liberality and prudence'. But there was a serious danger that, if Florence's present divisions went unchecked, someone far worse might emerge in future – and the city's liberty lost for good.

So, how could Florence be pulled back from the brink? For much of the last six years of his life, Machiavelli tried hard to devise a constitution capable of balancing the city's social classes. But even he knew that this, on its own, would not be enough. As he had already pointed out, any settlement would eventually be destroyed by vice. If social conflict was to be kept within 'acceptable' bounds, therefore, a dose of virtue would have to be injected into the body politic. The only problem was: how? It wouldn't be easy. If, as Machiavelli had claimed, men were naturally wicked, and prosperity only corrupted them further, it would be like flogging a dead horse. But he still thought it might be possible.

By looking carefully at Rome's period of liberty, Machiavelli identified four methods of reviving a state's *virtù*. The first was to minimise the disparities of wealth which had corrupted popular morals in the first place. The best way of doing this was by keeping the citizens poor. Even if they had little inclination towards virtue, their lack of resources would prevent them from corrupting either themselves or others. If this proved impractical, however, the same effect could be achieved by coming down hard on the rich. To some extent, Florence was already on the right track. Although it was perhaps not quite as 'equal' as some of the German states, Machiavelli believed that it still enjoyed *equalità* of a kind. All that was needed was to complete the process – and make it the basis of political life.

The second method was to make full use of the law. Here, Machiavelli was not thinking of law as an instrument of social control, but as a form of education. As he had already explained, men were naturally inclined to the bad. Unless there was something to stop them, they would invariably act in accordance with their worst impulses. What Florence needed to do, therefore, was to give its citizens a positive incentive to choose *virtù* instead. And what better incentive was there than the rule of law? By punishing those who harmed the state, and rewarding those who served it, Machiavelli argued, Florence could 'teach' men to be good.

A third was to nurture religious belief. If it was true that law could make men virtuous with punishments and rewards in this life, Machiavelli reasoned, then religion should be able to do exactly the same by promising salvation or damnation in the next. Indeed, given that it was grounded in the fear of an omnipotent God, it should be even more effective. Of course, this is not to say that Machiavelli was attempting to defend Christianity as it was then understood. He was bitterly critical of the Catholic Church for having weakened people's faith by meddling in temporal politics, and for glorifying values ('humility, abjectness', etc.) which made men weak and cowardly. Instead, he envisaged a Christianity which was more like Roman paganism. While remaining true to its core beliefs, the Church should interpret them in a more 'virile' manner – valorising courage, strength, and glory. And, at the same time, the Church itself should stay out of politics.

By far the most important way of cultivating *virtù*, however, was to have an outstanding leader. Though Machiavelli was generally pessimistic about the moral character of the common people, he was convinced that a truly exceptional figure could help them overcome their deficiencies – and restore balance to civil strife. There was no need for there to be someone like this around all the time. If a suitable *virtuoso* appeared once every ten years or so, that would be enough. There were various ways he could protect the people from corruption. He could, for example, inspire others with his example. Alternatively, if he had a particularly strong character, he could simply impose his virtue on them – either by cultivating a reputation for cruelty, or by being exceptionally kind. Most importantly, he could take steps to combat vice directly. If there was a conspiracy, for example, he would know how to diffuse it without provoking further unrest. Similarly, if opponents blocked him out of mere jealousy, he would have the foresight to dispose of them swiftly.

But while Rome had been blessed with many such figures in the period 493 to 133 BC, Florence had not been so lucky. In the 20 or so years before Medici's return, its two most prominent leaders – Fra Girolamo Savonarola (1452–1498) and Piero Soderini (1451–1522) – had been a bitter disappointment. They had not been kind or cruel enough to inspire *virtù* in others; they had failed to tackle their opponents; and, at times, they had been almost morbidly indecisive. As a consequence, the Florentines had slid ever deeper into corruption; social tensions had grown worse; a foreign army had invaded Tuscany; and – at the time Machiavelli was writing the *Discorsi* – liberty itself seemed to be slipping away.

Despite everything, Machiavelli still hoped that, if a suitable leader were to emerge, the situation might still be saved. Where such a person was to be found, however, was another matter. Of course, there was always a slim chance that one of the Medici might prove up to the task. But Machiavelli couldn't help thinking that Florence should look elsewhere. In the dedication to the *Discorsi*, he hinted that the best candidates were to be found among the young men on the fringes of political life. Granted, they weren't perfect. They were impulsive and, at times, a little crazy. But they were brave, idealistic, and true – the perfect people, in short, to build a rotten world anew.

Machiavelli intended the *Discorsi* to meet the specific challenges of his own times. But his dissection of civil strife nevertheless remains as compelling today as ever it did. As we confront the deep divisions afflicting our own society, we should perhaps console ourselves with the thought that, while conflict may be inevitable, it can still have a positive role to play – and that our best hope for the future lies with the next generation.

Aristotle with a Bust of Homer, Rembrandt
(Rembrandt van Rijn), 1653.
The Metropolitan Museum of Art, New York.

WHY APPLIED HISTORY MATTERS

Iskander Rehman

On a wintry day in January 1687, a small group of men huddled around a wooden table in an antechamber of the Louvre. Known as the '*immortels*', the 40-odd individuals were all members of the Académie Française – an institution created half a century prior by Cardinal Richelieu, with the aim of showcasing the resurgent nation's cultural prowess. Indeed, since the foundation of the institution in 1635, France had emerged as the most formidable power in Europe. Its combined economic, demographic and military might was unmatched. Under the aggressive leadership of Louis XIV, France had won a series of major victories, greatly enlarging its territories in the wake of a seemingly inexorable tide of conquest. And yet, in retrospect, it is clear that the French monarchy had already reached the high watermark of its power. Indeed, only a year before, a grouping of fellow European powers, disquieted by the Sun King's growing religious intolerance and expansionism, had coalesced to form a powerful new coalition – the League of Augsburg – with the express ambition of counterbalancing French hegemony on the continent. In early 1687, however, the dangers of hubristic overextension were far from readily apparent: for many of the august *académiciens*, it may have seemed that their country was at the very zenith of its power, with little to fear at home or abroad. This was an era of almost unabashed national self-confidence, one whose cultural productions were aureated with a shared sense of martial glory and grandeur.

On this particular occasion, the literary grandees had assembled in the bowels of the frigid palace to give thanks for the recovery of their monarch, who had just undergone a singularly unpleasant surgical procedure. A cloying panegyric was composed for the occasion by Charles Perrault, a writer and court favourite, and read out loud. Entitled 'The Century of Louis the Great', the poem made a brazen and controversial claim. Not only, argued its author, could France claim to rival in its splendour and intellectual achievements Augustan Rome, it had in fact already

surpassed it. The advent of modern scientific discoveries (such as the tele-
scope and microscope) and Cartesian rationalism heralded a new era of
progress, one which required a collective casting off of the crushing
weight of antiquity:

> Beautiful Antiquity was always venerable,
> But I never believed it was adorable.
> I see the ancients without bending my knee,
> They are great, yes, but men just as are we,
> And one can thus compare, without fear of being unfair,
> The Century of Louis to the fine century of Augustus…
> If we were to lift the specious veil
> Which prejudice puts before our eyes,
> And, tired of applauding a thousand gross errors,
> Were sometimes to use the lights of our reason,
> We would clearly see, without temerity,
> That one might not adore all antiquity.

For all their trailblazing talents, the ancients were also, Perrault argued,
the products of a more primitive, even barbaric, era. Their science had
been proven to be fatally flawed and their poetry could appear crude,
especially in comparison to the more polished verse of Perrault's contemporaries. Even the great Homer, Perrault boldly suggested, would have
benefited from being born in the seventeenth century, one in which 'a
hundred defects attributable to the century in which [he] was born' would
not mar his otherwise exquisite works.

The response to the poem seems, in the main, to have initially been
one of bemused befuddlement. Most of the other *immortels* engaged in
polite, if perhaps unenthusiastic, applause, while the famed playwright
Jean Racine – much to the author's vexation – thought that the poem was
an elaborate prank and that Perrault actually believed the opposite of
what he had written. The one exception was the great poet Nicolas
Boileau-Despréaux, more commonly known as Boileau, who – seething
and restless – had 'grumbled in an undertone' throughout the entire reci-
tation, before suddenly leaping to his feet and shouting that it was 'disgraceful for such a thing to be read, criticising the greatest men of antiquity'. This notorious breach in decorum has traditionally been viewed as
the starting point of an increasingly virulent intellectual debate over the

Portrait of Nicolas Boileau-Despreaux,
Jean Baptiste Santerre, 1690s.
Beaux-Arts Museum, Lyon.

merits of the classics, the notion of progress, and the value of applied history. Commonly known as the 'Quarrel of the Ancients and the Moderns', the controversy raged over almost a century, extending far beyond the salons of Paris to eventually engulf the entirety of the European 'Republic of Letters'.

In France, the Moderns were spearheaded, at various junctures, by influential figures such as Perrault, the Cartesian intellectual Bernard de Fontenelle, and the abbot Jean Terrasson. The Ancients, who resolutely opposed them, included literary icons such as Boileau and Jean de la Fontaine, and leading classicists such as the formidable Anne Dacier, one of history's greatest translators of the *Iliad*. Meanwhile in England, the quarrel was ignited by William Temple's famous *Essay upon Ancient and Modern Learning* of 1690, and its flames were then further fanned four years later by William Wotton's spirited response in his *Reflections upon Ancient and Modern Learning*.

As University of Chicago professor Larry Norman notes in his masterful study of the period, the quarrel was not a rigidly bifurcated dispute between partisans of tradition and champions of progress. Rather, it was a complex, multilayered and often passionate moment of collective intellectual reckoning:

> The conflict idea [ran] much deeper than a simple dispute unambiguously opposing clearly identified parties. This is true because partisans on either side were very often attracted to positions associated with their opponents. From contending principles, the two parties sometimes reached common conclusions; from common principles, contending positions. Indeed, and the point is capital, they agreed on what one might erroneously consider the essence of the quarrel: there was in fact little dispute that a vast historical evolution had considerably distanced modernity from antiquity, and more importantly, there was a consensus that 'authority' granted to the latter was largely superannuated… What the parties differed on, then, was not the deep fissure between antiquity and modernity, but instead the value to be granted those different times and, perhaps more fundamentally, the criteria for judging such value.

The Nature of the Quarrel

There comes a time, no doubt, when all rising great powers, in a fit of adolescent peevishness, lash out at key aspects of their intellectual heritage. Ancient Rome, after all, had long entertained something of a schizoid relationship with Greek culture, viewing it as both a wellspring of wisdom and a morally polluted foreign import. At the apogee of Rome's power, Virgil famously crowed that his empire had overtaken, in the glory of its achievements, ancient Hellas. The effeminate Greeks, he observed dismissively in the *Aeneid*, may have once pioneered the disciplines of rhetoric, astrology and sculpture, but their hardier Roman successors had mastered an altogether more useful set of 'imperial arts' in the course of their conquest of the Mediterranean basin. It was to Rome, and Rome alone, that the task fell 'with awful sway, to rule mankind, and make the world obey'.

Equally conflicted attitudes existed vis-à-vis European culture in the bustling coastal cities of nineteenth century America. Thus in 1837 Ralph Waldo Emerson gave a famous speech at Harvard, in which he argued in favour of an intellectual emancipation from the Old World, stating:

> Our [America's] day of dependence, our long apprenticeship to the learning of other lands, draws to a close. The millions that around us are rushing into life cannot always be fed on the sere remains of foreign harvests…We have listened too long to the courtly muses of Europe…The spirit of the American freeman is already suspected to be too timid, imitative, tame.

An American Supreme Court Justice, Oliver Wendell Holmes, later rapturously referred to Emerson's speech as 'America's declaration of intellectual independence', while the Romantic poet and critic James Russell Lowell observed: '[Whereas]…the Puritan Revolt had made us ecclesiastically and the Revolution politically, we were still socially and intellectually moored to English thought, till Emerson cut the cable and gave us a chance at the dangers and glories of the blue water.'

It was the somewhat predictable nature of these oedipal revolts against ancient authority that the seventeenth century French moralist Jean de la Bruyère lampooned in his collection of epigrams known as 'The Characters'. The Moderns, he quipped, were behaving like churlish infants, noting:

A man feeds on the ancients and intelligent moderns, he squeezes and drains them as much as possible, he stuffs his work with them, and when at last he becomes an author and thinks he can walk alone, he lifts up his voice against them, and ill-treats them, like those lusty children, grown strong through the healthy milk on which they have been fed, and who beat their wet-nurses.

The Moderns' critiques of the classics could not always be reduced to such crudely emancipatory efforts, however. Indeed, they often also incorporated a strong normative component, arguing that the pagan rusticity that characterised many of the ancient Greek and Roman traditions was morally as well as culturally inferior. Thus, the refined Perrault memorably took issue with the casual vulgarity of Homer's warrior-aristocrats, who laundered their own clothes and cooked their own food or – in the case of Odysseus – infiltrated Ithaca disguised as a beggar. 'One cannot see without indignation and disgust one of the heroes of the *Iliad* lie down at night amidst the pigs,' blustered Perrault. The brutish treatment of women was another source of indignation. Commenting on a passage of Theocritus in which a goatherd strikes his lover, the seventeenth century writer acidly remarked: '…it will be said that those were the manners of the times. Well they were depraved manners, and consequently that was a depraved age, very different from our own.'

Indeed, for Moderns such as Terrasson and Perrault, the prestige of the ancients had historically been tied to the supposed virtue of their heroes; yet these same heroes, in their cruelty, savagery and sexual licentiousness, often appeared anything but exemplary. Who could think, for example, that Achilles – that tenebrous warlord governed wholly by his selfish appetites and obsession for personal renown – could be held up as a paragon of aristocratic virtue? The modern, Christian world called for higher ethical standards, for more clearly didactic works, and therefore for a greater critical and emotional distancing from the oft-murky moral messaging contained in the classics. Then, of course, there was the inherent subversiveness of the political counter-models proffered by democratic Athens and republican Rome in an age of absolutist monarchy. The French Moderns were hardly the first to have drawn attention to the potentially insidious nature of some of the themes contained in the works of the ancients. Indeed, a few decades prior Hobbes had warned in *Leviathan*:

As to rebellion against monarchy, one of the most frequent causes of it is the reading of the books of policies and histories of the ancient Greeks and Romans...In sum, I cannot imagine how anything can be more prejudicial to a monarchy than the allowing of such books to be publicly read, without present applying such correctives of discreet masters as are fit to take away their venom.

In response to this onslaught of critiques, the Ancients argued that the great works of antiquity should be situated within their larger context, and as vivid depictions of past mores rather than as precise guides for moral (or political) instruction. The Moderns, by tying their assessment of the worth of the Classics to contemporary norms, were being short-sighted and displaying a form of temporal parochialism. The playwright Hilaire-Bernard de Longepierre's dispassionate plea for greater nuance in response to these spasms of moral outrage has a certain abiding power to it:

One must not believe that ideas of verisimilitude and decorum are the same in all ages. Must one not recognise that some of these ideas are founded on customs, on attitudes, on religion, etc...and that our own age is a very poor measure by which to ascertain conventions of decorum, which rest on foundations so unstable and variable? What a strange blindness, what unfair and inverted logic, to want to bring everything back to one's own time without ever allowing oneself to lose sight of it for one moment!

These rejoinders were echoed in the works of figures such as Jean Boivin, who did not hesitate, in his *Apologia for Homer*, to tie the Moderns' presentism and intellectual superciliousness to broader manifestations of intolerance. 'There has never been an age in history that did not believe itself enlightened, and more enlightened than any other age,' he observed, before acidly remarking that, 'Such a good opinion of oneself is habitually the result of ignorance.' To openly express such visceral distaste for one's distant forebears was not so dissimilar, he boldly ventured, to indulging in knee-jerk xenophobia vis-à-vis one's foreign contemporaries:

To be incapable of tolerating in men of another century, or from another century remote from our own, manners and morals

Buste of Thucydides, Ch. Winter, late nineteenth century. Rijksmuseum, Amsterdam.

different from those of men of the present century or of the country we live in, is to be incapable of tolerating a foreign appearance in a foreigner; it is to want a Turk, an Indian, or a Chinese to think and act like us and to have none of the flaws of their nation and all of the virtues of our own. As for me, what I like in the Chinese are Chinese mores and ways; and I would be most displeased with a painter who, promising to make me a portrait of the Chinese emperor, painted him dressed up as a Frenchman.

Contemporary Resonances

It is hard not to be struck, when perusing these reams of impassioned arguments and correspondence, by the eerie similarities with some of our current polemics over the study of the classics, or indeed of many of the texts long considered canonical in the history of Western statecraft. Just as in seventeenth-century France, bitter controversies now rage over the moral salubriousness of key figures in the history of political thought. Fevered debates swirl around whether one should 'cancel Aristotle' for his abhorrent views on slavery or rebrand university buildings named after David Hume because of the latter's comments on race. Meanwhile, American foreign policy pundits and political scientists have taken aim at some of their contemporaries' seeming obsession with quoting Thucydides, arguing that the works of a fifth-century BC Athenian no longer provide a useful or relevant guide for our supposedly more enlightened, evolved, and complex present. Thus, over the course of the summer an editor of the magazine *Foreign Policy*, in a much-discussed article, made the assertion that the study of Thucydides should be sidelined because 'conflicts between city-states in a backwater Eurasian promontory 2,400 years ago are an unreliable guide to modern geopolitics'. Noting that the epicentre of global geopolitical activity was now in Asia rather than Europe, the journalist argued in favour of a broader intellectual pivot toward the study of Asian diplomatic and military history. These arguments were reprised by a number of academics on social media, one of whom scoffed that the Peloponnesian War, fought 2500 years ago 'with swords and spears', was 'not a model for Sino-American rivalry', and that one might as well 'go back to when cavemen hit each other with clubs and rocks'.

At first glance, the discomfort and frustration lurking behind such sentiments may appear somewhat understandable. As the contemporary classicist Mary Beard has noted, studying the ancient world from our twenty-first century vantage point can be akin to '...walking on a tight-rope – a careful balancing act, which demands a very particular sort of imagination. If you look down on one side, everything does look reassuringly familiar, or can be made to seem so...On the other side of the tight-rope, however, is completely alien territory.'

This normatively alien territory, with its casual institutionalisation of slavery, infanticide, and teenage marriage, amongst other distressing practices, can naturally appear both repellent and foreign to a modern reader. A certain level of moral discomfort, however, should not, in and of itself, be viewed as justification for an abrupt intellectual untethering from some of the more foundational texts in the history of political thought. As Longepierre, Boivin, and other Ancients eloquently argued over three centuries ago, educated readers are perfectly capable of maintaining a certain critical distance when engaging with key texts. The main pitfall – one which should always be studiously avoided – is to read the text, or an excerpt of said text (say, the 'Melian Dialogue' in Thucydides' *Peloponnesian War*), in relative isolation.

Indeed, before analysing the work of any thinker, one should first acquire a fine-grained understanding of the cultural 'eco-system' and specific historical context within which said texts or ideas were produced. This approach should ideally be complemented – as Quentin Skinner and other members of the so-called Cambridge school have contended – by a granular study of the author's principal intellectual influences and contemporaries. When embarking on the study of a text that has proven to be hugely influential over the course of the centuries – such as Xenophon's *Cyropaedia* or Vegetius's *De Re Militari* – one should not hesitate to adopt a more philological approach, exploring how exactly that same text's meaning or message has been reinterpreted or repurposed. Much like a great wine, the meaning and value assigned to a foundational text can evolve over the course of time, as well as in accordance with the intellectual terroir within which it is resampled.

Provided one is willing to engage in such preliminary intellectual efforts, it is perfectly possible to, for instance, draw valuable insights from Aristotle's discussions of practical wisdom in the *Nicomachean Ethics* while utterly rejecting his theses on natural slavery in *Politics*. To suggest otherwise is infantilising. It underestimates our collective capacity for what Francesco Guicciardini in his *Ricordi* termed 'discretion' or 'discernment', ie the ability to delve into, and learn from the shared reservoir of human experience, all while retaining a 'perspicacious eye', by recognising the specificity of certain local and temporal conditions.

In his *Essays*, Montaigne advocated for a similar approach – one in line with the Renaissance-era emphasis on active reading. 'A dozen students have already caught syphilis', the earthy philosopher chortled, 'before they reach Aristotle's lessons on temperance.' Rather, a discerning reader should learn how to engage critically with a classical text, to 'pass everything through a sieve, and lodge nothing in his head on mere authority and trust.' Always one for colourful metaphors, Montaigne compared his more pedantic acquaintances to bloated figures who, holding forth at their dinner parties and lavish receptions, continuously belched out undigested fragments of knowledge in the hope of impressing a wide-eyed and gullible audience. An enlightened approach to learning, he argued, involved taking the time to more fully digest and metabolise one's acquired knowledge:

> We take other men's knowledge and opinions upon trust; which is an idle and superficial learning. We must make it our own. We are in this very like him, who having need of fire, went to a neighbour's house to fetch it, and finding a very good one there, sat down to warm himself without bringing any home…What good does it do us to have a stomach full of meat, if it is not digested, if it be not incorporated with us, if it does not nourish or support us?

Were Montaigne alive today, he would no doubt chuckle at the sheer volume of regurgitated Thucydides regularly splattered across various foreign policy outlets. Indeed, trotting out the same passages of the *History of the Peloponnesian War* when commenting on Sino-US rivalry has become something of a tired trope, not so dissimilar to those entrepreneurial self-help manuals that begin every chapter with the same circumlocutory quotes from Clausewitz or gnomish aphorisms from Sun Tzu. It can appear even more tiresome when this smattering of erudition serves as a fig-leaf for a lack of regional expertise, or to project a thin veneer of cultural sophistication.

The problem, however, is not that too many people draw on Thucydides, Clausewitz or Sun Tzu, but rather that they often do so superficially, self-servingly, and seem to not have fully read the texts in question. Unfortunately, the same charges can also often be levied at their critics – especially those in the field of political science – who frequently fail to properly engage with the relevant primary and secondary literature.

In this, those who now breezily dismiss the value of the classics differ greatly from the Moderns in *ancien régime* France or Restoration-era England, who all possessed, at least, a solid working knowledge of the texts whose relevance they were criticising. The similarities between them, perhaps, lie more in the self-satisfaction underlying some of the more knee-jerk dismissals of the relevance of ancient history to America's contemporary challenges. It is perhaps not a coincidence that this form of epochal exceptionalism, which so closely resembles that of the proud Moderns of the court of Louis XIV, has progressively become more, rather than less, prominent within America's intellectual class. Decades spent comfortably perched in a position of primacy, it seems, can sometimes lead to the spiritual equivalent of a torticollis, preventing one from looking backward as well as sideways.

Indeed, it takes an almost whimsical degree of self-regard to purport to devote one's life to the study of war and peace, and yet blithely affirm that a seminal figure such as Thucydides is no longer worthy of examination. The Athenian is one of the great pillars of the Western strategic and historiographical tradition and his work has inspired generation upon generation of political theorists and statesmen. Its enduring resonance is tied, precisely, to the universality and timelessness of some of its observations on politics, war, and the human condition. As Tufts University professor Daniel Drezner recently noted, the ancient historian's sweeping narrative constitutes a veritable 'Rosetta Stone of tragic narratives in world politics'. That *The History of the Peloponnesian War* has been occasionally plundered, misinterpreted, or crudely simplified should not be a reason for its sudden excision from international relations curricula. *Au contraire*, the solution to sloppy history or crude analogical reasoning is not to abandon the field of study in question, but to redouble one's efforts to acquire a more finely tuned sense of discernment. Whereas grand theories of international relations, much like philosophy, depend on universals and seek to teach by reason, history – in the words of Francesco Patrizi – 'depends on particulars and teaches through experience'.

It is also somewhat surprising that Thucydides should continue to remain such a focus of attention and controversy when there is a plethora of other classical historians or political philosophers who were equally – if not more – influential in the history of Western statecraft; and whose works could also be relied upon to furnish rich insights on contemporary challenges. Such as Polybius, the perceptive exile, on the virtues of historiography, the challenges of alliance management, and the dangers tied to unipolarity. Sallust, the saturnine stylist, on how Rome's destruction of its prime peer competitor Carthage, led to the dissipation of the Tiberine city-state's 'fear-rooted' internal consensus and eventually to decadence and overexpansion. Tacitus, the wry political operator, and ancient history's finest anatomist of life under authoritarian rule. One can only hypothesise that if Thucydides is so disproportionately cited, it is because his works often form the lone classical text shoehorned into contemporary international relations curricula. The net result is a sadly impoverished intellectual debate: one which could greatly benefit from a more interdisciplinary exchange of ideas and from a reinvigorated effort to engage in applied history.

The Need for Applied History

For centuries, a solid grounding in history was considered essential both to the conduct of statecraft, and to the prosecution of military strategy. From the Ancient Greeks to the Victorians, the careful study of past events lay at the heart of 'practical wisdom', or prudence, and the mastering of such a historical *techne* was perceived as one of the finest political arts. Not only did history teach humility, it was also a school of statesmanship, that provided what American political scientist Marc Trachtenberg called a mental 'workshop within which basic ideas about core policy issues [could] be hammered out', thus enhancing future strategic performance. As Polybius famously noted in *The Histories*:

> There are two ways by which all men can reform themselves, the one through their own mischances, and the other through those of others...For it is the mental transference of similar circumstances to our own times that gives us the means of forming presentiments of what is about to happen, and enables us at certain times to take precautions and at others, by reproducing former conditions, to face with more confidence the difficulties that menace us.

Following pages: Battle order in a plain, engraving from *The Histories* by Polybius, Volume IV, 1774.

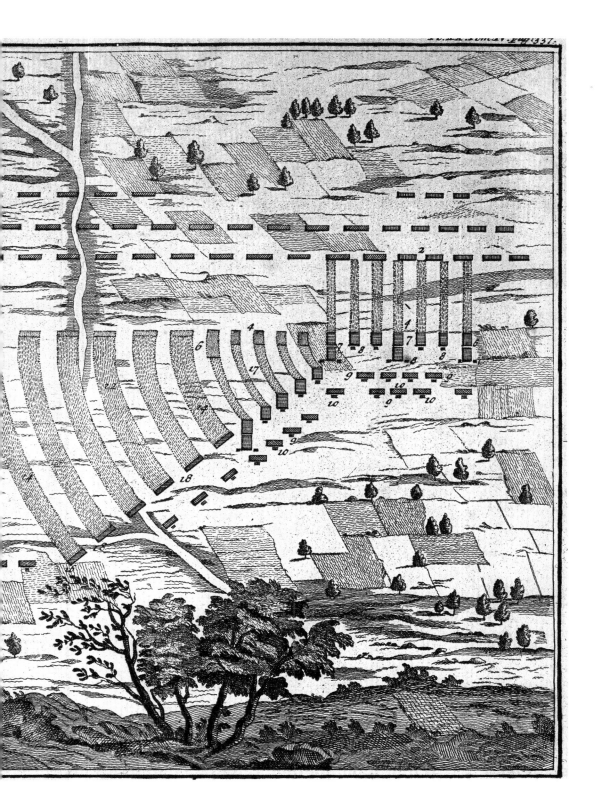

And indeed, for statesmen grappling with the uncertainty of their present circumstances, the business of liaising between the universal and the particular has often been conceptualised in terms of a temporal process, with the hope that the lessons of yesteryear hold the promise of better ascertaining future outcomes. As Yaacov Vertzberger has rightly observed, history teaches by analogy, enlightens by metaphor, and educates by extrapolation; but analogy can mislead, metaphor can be misplaced and extrapolation misguided. The acquisition of a historical sensibility should thus go hand in hand with a certain degree of intellectual caution – one that avoids succumbing to deterministic historical narratives, and that does not systematically rely on analogical reasoning as a means of predictive inference.

Perhaps most importantly, the accomplished historian is a skilled manager of complexity and a processor of information – someone trained to detect patterns of cause and effect. The great Harvard historian John Clive thus once wondered whether '...historians, especially those dealing with abstract entities like groups and classes and movements, have to possess a special metaphorical capacity, a plastic or tactile imagination that can detect shapes or configurations where others less gifted see only jumble and confusion.'

If so, then it would seem as though the historically trained mind reflects many of the mental processes most prized by generals and statesmen. Political and military judgment, like historical study, demands a capacity for integration, for perceiving qualitative similarities and differences, and, as the war studies specialist John Stone puts it, a 'sense of the unique fashion in which various factors combine in the particular situation'.

And yet despite the seemingly obvious benefits to be derived from its study, applied history appears to have fallen out of favour. As much of American political science has become more 'positivist' in its intellectual leanings – with a heightened focus on quantitative methods, and theoretical abstraction – it has also become more narrowly self-referential. When contemporary political scientists do draw on military history, they often do so in a limited and self-serving way, retroactively selecting case studies that appear to confirm their parsimonious theories. The past is thus often viewed as a 'treasure house, to be plundered in search of illustrative effect, rather than being examined and analysed for its own sake', in the words of the historian John Gooch. This dispiriting state of affairs, however, should not solely be attributed to the evolution of political science. Indeed, within the embattled academic field of history itself, the study of military and diplomatic history has been shunted to the sidelines, and the production of policy-relevant works of historical analysis is often frowned upon. On popular national security or foreign policy websites, military and diplomatic historians remain heavily outnumbered by political scientists.

Meanwhile, many of the most well-examined case studies in the security studies literature – from America's approach to carrier warfare to the Wehrmacht's adoption of the *blitzkrieg* strategy during the Second World War – are by now overly familiar. Vast spans of military history, from late antiquity to the early modern era, are considered less relevant to contemporary concerns and almost uniformly ignored, with contemporary international relations scholars drawing the overwhelming majority of their historical case studies from the twentieth or twenty-first centuries. The great French historian Marc Bloch famously inveighed against this tendency for analysts to consider only the more recent historical periods to be the most relevant, caustically asking:

> What would one think of the geophysicist who, satisfied with having computed their remoteness to a fraction of an inch, would then conclude that the influence of the moon upon the earth is far greater than that of the sun? Neither in outer space, nor in time, can the potency of a force be measured by the single dimension of distance.

One could apply the same metaphorical association – of distance versus relevance – to geography as well as time. Granted, there is most definitely, as scholars such as David Kang have repeatedly urged, a pressing need for more substantive work focused on Asian diplomatic and military history. Acquiring a better understanding of China and India's military pasts, along with seminal texts such as the *Arthashastra* or *The Three Kingdoms*, for example, is essential to understanding both Asian behemoths' respective strategic cultures and ideational outlook. That being said, the oft-subsidiary assumption that one should automatically dismiss certain periods in history or strategic traditions as irrelevant to contemporary challenges in Asia, is not only short-sighted, but also somewhat disconcerting. Is the underlying premise of such culturally freighted arguments that the lessons to be derived from European history are somehow solely for Europeans, and the lessons and insights from Asian history only for Asians? Can we not somehow all pool and learn from our collective historical experiences rather than hive them off into our respective sub-disciplinary corners?

Moreover, there is an additional risk nested within such culturalist assumptions: that of falling victim to the more insidious variant of regional essentialism promoted by authoritarian state actors such the People's Republic of China. Indeed, Beijing has long insisted that its supposedly exceptional historical trajectory entitles it to an unprecedented degree of deference on the basis of a so-called 'different historical model of international relations'. It is not immediately apparent, however, that China's much-touted 'tributary model' of international relations provides a better repository of insights into its current behaviour in the South China Sea, than, say – the Valois and Plantagenet dynasties' sophisticated use of lawfare for purposes of territorial contestation in the fraught decades leading up to the Hundred Years War. Lessons can be gleaned and applied across different cultures as well as across different periods. There are most certainly rich seams of world history that remain woefully underexplored, but the default posture should not be to argue in favour of further disciplinary siloisation, but rather to read more, to read deeper, and to read across traditions.

Breaking through Cobwebs of Learning: the importance of a more humanist approach to the study of international relations
In 1704, Jonathan Swift published a mordant satire on the 'Quarrel of the Ancients and Moderns' entitled *The Battle of the Books*. Written in the form of a mock epic, and set in the King's Library of St James's Palace, it described a war between two armies of books – the Ancients and the Moderns – over a real estate squabble far away on Mount Parnassus, the home of the Muses in Greek mythology. The neighbourly quarrel begins when the Moderns complain that the soaring heights of the Ancients' ancestral land obstruct their view, and demand that their august predecessors 'remove themselves down to the lower summit, which the moderns would graciously surrender to them'. The Ancients are both baffled and indignant, pointing out 'how little they expected such a message from a colony whom they had admitted, out of their own free grace, to so near a neighbourhood'. Moreover, the Ancients' elevated neighbourhood had long provided the very shade and shelter that allowed the ungrateful

Moderns to flourish in the first place. As the dispute grows in intensity, leading to 'whole rivulets of ink being exhausted', it begins to spread to public libraries such as at St James, where the books come to life and engage in an unseemly brawl.

Swift is far from an impartial narrator, and his own intellectual sensitivities skew heavily toward those of the Ancients. His bias is made most evident during the highlight of the narrative, which consists in a public battle of wits between the library's resident spider and a visiting bee which, in the course of its merry itinerancy, careens through a meticulously erected cobweb. Each critter serves as the figurative champion for the two papered hosts facing off on the bookshelves below.

The spider – representing the Moderns – derides the bee's cross-disciplinary and supposedly indiscriminatory approach, his dependence on all manners of foreign sustenance, and describes his opponent as a 'vagabond without house or home, without stock or inheritance'. The self-important arachnid 'having swelled himself into the size and posture of a disputant', and 'fully predetermined his mind against all conviction', proudly draws attention to his intellectual autonomy and to the mathematical precision of his cobwebs, which are clearly the fruit of Cartesian reason and the scientific method:

> Your livelihood is a universal plunder upon nature; a freebooter over fields and gardens; and for the sake of stealing, will rob a nettle as easily as a violet. Whereas I am a domestic animal, furnished with a native stock within myself. This large [cobweb] castle, to show my improvements in the mathematics, is all built with my own hands, and the materials extracted altogether out of my own person.

The bee remains unflappable, and his response, in its searing wit, constitutes one of the more memorable defences of the humanist approach to wisdom and learning. Conceding that, with regard to the spider's 'skill in architecture and mathematics', he had little to say, the Ancients' apian defender concludes by posing the following query:

> ...the question comes all to this; whether it is the nobler being of the two, that which, by a lazy contemplation of four inches round, by an overweening pride, feeding and engendering on itself, turns all into excrement and venom, producing nothing at all but flybane and

cobweb; or that which, by a universal range, with long search, much study and judgment, and distinction of things, brings home honey and wax.

In short, it is both humbler and more worthwhile to view the pursuit of political and literary wisdom as a continuous, wide-ranging journey across time and disciplines, rather than as an immediately achievable and scientifically bounded endeavour. Less parsimonious theories, methodological fetishism and disciplinary prejudices, suggests Swift. Rather, the path to excellence resides in a combination of curiosity and humility: one which recognises the immense debt owed to one's intellectual forebears, as well as the fact that in some fields of human endeavour there are no monocausal explanations or elegant theoretical solutions. Without such an attitude toward knowledge, one risks spinning increasingly elaborate – but ultimately flimsy – designs from one's own guts and producing an endless stream of banalities. Indeed, if one opts to ignore the wealth of insights already contained in canonical texts, how can one be sure that one is not merely restating what has already been articulated by one's predecessors, and perhaps even with far more sophistication and eloquence? International relations theories can certainly be of use in momentarily simplifying a complex world, much as two-dimensional paper maps can help guide the befuddled traveller. An overreliance on such mental crutches, however, can cause one to durably lose one's sense of orientation.

From Petrarch to Ben Jonson, the allegory of the bee and of its peripatetic existence had long been used by humanist theorists of knowledge. Perhaps the earliest, and most famous, example is contained in the writings of Seneca, in his 'Moral Letters to Lucilius', when the Roman scholar-practitioner described how true wisdom could only stem from extensive reading, and from a slow, almost alchemical process of intellectual distillation:

> We [scholars] also, I say, ought to copy those bees, and sift whatever we have gathered from a varied course of reading…Then, by applying the supervising care with which our nature has endowed us – in other words, our natural gifts – we should so blend these several flavours into one delicious compound that even though it betrays its origin, yet nevertheless it is clearly a different thing from whence it came.

This is where applied history, with its prudential rejection of presentism, teleological certainty, and overweening positivism, can prove most useful. It furnishes a healthy scepticism in the face of those who, starting from grand theories or first principles, are determined to engineer tidy sets of explanations applicable across all circumstances. It recognises that threads of wisdom are woven throughout the tapestry of history, and that our epoch is not necessarily more complex, unique or enlightened than any other. Last but not least, it renews with the humanist belief – so dear to figures such as Montaigne, Charron or Locke – that there is an abiding beauty in the expression of doubt, and in the recognition of complexity. And lest one fear that – by detaching oneself from one's snug disciplinary harness – one's thoughts might drown in the vast ocean of past human endeavour, the great, churning wake left by figures such as Thucydides can always help guide us to shore. For as Francis Bacon once lyrically expounded:

> ...the images of men's wits and knowledges remain in books, exempted from the wrong of time, and capable of perpetual renovation. Neither are they fit to be called images, because they generate still, and cast their seeds in the minds of others, provoking and causing infinite actions and opinions in succeeding ages; so that, if the invention of a ship was thought so noble...how much more are (such works) to be magnified, which, as ships, pass through the vast seas of time, and make ages so distant to participate of the wisdom, illuminations, and inventions, the one of the other.

CULTURE AND CRISIS

Westminster Bridge during lockdown, April 2020.

THE EMPTY METROPOLIS

Tom Holland

To Westminster Bridge

On Easter morning, my wife and I got up early, left our house in south London, and walked to Westminster Bridge. We arrived there just in time for sunrise. The bridge was completely empty. No cars, no cyclists, no pedestrians: just us. We stood there and admired the view. On the south bank loomed the great concrete cube of St Thomas's Hospital, where Boris Johnson, the prime minister, had just spent his third night in intensive care. On the far bank rose Big Ben, muffled by scaffolding. Looking eastwards, the Thames appeared preternaturally still. The city looked as beautiful as once, more than 200 years ago, it had appeared to Wordsworth: 'All bright and glittering in the smokeless air.'

But if it was beautiful, so also was it chilling. By 12 April, London had been in lockdown for three weeks. Infection was everywhere: across the city, across the country, across the world. If, in St Thomas's, there had been someone who for the past month had been lying in a coma, and that person had woken up abruptly, and left the hospital, and wandered out onto Westminster Bridge, how bewildering the silence would have seemed. 'Dear God! the very houses seem asleep' – but now, in a city immensely vaster than the one Wordsworth knew, immensely more full of people, the houses seemed dead. It required no great feat of imagination, that Easter dawn, to gaze at London spread out before us, and to imagine it one vast tomb.

'How unreal it all is,' people kept saying, 'how like a film.' The world might not have experienced a pandemic on the scale of Covid-19 in over a century, and yet there seemed, for all that, a haunting sense of familiarity about its progress. The remorseless spread of infection across the globe, tracked by maps, and arrows, and graphs; the stilling of airports and motorways; the spectacle of empty streets in the world's most iconic cities: we had seen all these things in films many times before. We found ourselves trapped inside a familiar story, following the lines of a narrative that has been written time and again. The best guide to where this crisis may take us, to the rhythms it is bound to follow, lies not, perhaps, in briefing papers written by epidemiologists and economists, but in fictions. These, in 2020, can strike us with the force of familiarity because it was only in fictions that people writing in the years prior to 2020 could supply narrative accounts of what the twenty-first century might look like when swept by a pandemic. Even so, the authors of these fictions did not have to draw on any particular powers of prophecy to predict how society might respond. Successful fictions have roots that reach deep into human nature, and therefore into all the various ways in which it has manifested itself over the course of history. Visions of the future are invariably mirrors held up to the past.

When Cillian Murphy's character in the 2002 horror film *28 Days Later* wakes up in St Thomas's Hospital, crosses an empty Westminster Bridge, and wanders through a silent London, it is to discover that almost everyone in the country has been infected by an Ebola-like virus that turns its victims into ravening zombies. He and three other survivors do what anyone would do in such a situation: run for the hills. Over the course of the film, they hunker down variously in a tower block, in a stately home converted into a military stockade, and in a Lake District cottage. Brilliantly though *28 Days Later* may rework the clichés of the zombie movie, it still depends for its power on the instinct without which there would never have been a zombie myth in the first place. The urge to flee infection, to put up barricades against the infected, is as primordial as civilisation itself. 'Everybody's looks', wrote Samuel Pepys in 1665, as plague ravaged London, 'is of death, and nothing else; and few people going up and down, that the town is a place distressed and forsaken.' Boccaccio's *Decameron*, written in the immediate aftermath of the Black Death, has as its framing device the flight of ten young men and women from plague-ravaged Florence to a villa, where they remain sufficiently proof against the buboes to tell a hundred tales. A millennium and more before, in Roman Alexandria, those with sufficient resources had likewise fled the onset of epidemic: 'At the first appearance of the disease, they pushed the sufferers away and fled from their dearest, throwing them into the roads before they were dead and treating unburied corpses as dirt, hoping thereby to avert the spread and contagion of the fatal disease.'

Sure enough, as SARS-CoV-2 began to spread around the globe, it was those countries that pulled up the drawbridge fastest that tended to suffer the fewest deaths. The memory of this, in a world that had been growing suspicious of globalisation even prior to the onset of Covid-19, is unlikely to be one that fades any time soon. Even so, as fans of zombie films know all too well, the idea that anywhere in a time of infection can truly serve as a sanctuary is delusory. Peril can lurk just as well within a refuge as beyond its walls. In *28 Days Later*, the soldiers who welcome the film's protagonists to the ring-fenced stately home turn out to be rapists, and their commander a psychopath. Nor, in a horror film, is there ever any real prospect of holding the line. It is pretty much a rule of the genre that any defence capable of being breached will be breached. Retreat to an abbey, weld the doors shut, party without a care in the world, yet in the end the Red Death will always get through.

This is not to suggest that Darkness and Decay and Covid-19 will hold illimitable dominion over all. Leaving Westminster Bridge, walking along the Thames, we began to find ourselves passed by the odd runner, and in the City by the occasional car. Looping back to Trafalgar Square, we found no toppled double-decker bus – as Cillian Murphy's character had done in *28 Days Later* – blocking the road in Whitehall. Yet to wake up from a nightmare is not always to escape its shadow. Horror films, by giving shape to fears that may lurk inchoate or unarticulated in the collective subconscious, provide as good a guide as any to the terrors that this crisis is bound to leave in its wake. Even should a vaccine be discovered, even should herd immunity be obtained, even should the virus end up burning itself it out, the memories of the pandemic will not quickly fade. Instead – much like the scarring that can be left on the lungs of someone who has suffered badly from Covid-19 – dread of infection and suspicion of the infected look likely to remain as a permanent scarring on the mind.

To Primrose Hill

Nineteen days later, we got up even earlier than we had done on Easter morning, and walked to Putney. Here, in H G Wells' 1898 novel *The War of the Worlds*, an artilleryman camps out amid a great desolation of houses and contemplates a new normal. Martians, after landing outside London,

Following pages: The Banquet in the Pine Forest, third painting in the series *The Story of Nastagio degli Onesti*, Sandro Botticelli, 1483. Museo del Prado, Madrid.

have conquered the city, and scoured it almost entirely clean of human life. How, then, are people to survive? By retreating underground, by living like rats in the city's drains. So, at any rate, the artilleryman tells the narrator of Wells' novel. 'There won't be any more blessed concerts for a million years or so; there won't be any Royal Academy of Arts, and no nice little feeds at restaurants.' But the narrator, although initially convinced by the argument, soon comes to realise that he has no wish to live under such a permanent lockdown. Instead, abandoning the artilleryman and crossing the Thames into Fulham, he walks through the dead city, heading for Primrose Hill, where the Martians have made their camp.

The account of what he sees along the route – which includes, in an eerie foreshadowing of *28 Days Later*, a toppled bus – is sufficiently detailed that we, following in his footsteps, found it an easy thing to trace. By midday, we had reached Primrose Hill. Here, in Wells' novel, the narrator discovers that the world is saved: that the Martians, with none of the immunity to terrestrial diseases that humans over many millennia have developed, have succumbed to pathogens. 'All about the pit, & saved as by a miracle from everlasting destruction, stretched the great Mother of Cities. Those who have only seen London veiled in her sombre robes of smoke can scarcely imagine the naked clearness & beauty of the silent wilderness of houses.' We did as the narrator had done: sat and enjoyed the view.

People who would once have looked to the heavens for salvation from pandemic, by offering sacrifice or raising prayers, now hang on the words of virologists. Governments, struggling to defeat an adversary they barely understand, insist that they are following 'the science'. Scientists themselves, standing before the cameras as they guide the fate of nations, have become celebrities. People root for their various epidemiological models as they might cheer on football teams, debate their looks, gossip about their affairs. We have come to live in a world in which almost everything we do – whether we can travel, or go out for a meal, or visit our parents – is determined by 'the science'.

Does this mean, then, that the future is one that will be governed by a cool and objective rationality? Wells, a century ago and more, scorned the claims of churches and mosques to offer any guide to the purposes of the universe. Both, in the Martians' initial assault on Woking, are flattened much as a man might flatten an ant-heap. A curate, hailing 'the

Last Judgment, designed by Janos Stein and executed by mosaic master Miksa Roth, 1904–1908. Kerepesi Cemetery, Budapest.

great and terrible day of the Lord', goes steadily insane. Far from being saved, he ends up drained by a Martian of his blood. Yet Wells, despite rejecting Christianity, could not help but bear witness to its stamp. Shadowy throughout *The War of the Worlds*, but a constant presence for all that, is the sense that the British Empire, the prime target of the Martian war-machines, is reaping what it has sown. 'The Tasmanians,' the narrator writes, 'in spite of their human likeness, were entirely swept out of existence in a war of extermination waged by European immigrants, in the space of fifty years. Are we such apostles of mercy as to complain if the Martians warred in the same spirit?' It is the status of London as the greatest and richest city on the face of the earth that makes her downfall so salutary. So Isaiah had foretold the downfall of Babylon; so St John had foretold the downfall of Rome. That a day of judgement will come when cities grown fat on the exploitation of the far-flung places of the world will be humbled into the dust is an assumption so deeply rooted in the soil of Christian culture that not even Wells, in the late nineteenth century, could escape it. Nor, in the early twenty-first century, can we.

The current crisis, far from calming the apocalyptic strain in our collective imaginings, seems bound only to stoke it. In the book of Revelation, Rome was portrayed as a monstrous vampire, engorged with the lifeblood of the entire world. Today, there are plenty who conceive of the great centres of twenty-first century civilisation in very similar terms. The hyper-connectivity of contemporary capitalism, combined with the steady degradation of ecosystems across the world, is providing an ideal opportunity for novel pathogens to come into contact with humans, and then, having done so, to spread faster and further than they have ever done before. It is not hard to see why many of us, contemplating the impact of Covid-19, should see it much as plague was understood in ancient times: as a judgement upon us for our sins.

Some, however, go even further. That the Himalayas have lately been visible from India for the first time in 30 years, that boars have begun venturing into European towns, that bird song is to be heard in cities rather than the din of planes and cars: all these developments of the past months have helped to foster a sense among a radical minority that SARS-CoV-2, far from serving a baneful purpose, may well be on the side of the angels. 'Coronavirus is Earth's vaccine,' as a popular meme has it, 'We are the virus.' But this, perhaps, seen through the prism of Wells' novel, might be given a different formulation. In addition to renewing humanity's faith in science, Covid-19 is likely as well to supercharge the opposite: a dread that our technological prowess, and all the appetites it sustains, threatens the planet with ruin. In which case we would not be the virus. We would be the Martians.

To Talbot Yard

Twenty-five days later, I walked to Talbot Yard, a narrow thoroughfare just south of London Bridge. My aim in heading there was to embark on a pilgrimage. Or at least a kind of pilgrimage. It was certainly nothing that could compensate me for the walk that, at the end of the previous year, before either I or my brother had ever heard of Wuhan, the pair of us had scheduled for the fortnight after Easter. As part of a campaign against a government scheme to build a monstrously intrusive road development through the Stonehenge landscape (a World Heritage Site, no less!), our plan had been to hike from Dover all the way to Stonehenge itself. The prospect of taking to the Downs, following prehistoric trails, breathing in the fresh air of spring, had been something that both of us had been looking forward to eagerly all winter. Until, of course, Covid-19 had intervened.

Regret for what might have been had plunged me into gloom the moment the lockdown began. Depressed not to be following an ancient pilgrimage route across Kent in the month of April, I had turned for consolation to the most famous account of such a journey: 'Whan that Aprill with his shoures soote…' So begins the most celebrated work of medieval English literature. *The Canterbury Tales*, Geoffrey Chaucer's riff on the model established a few decades earlier by Boccaccio, is a collection of short stories told by people who, as in the *Decameron*, have left their homes, and are departing a city. Chaucer's narrators, however, are no fugitives. Their aim, rather than hunkering down, is to enjoy the closest that most people in the fourteenth century came to going on a holiday. Begun in 1386, almost four decades after the arrival of the Black Death in England, it portrayed a society in which people drawn from every background and class have not the slightest compunction about meeting up in a London tavern, then heading off together for Canterbury on pilgrimage.

Did this mean, however, that Chaucer had written a poem from which the shadow of pestilence had been lifted? I had always assumed so; but now, reading it in the shadow of pandemic, I found myself not so sure.

Under lockdown, I was alert in a way I had never been before to the joy that might be taken in the simplest pleasures: going for a drink in a pub, leaving a city for the countryside, breathing in clear air. Would Chaucer's pilgrims have taken a similar joy in them? Perhaps. The Black Death, although it had first arrived on England's shores in 1348, had returned numerous times since. A decade before Chaucer embarked on *The Canterbury Tales*, it had raged all winter across London. In 1378, it had paid a fifth visitation to England, stripping entire regions 'of their best men'. From that year on, chroniclers no longer recorded its arrival and departure – not because it had ceased to infect people, but because it had become endemic.

To live in London, then, in the final decades of the fourteenth century, was to live in constant dread of the effects of epidemic. Chaucer, who as a child had lost large numbers of his relatives to the initial onset of the plague, had grown up in the full consciousness of the great reaping that had claimed a third, or perhaps a half, of all Christendom. The decades might have passed, and the inferno of infection with them; but the bush fires continued to smoulder. What joy, then, when April arrived with its 'shoures soote', to bid farewell to a city that might well have been rotten with plague the whole winter, to feel the 'sweete breeth' of the open road in spring, and to head for the shrine of that blissful martyr St Thomas Beckett, 'that hem hath holpen whan that they were seeke.' It might well have seemed a gesture of defiance. It might well have seemed a gesture of hope.

Arriving at Talbot Yard, where the tavern in which Chaucer met with his fellow pilgrims had once stood, I could not have a drink, nor could I mingle with strangers, nor could I embark on the 60-mile road to Canterbury. But I felt cheered to be there, all the same. Of the three walks I had taken across London since the lockdown began, this, the final one, seemed to point towards the surest future. The lockdown was bound to end. Society would renew its rhythms. My brother and I – no matter how late – would get to do our pilgrimage.

Life, I dared to hope, would find a way.

Adoration of the Magi, Nicola Pisano,
1257–1260. Baptistery of San Giovanni, Pisa.

CRISIS AND THE CREATION OF GREAT ART

Andrew Graham-Dixon

S ocial crisis has often been a catalyst for artistic change, so much so that I wonder if there might be room for an alternative history of art. The history I have in mind would consider the development of painting and sculpture (and for that matter architecture) not as a gradual metamorphosis of styles – from medieval to renaissance to baroque and beyond – but as a series of convulsive responses to the cataclysms of the historical past.

This is certainly, I think, a fruitful way to think about the origins of Italian Renaissance art, which might reasonably be regarded as the fountainhead of the Western art tradition as a whole. No one can question that a great change swept through the painting and sculpture of Italy from the early thirteenth century to the middle of the fifteenth century. In short, a new art was born at that time: one that turned away from the extreme stylisation of Gothic, on the one hand, and the transcendent abstractions of Byzantium, on the other. This new art emphasised the suffering humanity of the adult Christ, dying on the cross, just as it emphasised the helplessness of the infant Christ in the manger, newborn baby of a refugee family forced to flee from a tyranny so severe that it condoned the massacre of innocent children. It made visible the pain of his mother, forced to witness the torture and death of her son, taken from her at a cruelly young age.

This art of pain, pathos and drama looked new and unfamiliar to late medieval eyes, although it drew inspiration from the distant past. It was rooted in a naturalism for which the chief precedent was the statuary of ancient Roman times, which survived in abundance, albeit often rather damaged, all over Italy. It is no coincidence that the greatest innovators in the field of early Renaissance sculpture, the father-and-son team of Nicola and Giovanni Pisano, came from Pisa (whence they took their name), where such remains were particularly numerous and well preserved. They can still be seen today, in the form of the numerous sarcophagi carved with classical myths and legends that line the Campo Santo, a cloister erected on the site of an ancient Roman burial ground, the relics of which were preserved as curiosities from another world.

Looking at the masterpieces of the Pisano workshop, such as Nicola's mid-thirteenth century bas-relief of *The Adoration of the Magi*, which decorates the pulpit in Pisa's Baptistry, or Giovanni's slightly later relief of *The Massacre of the Innocents*, on a similar pulpit in the church of Sant'Andrea in Pistoia, it is clear that they borrowed from the sarcophagi of their home town so extensively as to have regarded the Roman sculpture of ancient Rome as their art school, or academy. Nicola's Virgin Mary resembles a Roman goddess; Giovanni's tangle of agonised mothers resisting Herod's death squad recall the struggling bodies of the Trojan priest Laocoon and his sons, fighting off serpents. What Rome gave to Pisano, father and son, was a new and distinctly un-medieval sense of the human body as it might be realised in art: a body endowed with substance and flesh; a body capable of movement; a body realised in art, but so convincingly realised as to compel belief.

The innovations of Nicola and Giovanni Pisano, in sculpture, were shortly followed by Giotto's great leap in painting. The two were not unconnected: Giotto knew and admired the work of his predecessors from Pisa, so much so that their work might have been his own art school. The figures who animate the walls of the Arena Chapel in Padua, Giotto's most perfectly preserved cycle of frescoes, have such weight and monumentality that they look less like real people (to my eyes) than sculptures come to life. In scenes such as the *Lamentation*, the emotional effect is all the stronger for this: when Mary grieves, it is as if a statue has burst into tears.

The great shift in form and sensibility embodied by such work is clear and obvious. But what lay behind it? What was its cause? The question goes unanswered in many histories of art, even many specialist studies of the Renaissance. The most compelling explanation is that the artists of the period were responding, with great urgency, to a social emergency.

The late twelfth and early thirteenth centuries were a time of wrenching change in Italy. The feudal social structures of the Middle Ages were collapsing and a new mercantile society was emerging. The process has been compared to a mini-industrial revolution, a phrase which does scant justice to the extent of upheaval facing many, especially the poor, at the time. In the flourishing cities of Tuscany, Florence in particular, new methods of textile production led to a sudden and massive expansion in

Lamentation over the Dead Christ, Giotto (Giotto
di Bondone), 1304–1306. Cappella degli
Scrovegni, Padua.

manufacturing. Large factories and workshops were established around the river Arno and its tributaries, and many thousands of impoverished agricultural labourers – their plight worsened by successive crop failures, repeated outbreaks of plague and resulting widespread famine – flocked to the cities in search of work. They were paid a pittance, but that pittance was still preferable to the total uncertainty of life in their old peasant communities. The new textile industrialists needed their labour but were not prepared to house them. There was no space for these crowds of wage-seeking refugees in the medieval warren of streets that made up the cities of the time. So they lived outside the walls, in vast makeshift settlements of wood and canvas: dwelling places of the terminally desperate that were Renaissance equivalents to the shanty towns of modern cities like Mumbai or Mexico City. They had little food and poor shelter. Disease was rife, healthcare virtually non-existent.

The poor in every crisis need their spokesman, and in early thirteenth-century Italy that spokesman was – it has often been so – a man born into the very ranks of those responsible for their plight. Francis of Assisi was the son of a wealthy textile merchant, who renounced his birthright to take up the life of an itinerant friar ministering to the needs, above all, of the new urban poor. The essentials of his legend are well known: his calling to faith by an image of Christ which miraculously spoke to him in a tumbledown church; his charismatic preaching; his communing with nature, recorded in lyric poems known as 'The Flowers of Francis'; his receiving of the stigmata, miraculous wounds like those of the crucifixion, burned into his flesh during a retreat on Mount Averna. Less well known is the transformative effect of his teachings on the art and architecture of the Christian church in Italy.

Francis recognised that the poor of his time needed an image of Christ – and an idea of Christ – very different from that which prevailed in the churches of the day. They needed a Christ in whom they could really believe, a Christ who could allow them to dream that their own sufferings, like his, were a path to redemption; a Christ whose story they could follow, scene by scene, as if in a comic book, and in so doing find consolation for their own pain and suffering. Francis's spiritual revolution led to a corresponding revolution not just in the imagery of the church but in the very structure of churches themselves, as buildings.

His conviction that the image of Christ should be made more immediate, more real, more visceral, had its most immediate effect on depictions of that central event of the Christian story, the crucifixion. Before Francis, it was customary for artists to depict Christ on the cross as a smiling, beatific figure, unscathed by his ordeal: transcending his death before it has even happened. This type of image, perfected over centuries by generations of painters working in what art historians have called the Italo-Byzantine style, was known as the *Christus Triumphans*, Christ Triumphant. After the impact of Francis's teachings is felt, the image of Christ on the cross changes accordingly. Artists no longer make him look detached from the instrument of his torture. He writhes against the nails that pierce him, his body assuming the serpentine contours of agony. His brow furrows and his gaze loses its serenity, becoming tormented and anxious. Sometimes his eyes are tight shut, screwed up in anguish. Tears run from his cheeks, and his wounds bleed. This post-Franciscan image of the crucifixion was known as the *Christus Patiens*, Christ Suffering.

The best place I know to see and feel this transition, from a triumphant to a suffering Christ, is the *Sala dei Crocifissi* in the little visited Pinacoteca of Pisa, 'the room of the crosses', where a number of crucifixes from the twelfth to the fourteenth century, which once stood in modest local churches, have been gathered and planted in the gallery floor like so many trees. What they collectively reveal, in shades of feeling that move inexorably from serenity to agony in the course of just a few decades, is the 'before, and 'after, of art in the time of St Francis. The new agonised Christ was the exemplary image, the figurehead so to speak, of troubled times. This was not just powerful art, it was also helpful, and healing. The idea that their God had suffered as they suffered was a source of great consolation – as Francis knew it would be – to those struggling to make sense of lives that might easily have seemed hopeless.

Francis, together with the other charismatic friar of the period, St Dominic, also enacted a revolution in church building. The cathedrals and baptistries of great Italian cities such as Florence were built with a Byzantine sense of magnificence and otherworldliness: their construction was of fine polychrome marble while their decoration, carried out by teams of mosaicists from the Greek east, might take half a century or more. But Francis and Dominic (and their followers) needed to build many new churches, and they needed to build them quickly. The people they wanted to help could not wait 50 years to be saved. The average length of life for a man from the new urban underclass was somewhere in the early thirties (a lifespan not much longer than that of Jesus Christ).

Sala dei Crocifissi.
Museo Nazionale di San Matteo, Pisa.

So the Franciscans and Dominicans built not in marble, but in brick, raising their churches on simple post-and-lintel frameworks of timber. The simplicity of the resulting structures is still striking today. They are rather like boxes in cruciform shape, designed to accommodate as many people as possible.

Under the influence of the friars, who well understood the power of the image, these churches became boxes filled with stories: the stories of the New Testament, told by painters in pictures of great clarity, as sharp in colour as in emotion, so that people who could not read might nonetheless be touched by the truths of the Bible. The church walls were plastered and fresco cycles were painted into the wet plaster. Fresco was preferred to mosaic for the same reasons that brick was chosen over marble: cheapness and speed. Such was the genius with which successive generations of Italian painters employed the medium that it was eventually adopted everywhere, even in churches or chapels intended for the rich and powerful, rather than the poor (the Sistine Chapel, painted in fresco by Michelangelo, is a case in point). But its origins lie in a particular response to the plight of a particular group of people, who were poor through and through. Fresco itself is dirt-poor, being after all no more than earth pigment fixed to a wall: the original *arte povera*.

Using such methods, an entire church for a congregation of thousands could be built and painted in less than a year. Such large churches were totally different in appearance and in kind from the large churches that had preceded them, which were built over many decades or even centuries and dedicated to the glory of God. These new churches turned those old priorities upside down. They were not built for God but for men and women who needed God in their lives, or at the very least the experience of Christian mercy. They were emergency refuges as well as places of worship. Every Franciscan foundation contained a hospital and a pharmacy, as well as a soup kitchen, so when famine came or when plague struck – as it did with depressing regularity throughout the thirteenth and fourteenth centuries, sometimes carrying off as much as half of a city's population – the friars would at least be in a position to help.

The locations of these churches also expressed the intentions behind them. Stand outside more or less any great Franciscan or Dominican urban church from the thirteenth or fourteenth centuries and you will, almost invariably, find yourself on what was once the perimeter of the city: this is true, for example, of the Franciscan churches of Santa Croce in Florence and San Francesco in Pistoia, as it is of San Domenico in Siena. Why should this be so? Because these churches were not built to serve the city dwellers but the migrant labourers huddled in makeshift housing at the edges of the city. To save people living at the margins of society, Francis taught, you have to make your dwelling with them.

In essence, Francis's message was clear and straightforward. He believed passionately that Christianity was a religion of and for the poor: had Christ himself not favoured simple folk like Peter the fisherman when choosing his disciples? Had he not preached to the poor, and fed them with loaves and fishes? Had he not said that the meek will inherit the earth, and that it would be easier for a camel to pass though the eye of a needle than for a rich man to get to heaven? Therefore the Church itself should avoid ostentation and magnificence and should minister above all to the poor – to whom Francis and his followers referred as 'the living images of Christ'. Religious art, accordingly, should speak the language of those poor people. It should be direct and immediate and easy to understand. It should be realistic, in order to compel belief in the stories of the Bible: because belief in those stories is faith, and faith is what saves.

The conviction with which Francis and his likeminded contemporaries preached that message was the driving force behind Renaissance art in its earliest and most vital phase. And all of it – Francis's personal sense of mission, as well as the new buildings, the new paintings and sculptures created to serve that sense of mission – was born out of a moment of crisis.

Much the same might be said of many other great shifts in the history of art. Would Dutch art of the so-called Golden Age, with its peaceful landscapes and gentle celebrations of domestic life, breathe the same air of nervous and idealistic optimism had it not been for the 80 years of war with Spain that preceded it? Could the turbulence of French Romanticism have ever stirred into being had it not been for the upheavals of the French Revolution and the Napoleonic wars? Could the English Gothic style have developed its own peculiarities – seesawing between morbid nostalgia for the medieval past and visions of a dystopian future – had it not been for the trauma of the Industrial Revolution, the birth of the modern metropolis and with it the spectre of a new, nineteenth-century urban poor?

I am sure there are lessons to be drawn from all this, but I personally do not subscribe to what might be called 'the cuckoo clock argument' – the glib idea put forward by Orson Welles in *The Third Man*, that tumult and conflict (as in Italy under the Borgias) produce great art, while peace and understanding (as in Switzerland) produce only trivia like cuckoo clocks. Thinking like that leads to another glib misconception, namely the belief that good or interesting art is a silver lining to every cloud of crisis. The times might have been bad, but look on the bright side: at least they produced some good books to read and some wonderful pictures to look at. I think that is the wrong way to see it. The truth is more complicated.

Moments of crisis have a way of making people – some people, at least – rethink their lives, re-evaluate their relationships with others and reconsider their values. At such moments art is naturally revitalised and is almost bound to ask searching questions with fresh intensity – for the simple reason that art is always the mirror of a broader human consciousness. I would be very surprised if our own, current crisis did not yield similar results. I also think that although our troubles cannot be equated with those facing thirteenth-century Italy, many of St Francis's beliefs deserve renewed consideration. What he had to say about the inequality between rich and poor, and about man's relationship to the natural world, seems as true today as it did 800 years ago.

The southern facade of Castle Howard,
near York, England.

THE COUNTRY HOUSE IN DECLINE

Clive Aslet

Rats are supposed to leave a sinking ship; in 1977, I joined one. Although the country house was, people thought, holed beneath the waterline, I became an architectural writer for the magazine *Country Life*, which was dedicated to that very subject. Since its foundation in 1897, *Country Life* had celebrated the architecture, collections, gardens, horses, dogs, families, traditions and arcana of country houses. Each issue contained a long, scholarly article on one of these great buildings, describing its evolution, usually over centuries, and the characters who had built it. How grand, how apparently – but the whole edifice was tottering.

For the 1970s was a calamitous era for country houses. The extent of the catastrophe that had overtaken them was made painfully clear by an exhibition at the Victoria and Albert Museum, 'The Destruction of the Country House'; this revealed that more than 1,000 country houses had been demolished in the course of the twentieth century. Visitors were greeted by the erudite voice of Sir John Summerson, curator of the Sir John Soane Museum, intoning the roll call of losses. Later, the V&A's director, Sir Roy Strong, would remember: 'Many was the time I stood in that exhibition watching the tears stream down the visitors' faces as they battled to come to terms with all that had gone.'

Admittedly I had a temperamental affinity for lost causes and would certainly have galloped into battle with Prince Rupert of the Rhine if I had been living at the time of the English Civil War, irrespective of the ultimate Roundhead victory. (Although in reality I wouldn't have been a cavalier on horseback but an unglamorous pikeman, possibly consigned to the forward position called a Forlorn Hope.) But I don't think my decision to join *Country Life*, at which I remained, in one capacity or another, for nearly 40 years, was the result of an economic death wish. The fact was I had been to university during the mid-1970s. What if Britain was up the spout, the sick man of Europe? We were 18. There were more important things in our lives. We hadn't known any different. Later, country house doors opened for me and I loved the many layers of culture I found inside. But the state of the country house symbolised Britain's failure to hold its head up in the world. Owners were struggling to keep the roof on and the taxman at bay.

There is a divide in political life between those who remember the 1970s and those who don't. To most people who were alive during that dreary decade, it felt like a horrible dream – the sort in which you can see a disaster unfolding but are powerless to influence events. Britain was a democracy, not a totalitarian state, but personal ambition seemed to be frustrated almost as often as it was in the Soviet Union. I was lucky in moving to London; as a journalist, I could claim that the telephone was an essential tool of my trade. As a result, it took only a fortnight to get one installed, whereas friends who could not play this card had to wait months. The trains which I took frequently often broke down. Every news bulletin contained details of a new strike. Secondary action meant that a strike by one union could be backed up by others: should the management of British Leyland have contrived to get a car off the production line, after the Amalgamated Engineering Workers had downed tools, ASLEF, the train drivers' union, could refuse to transport it. It was an anarchic, grey decade.

Cambridge, where I read first English, in a faculty riven by ideological conflict, and then, more comfortingly, history of art, reflected the times. Student politics had sunk to a low ebb but protest remained the default position. The heroic age of left-wing agitation, whose ultimate expression had been, in 1970, a riot outside the Garden House Hotel, on the basis that a Greek-themed evening might have given succour to the junta of colonels that formed the Greek government, might have passed but students remained exercised by the university's failure to provide creche facilities for the small number of students with babies – a cause pursued by the Nursery Action Group, with the appropriate acronym of NAG.

When Prince Philip visited as chancellor of the university, their chants were drowned out by the pealing of the bells of Great St Mary's. My college, Peterhouse, rebelled against the zeitgeist – not that the Peterhouse fellows who influenced me believed in zeitgeists, or any other aspect of Hegelian determinism; au contraire. The history don Maurice Cowling was regarded as the eminence grise behind Thatcherism, as it became; the art historian David Watkin set his face against the tyranny of the

People in London using candles to read
newspaper headlines about the continuing
miners' strike, 1972.

modern movement. The philosopher Roger Scruton, who passed through as a junior fellow, later described how the few conservatives in academe would catch each other's eyes across the room like the homosexuals in Proust. The student body made a stand by founding dining societies and wearing white tie.

In one respect, Peterhouse was lucky. In that age of power cuts and rationing of electricity usage, the lights never went out. On the other side of Trumpington Street stood the polychromatic glory of the old Addenbrookes Hospital, yet to move to the new site, with the rabbits' ear chimneys that are visible from the train (now described as 'iconic' by the Cambridge University Hospitals NHS Foundation Trust. Actually, you couldn't see the colours of the 1860s façade until the building was reimagined as the Judge Business School, when the brickwork was cleaned of grime and more vibrancy added by the post-modernist architect John Outram). We were on the same circuit – a matter of some disappointment to those of us who had invested heavily in candles, in the expectation of using them for Georgian soirées. That was during the Tory Prime Minister Ted Heath's unhappy three-day week, when the working population was compelled to go part time, with none of the billions in compensation recently provided for lockdown. The National Union of Mineworkers was at the bottom of it. Soon, Heath was fighting one of the numerous elections of the period on the slogan: Who governs Britain? He lost. Whoever governed Britain, it wasn't him.

Misery for all, but a disproportionate dose for country houses – those big, unwieldy, ancient, labour-intensive, remote and, many thought, anachronistic dwellings, stuffed with treasures, a steady stream of which was reaching the salerooms. Today, Covid-19 is an accelerator of change. In the 1970s, it was OPEC – the Organisation of the Petroleum Exporting Countries – which, resentful of Western support for Israel during the Yom Kippur War, imposed an oil embargo. The price of oil rose by 300%. Inflation skyrocketed. For country house owners the consequences were dire. Since 6,000 miles of railway line had been axed during the 1960s by Dr Beeching, the efficiency wonk who chaired British Railways, many stately piles could only be reached by car. On arrival, they might quite literally be below zero, since oil was the fuel of choice for heating them. I once visited a country house the morning after the heavy cast iron radiators and pipes, an epic legacy of Victorian plumbing, had exploded like artillery shells because the water inside them had frozen. With Britain in decline, the future of the great domestic creations that had housed the titans of industry and empire of previous ages looked bleak. The writing was on the wall, spelt out in stains from leaking roofs and the fungal spores of dry rot.

Problems had been gathering for three-quarters of a century. Film makers like Joseph Losey, director of *The Go-Between*, nostalgically evoked the Edwardian decade as a time of Indian summers and white dresses, but unease was already being felt by some country house owners. They were having difficulty in finding servants. This may seem strange, when one considers that, in terms of absolute numbers, peak servant was reached in the 1901 census, when about 1.7 million women worked in domestic service; but as a proportion of the growing population, this enormous figure was evidence of decline. Ten years later, it had fallen to about 1.35m. The servant question or even crisis, as it was beginning to be called, caused not only a practical problem but an ethical reaction. As a character in Mrs Humphry Ward's *The Marriage of William Ashe* of 1905 put it, 'people are beginning to be ashamed of enormous houses and troops of servants.'

Another harbinger of doom came in 1909, with Lloyd George's 'People's Budget'. It called for taxes on the sale of land, higher death duties and a supertax on incomes above £3,000. The measures were bitterly opposed by the House of Lords, as the bastion of the landed interest; but the upper house was defeated and its powers reduced. To the Duke of Bedford, this was tantamount to socialism and in 1911 he announced that he would sell his estate in Devon. This became the first of an avalanche of sales across the country which gathered pace after the war when it is said that a quarter of England changed hands: a transfer of ownership comparable to the dissolution of the monasteries.

During the First World War, 17% of British officers were killed, compared to 12% of ordinary soldiers. All those young subalterns leading their men from the front made a conspicuous target in their jodhpurs and top boots, with pistols rather than rifles in their hand; Eton's war memorial bears a thousand names. They were often sons of country houses. Taxation increased again, incomes stagnated. Agriculture, depressed since the 1870s, briefly revived while Britain was blockaded, but after 1918 it fell back again, and the prestige of owning land hardly compensated for the responsibilities. By the time P G Wodehouse published *Thank You, Jeeves* in 1934, the plight of the fifth Baron Chuffnell of Chuffnell Regis

Egginton Hall, Derbyshire, demolished in 1955.
The photograph shows nurses and convalescent
soldiers in the grounds during WWI when the
house was used as a Red Cross hospital.

– Bertie Wooster's friend Chuffy – was to be pitied. 'He's dashed hard up, poor bloke, like most fellows who own land, and only lives at Chuffnell Hall because he's stuck with it and can't afford to live anywhere else…But who wants to buy a house that size in these times?' The 'times' were those of the slump, as Britain called the Great Depression. When Noel Coward wrote 'The Stately Homes of England' in 1938, sung by Lords Elderley, Borrowmere, Sickert and Camp in the musical *Operette*, the picture was of a bankrupt class, bereft of ideas and relevance.

The Second World War seemed to deliver the *coup de grâce* to a culture and way of life – think of Eveyln Waugh's *Brideshead Revisited*. Country houses that had been requisitioned to become schools, hospitals or military bases were not usually handed back in the condition in which their owners had left them, not least because no repairs had been undertaken for six years. Horror stories abound of mahogany furniture smashed to make kindling or taps being deliberately left on when the troops left, bringing down plaster ceilings (that happened at Egginton Hall in Derbyshire; the family had to demolish the house and move into the stables.) Under the reforming Attlee government of 1945, it was difficult to see that the country house had a continuing purpose. Woburn and Longleat reinvented themselves as visitor attractions for the mass holiday market but that option was not open to all; nor did it sit comfortably with the long-held image of the country house as an Arcadia that provided refuse from the tumult of life outside its bounds. It was becoming nothing but a worry. And so the demolitions, which had begun earlier in the century, gathered pace. When in 1982 Yale University Press published my first book, on country house architecture of the period 1890– 1939, I called it *The Last Country Houses*. I couldn't imagine houses on the scale of, say, Tylney Hall in Hampshire, built in 1898 for the 'randlord' Sir Lionel Phillips, banished from South Africa for his part in the Jamestown Raid, ever being needed again; it had six rooms for visiting valets.

But wait. Time has shown that my pessimism was misplaced. After an initial grinding of gears, Mrs Thatcher's premiership put Britain's Austin Metro back into gear; revving noisily and threatening to boil over, it climbed out of the slough of despond onto the sunlit uplands. The recovery was mirrored by the country house. In 1979, after the winter of discontent, when rubbish went uncollected and the dead unburied, the most desirable property in Britain, as displayed in the advertising pages of

Country Life, was a convenient modern house, close to a golf course and not too far from London. Large stately homes in remote counties were branded with the dread words: 'suitable for institutional use'. A decade later saw a transformation: now advertisements offered landed estates with sporting rights, beyond the Home Counties – and the more architecturally show-stopping the house was, the better.

In 1985, 'The Treasure Houses of Britain' exhibition, a spectacular celebration of the collections still found in privately owned country houses, opened in Washington DC and the 'country house look' swept the world. Admittedly Tylney Hall remains a hotel but other country houses that used to be schools were taken back into family use and many new ones erected.

The love affair with the country house has continued into the twenty-first century, albeit in different clothes – minimalism around 2000, wild-flower meadows and rewilding now. Not even the financial crisis of 2007–08 dented the determination of some clients to build or restore. The Covid-19 crisis has made the countryside seem more desirable than ever. Who knows what the future will hold? Some change in taste, perhaps, which cannot as yet be foreseen. So it's worth reflecting on the 1970s, when all hope seemed to be lost. The 'Destruction of the Country House' exhibition was right to highlight the toll of loss. But let's pause and remember, as we weren't inclined to do then, that Britain's country houses had suffered previous buffets. Nearly all the immense houses of the Lancastrian nobility disappeared after it lost the Wars of the Roses. Another wave of destruction accompanied the English Civil War, with the slighting of castles and wrecking of gentlemen's seats. Then there's the usual wastage caused by extravagance or a dud heir. The first Duke of Chandos's princely Canons Park, in Essex, lasted a mere 23 years after its completion before the second Duke broke it up. Numerous Tudor country houses were replaced in the Georgian period because their facades no longer fitted. Scholars might mourn the country houses that have gone, but their replacements might have been better. Life moves on.

And perhaps the shell represented by the house is, in the end, secondary to the life that inhabits it. The orthodoxy of the 1970s was not just that the country house had no role but that the tradition it represented was backward-looking, uncreative, evil. Today, other attacks are being made on cultural life; statues are metaphorically or literally pushed off their pedestals, with the fervour of the iconoclasts of Tudor and Cromwellian years. The 1970s should give hope to the defenders of the old faith. Like a phoenix, the country house has succeeded, against all predictions, in rising from its own ashes. Tradition, the indomitability of the human spirit and the sheer bloody-minded stubbornness of some owners, who refused to give up, have won through.

Poster for John Hughes' *The Breakfast Club*, 1985.

JOHN HUGHES – MAKING AND UNMAKING THE AMERICAN DREAM

Johan Hakelius

If you grew up in the eighties, John Hughes was probably part of your life. Within just three years, starting in 1984, he wrote and/or directed *Sixteen Candles*, *The Breakfast Club*, *Ferris Bueller's Day Off*, *Pretty in Pink* and *Some Kind of Wonderful*. Each of these movies became almost instant classics. They redefined what a teen movie could be. They were the first American teen flicks with decent soundtracks, featuring The Specials, The Jesus and Mary Chain, The Smiths, Simple Minds, The Psychedelic Furs, New Order, OMD and many others. In a sense they re-established and updated the American dream for a new generation.

Molly Ringwald, the American actress forever remembered as one of Hughes' 1980s teen heroines, revisited her early career in an article in *The New Yorker* a couple of years ago. It was in the midst of the #MeToo fever. The piece came across as a hesitant one-woman wrestling match. On the one hand her mentor had a unique understanding of the 'minutiae of high school' from a 'female point of view'. He really 'wanted people to take teens seriously'. On the other hand, she noted that he didn't cut out the scene in *The Breakfast Club* when the bad boy Bender – and all the viewers – get to take a peek up Molly Ringwald's character Claire's skirt.

Ringwald explains in detail how worried she was to let her ten-year-old daughter watch the movie. She spoke to friends about it in advance. She explained to her daughter that the person in the underwear actually was someone else: an unnamed actress well out of her teens, hired for that particular purpose. She felt troubled after showing the movie to her daughter, even though her daughter seems to have taken it all in her stride.

'Back then,' Ringwald writes, citing her youth and the standards of the time, 'I was only vaguely aware of how inappropriate much of John's writing was.' Wasn't there a date rape made into a joke in *Sixteen Candles*? Wasn't there an indefensible use of homophobic language? And where are the people of colour to be found? To top it all, the pieces Hughes wrote for *National Lampoon* are just coarse and disturbing.

However, Ringwald recognised that Hughes had an ability to speak to teenagers, regardless of colour, sexual preferences or gender. She was astonished when a gay African American, growing up in Cincinnati, told her that Hughes' movies 'saved him'. Are experiences like that 'enough to make up for the impropriety of the films?' Ringwald's text is a perfect example of how an over-politicised age loses its ability to gain inspiration or understanding from a common cultural heritage. Cultural expressions handed to us through time are almost always permeated with values and mores that most of us reject. Why should that be a problem and what does that really tell us about John Hughes?

The American journalist Michael Weiss, who usually keeps himself busy with foreign policy and geopolitics, found a seemingly perfect John Hughes put-down almost 15 years ago. His article in *Slate* magazine in the fall of 2006 questioned whether John Hughes' teen movies actually favoured teen rebellion, or whether Hughes was really a Hollywood take on Norman Rockwell. Someone who liked to celebrate the 'moral victory of the underdog', but essentially was a family values guy who didn't really champion the underprivileged. A Reaganite, possibly.

The article was captioned 'Some kind of Republican'.

When John Hughes left the advertising industry and joined *National Lampoon* at its peak in the late 1970s, the Republican party reptile P J O'Rourke was the magazine's managing editor. Hughes and O'Rourke co-wrote several items, including a legendary full-fledged parody of a midwestern Sunday newspaper. It even had a spoof colour ad circular.

They shared their experience of middle America: O'Rourke grew up in Toledo, Ohio; Hughes in Grosse Pointe, Michigan and Northbrook, a fairly affluent suburb north of Chicago. Both of them liked to reconnect to that world. Hughes dropped out of university, but he had a steady life-style. He got married at twenty, got out there to make a living and stuck to his marriage until his premature death in 2009.

He didn't much like the conceitedness of his own baby-boomer gener-ation. If his movies had a soft, idealistic spot for anyone going through puberty, it did not extend to people who never got out of puberty. Like O'Rourke, Hughes was in certain respects a sceptic, just as inevitably bound to be a contrarian within the counterculture. In the original screenplay to *Ferris Bueller's Day Off* Ferris tells the story of an uncle who went to Canada during the Vietnam war to avoid getting drafted, but now

Left to right: Annie Potts, John Hughes and Molly
Ringwald on the set of *Pretty in Pink*, 1986.

says he feels guilty he didn't go. Ferris puts him on the spot: 'What's the deal, Uncle Jeff? In wartime you want to be a pacifist and in peacetime you want to be a soldier. It took you twenty years to find out you don't believe in anything?' Ferris gets grounded. His conclusion: 'Be careful when you deal with old hippies. They can be real touchy.'

Hughes wasn't even a Hollywood man. After only a few years in Tinseltown he moved back to the Midwest and bought a farm, like the Roman general Cincinnatus returning to his plough. He didn't move to New York when he worked for the *Lampoon*. Hughes was not a coastal man; he was loyal to 'fly-over country'.

Of course, there was a Republican streak. For God's sake, the man wore Brooks Brothers.

Indeed, the fact that Hughes had this middle-America, Republican leaning makes his films far more complex than agitprop stories of 'teen rebellion'. There's something particularly interesting about Hughes' ability to marry the idyllic with harsh reality. The setting – in the teen movies almost always a fictional suburb of Chicago – has all the trappings of the American dream, but it's not ironic or meant to be perceived as a fake façade, hiding terrible secrets. The dream is truly there and it's real. At the same time, so are poverty, violent parents, suicide, alcoholism, estrangement, injustice.

The basic premise for any Hughes movie is, quite simply, anti-utopian. There is no belief in a perfect world. There is no dream of 'a new man'. It's not implied that the teen heroes will grow up and change the world to become something entirely different. It seems much more likely that they will grab the baton handed over by their elders and continue the relay, hopefully avoiding the fate of Richard Vernon, the bitter school principal in *The Breakfast Club*, or Ed Rooney, the vindictive headmaster in *Ferris Bueller's Day Off.*

It's no surprise that John Hughes has often been called 'the Capra of the eighties' or 'the Capra of teendom'. In his films, Frank Capra sided with ordinary people. Life takes place within civil society, the 'little platoons', and figures of authority, whether they represent politics, big business or something else, are always faintly or even outrageously ludicrous. In that, as in many other respects, Hughes and Capra are on the same page. They both made movies that are very American, even patriotic.

The teens in his movies live in a world of progress. It's a bygone 80s world that has just been introduced to MTV, the VCR, the Walkman and many other inventions that added up to a wave of liberation for Western teenagers. And there's something else: just a faint whiff of a sense of relief and sprouting pride, a Reaganesque confidence after a couple of decades of self-doubt. America was, in a quiet way, becoming great again.

It makes you wonder: how did we end up here? Something must have gone wrong.

What makes John Hughes' movies transcend their particular place in time, even though the clothes, the music, the hair and the make-up are unmistakably 80s, is that they're existential, not political. They are about humans, not ideologies. As Ferris Bueller says early on in his movie: 'Isms, in my opinion, are not good. A person should not believe in an -ism, he should believe in himself.'

Hughes' movies are wittingly apolitical. They deal with a host of problems, like economic differences, education and drugs, that are commonly addressed in a political way, but Hughes instead addresses them from a social and individual point of view. These movies are not indignant about obvious injustices. They do not try to mobilise their audience to become activists for this or that cause. They simply describe an imperfect world and tell us the story of how a group of individuals deals with its imperfections. It's not about changing society and rebelling against 'the system', it's about growing as an individual: to face up to your unloving father, even though there's hardly a chance that he will get his priorities right after a showdown. To see what, or rather who, is in front of you, instead of reaching for a prestigious prize that really only exists in your own mind. To recognise that differences aren't necessarily chasms between people, but rather can be the starting point for an interesting friendship.

In that sense Hughes' work is part of a classical tradition. It also makes him odd, for some probably unintelligible in this brutally politicised and thus polarised time. Molly Ringwald's inability to get to grips with her own feelings for Hughes and her work for him probably reflects that change. It is as if she's trying to remember a world that she knows used to be there, because she was part of it, but somehow it eludes her. From this place in time she simply can't get a firm grip on the world as it was 35 years ago. It seems unreal, fantastic, unfathomable. More like another planet, than another time.

John Hughes, like Frank Capra, obviously loved America. But that America isn't a place as much as a frame of mind. It's that tightrope that requires you to keep your balance between the matter of fact and soppy idealism. It's the belief in solving your problems yourself, instead of turning them into societal issues and demanding that others need to solve them for you. It's recognising differences, without necessarily seeing them as injustices or even problems. It's about minding your own business and caring about others, but not demanding that others have a duty to mind your business on your terms. And it's a frame of mind that doesn't lure you into turning everything into politics.

America has become a less multi-dimensional society. Left to right, politics has become the supreme, for some the only, way of looking at life. The students in detention in *The Breakfast Club* would never find their common ground in the current American setting, they would be too busy insisting on the interpretative prerogative of their own identities. And the gentle, civic-minded, character-based and at heart apolitical idea of what is great about America, that fuelled Reaganism in the 80s, has turned into Trumpism: a harsh, despotic, mean and politically boundless street-fight. It's trying to make America great again by scoffing at everything that is great about America.

In America today, everything is politics. It's a country hell-bent on picking a fight with itself, at any cost. It has stopped being interested in itself. It has stopped revelling in its kaleidoscopic diversity and has started to use diversity as a tool for moral extortion or a reason for fear.

America has lost its way. Maybe even its soul. If Americans want to find it again, they could do worse than to start with John Hughes.

THE PANDEMIC
IN HISTORY

Quarantine at sea. Hundreds of passengers
onboard the Diamond Princess cruise ship tested
positive for coronavirus in February 2020, and
remained onboard in quarantine for two weeks.

2020 – PUTTING OUR PANDEMIC
IN PERSPECTIVE

Lincoln Paine

Historians are masters of teasing momentous events from apparently insignificant details. The most obvious such effort is Ray Huang's *1587, A Year of No Significance: the Ming Dynasty in decline*, which considered a number of little examined incidents and trends that took place in or began in 1587 and that, in hindsight, anticipated the collapse of the Ming Dynasty two or three generations later. In choosing what to expand upon in his study, Huang, writing in 1981, had the benefit of nearly four centuries of research, debate, and interpretation. We can be sure that his choices would have been wildly different had he been writing in 1587.

Predicting the future is a mug's game, but even accounting for the distortion caused by capturing one's own likeness in an historical selfie, it seems a safe bet that 2020 will never be regarded as a year of no significance. The coronavirus pandemic has affected the entire world more quickly and comprehensively than any other single event in human history. Given the universality of its impact, it is hardly surprising that reminders of the past are everywhere, especially with respect to the ways in which individuals, communities, and governments have framed their responses in terms of personal behaviour, health science, and public policy. The media, medical and economic environments of 2020 may look nothing like they did a century or 500 years ago, but the range of human impulses that animate them are familiar.

The disease's worldwide diffusion was sparked by international travel, and public attention to the contagion was first drawn by the plight of cruise ships. Thus it seems fitting to consider our reactions to the coronavirus against a backdrop of maritime trade, which, until the start of the jet age 60 years ago, was the fastest and most direct line of transmission for pandemic viruses and therefore a primary focus of governmental concern and public interest. It is quickly evident, however, that policies intended to contain or alleviate the stress of disease very often reveal or further rend tears in the social fabric, between haves and have-nots; between knowledge, belief, and ignorance; between us and them.

Before the widespread acceptance of germ theory – the idea that many diseases are caused by microscopic pathogens – little was known about the pathology, cure, or containment of diseases. The first pathogen identified was *Mycobacterium leprae*, which gives rise to leprosy (Hansen's disease), in 1873. While leprosy and plague now refer to specific diseases, historical sources tend to use these terms as catch-all descriptors for a variety of ailments with similar characteristics. People likewise treated infected people with a broad brush, and they divined early on that segregating the sick – particularly if their disease was notably disfiguring or fatal – from the healthy was one way to prevent the spread of illness.

Ancient Indian texts regarded leprosy and similar skin ailments as contagious and advised against close contact with people so afflicted or their belongings. The Book of Numbers explicitly recommends keeping 'out of the camp every leper, and every one having a discharge' to prevent their infecting those not so afflicted. Less well known is a more comprehensive approach towards communicable disease described in the Chinese *Han Shu* ('Book of Han'): 'In 2 AD, after the drought and locust plague occurred, people were infected with the plague. The local government told them to leave their homes, go to a special institution, take medicine for medical treatment and receive isolation treatment.'

Leprosy was widespread across Eurasia in the medieval period, and there are abundant references to it in European writings. The earliest known leper house was established in the fourth century, and judging from contemporary estimates, there were hundreds if not thousands of leprosaria across Christendom in the thirteenth century. Not all lepers were confined to leprosaria and not all leprosaria housed only lepers. The most famous was the hospice of St. Lazarus, established outside the walls of Jerusalem at the start of the first crusade in the twelfth century. Lazarus was the patron saint of lepers and beggars, described in the Book of Luke, and such institutions were commonly called 'lazarettes' or 'lazar houses' in his honour. Despite enormous advances in our understanding of epidemiology – and, indeed, of the nature and causes of poverty – the equation of physical ill-health with financial ill-health embodied in the person of St Lazarus has long infected societal responses to communicable disease.

The most widely used term for isolating people for medical reasons is quarantine, a practice that has its roots in the maritime cities of southern

A burial scene captured in the illumination
Black Death at Tournai, 1349, from *Chronique et
annales de Gilles le Muisit*.

Europe in the decades following the Black Death (1346–53), the first and most virulent episode of the second plague pandemic caused by the bacterium *Pestis yersinia*. (The first pandemic was Justinian's plague, which ravaged the Mediterranean from about 541 to 750 AD. The second lasted until the nineteenth century, which is when the third pandemic started.) The Black Death has received the most notice in large part because Western historians have long considered it a watershed crisis in European history, a portal from the medieval world to modernity, although the validity of this claim has come under scrutiny. Not all parts of Europe were affected in the same way and, while the Black Death had catastrophic effects across Eurasia and parts of Africa, other regions did not share Europe's economic or technological trajectory.

It is said that the Black Death spurred advances in health policy, but various cities had begun implementing sanitary initiatives well before the plague hit, and tactics like quarantine were not implemented until decades afterwards and in response to briefer, less traumatic pandemic aftershocks. While quarantine today can apply to individuals, households, and larger aggregations of people, quarantine originally referred to the practice of detaining ships before allowing them to land their passengers, cargo, or crew. In 1377, the Great Council of Ragusa (Dubrovnik) held ships for 30 days if their port of origin was experiencing an outbreak of the plague. In 1383, the port of Marseilles started to keep ships for 40 days (*quarantina giorni*). Although the duration of quarantine varied from port to port and would depend on the disease, the term quarantine stuck, in part because a period of 40 days has a rich Biblical pedigree, including the duration of the flood, Moses' stay on Mount Sinai, the temptation of Christ, and the season of Lent. Ships carrying infected people flew a quarantine flag. Today, this is the international signal flag for the letter L, four squares alternating yellow and black. Upon reaching a port, the captain was interviewed about the health of his passengers and crew, and the nature and condition of the cargo, which for many centuries was considered a potential vector of contagious disease.

By 1470, at least seven northern Italian cities had determined that lazarettes were essential to any programme for containing the plague. Inasmuch as quarantine is a form of segregation, it is only a short step to discrimination, which has taken many forms in the history of disease. The most common divisions are between rich and poor, and between residents and foreigners. The more affluent have always had an advantage in being able to flee hotbeds of disease for more salubrious and less crowded estates outside of cities, thus consigning the masses to bear the brunt of whatever illness is raging. And while riches do not necessarily confer immunity against disease, they can render one immune from rules designed to protect public health. In fifteenth-century Italy, officials frequently gave merchants, ambassadors, and the rich preferential treatment even if they arrived from places where the plague was known to be raging, but they were quick to ban the poor on the suspicion they might be unhealthy.

A more modern example of economic inequality affecting community response to epidemics took place on the eve of the American Revolution. In 1764, the city of Boston suffered one of its recurring bouts of smallpox, which had ravaged Massachusetts since before the Pilgrims landed in 1621. Nearly 5,000 people were inoculated against the disease, of whom only 46 died, or one in 109; of the 669 people who were infected by smallpox, the death rate was one in five. Smallpox broke out again a decade later, and leaders in the neighbouring port of Marblehead opposed mass inoculation on the grounds of cost, in favour of building a privately funded inoculation hospital. Voters approved the latter option in the belief it would serve the common good, only to discover that inoculations would cost the equivalent of several months' pay for the average worker. When it turned out that the authorities and patients at 'Castle Pox' were not observing their own rules on isolation, protestors turned violent and ultimately put it to the torch. Chastened by their experience, when smallpox returned in 1777, the town voted to 'goe into inoculation' as Boston had done thirteen years before.

If the struggle over Castle Pox set a rich elite against a poor majority, the broader contours of the debate over quarantine for much of the following century pitted commercial interests against public health, although the contest mirrored disagreements over epidemiology within the medical establishment. Most doctors of the time believed in miasma theory, which had a classical pedigree going back to the writings of Hippocrates and Galen. This held that diseases arise from and are spread by bad air – literally *mal'aria* – emanating from rotting organic matter. (Malaria as we know it today was attributed to the fetid tropical air of West Africa, home of the Anopheles mosquito, which transmits the parasite responsible for the most virulent form of malaria.)

Among the most influential exponents of miasma theory in the United

States was Benjamin Rush. The eminent doctor and signer of the Declaration of Independence maintained that the yellow fever outbreak that devastated Philadelphia in 1793 resulted from a load of coffee beans that had been left on a dock and 'putrefied there to the great annoyance of the whole neighbourhood.' Thanks to miasma theory, coffee and animal hides – both of which are especially susceptible to decay – were among the items most likely to be quarantined at Philadelphia. A third was rags, used in paper making, though less because they might rot than because of their identification with rag pickers, an impoverished class of people wherever they were, and the possibility that the rags might have originated as slum dwellers' clothes.

When it came to infectious diseases like yellow fever and cholera, doctors fell into one of two groups: contagionists, also called importationists or quarantinists, and anticontagionists, known as localists or sanitarians. Contagionists believed that diseases could be introduced to a community – from the West Indies in the case of yellow fever – and that one way to prevent this was by quarantine. Anticontagionists considered epidemic diseases to be of local origin and thought they erupted spontaneously and that the only way to reduce the risk of epidemics was through improved sanitation. The economic implications of this view were significant, for if disease originated locally, quarantine and the interruption of trade were unnecessary. Not surprisingly, localism was favoured by laissez-faire proponents of free trade opposed to what they perceived as government overreach. As Dr Benjamin B Strobel noted, 'It is the object and interest of all commercial communities, to establish, if possible, the non-contagious character of all diseases; and for the very plain reason, that the restrictions necessary to prevent the extension of such diseases, are calculated to interrupt free intercourse between commercial cities.'

Since the turn of the nineteenth century, the Medical Society of South Carolina had argued that yellow fever was not contagious and that quarantine was unnecessary to prevent the disease from spreading. Nonetheless, an 1840 law stipulated that ships with sick passengers or crew had to remain at the quarantine anchorage for twenty days. Although the science was as yet unproven, Strobel believed that if a disease did arrive from somewhere else, there was a moral imperative to exercise all caution to keep it at bay. He went on to ask, in words eerily familiar in the age of Covid-19, 'Dare we place the life-blood of our fellow men in one scale, and coldly calculate how many pounds, shillings, and pence in the other shall preponderate?'

As it happens, yellow fever is not contagious via casual person to person contact. It is spread via Aedes mosquitos passing a virus between an infected person and an uninfected one. People who recover from yellow fever have a lifetime immunity to it and are considered 'acclimated'. Quarantine measures were effective in keeping yellow fever away from susceptible populations because the anchorage was farther from shore than mosquitoes can fly, but anticontagionists secured the repeal of the 1840 quarantine law, anyway. This, combined with an influx of unacclimated Irish and German immigrants, meant the port suffered from repeated outbreaks of yellow fever that escalated in severity in the decades before the Civil War.

Discrimination against people susceptible to disease on the basis of social status was not always a given. Cholera, which spread through water and food, reached the United States in 1832. On overcrowded and unsanitary immigrant ships and steamboats, drinking water was put in communal barrels for the use of passengers and crew. People ladled out their share with their mug or cup, and thus shared the *Vibrio cholerae* bacteria with which they were infected, or picked them up from someone else. An acute disease, cholera can kill its victims within 12 hours of ingestion. Although it was widely associated with immigrants, the mass of whom were poor, its effects were not limited to them and it was widely feared. Yet despite anxiety about the disease, antebellum Americans were well-disposed towards immigration, and during an outbreak in St Paul, Minnesota, in 1854, the town council buried reports of cholera for fear the news would deter immigrants who were badly needed in the state's rapidly expanding forestry and other industries.

Few people were willing to show such largesse later in the century, when disease, illness, and poverty became tools for suppressing immigration, and the threat of disease became an excuse to discriminate against the foreign-born. There was nothing new in this. During the second plague pandemic, Europe witnessed countless attacks on beggars, lepers, foreigners, and Jews. But by the mid-eighteenth century, Europeans (and subsequently Americans) had fixated on a nebulous East in an exercise historian Nükhet Varlık has described as 'epidemiological orientalism'. Writing for Diderot and D'Alembert's *Encyclopédie* (1751–72), the physician and scholar Louis de Jaucourt declared: 'Plague comes to us from

Following pages: Sentiment towards the cholera outbreak illustrated in an issue of *Puck* in 1883.

THE KIND OF "ASSISTED EMIG

CAN NOT AFFORD TO ADMIT.

Asia, and for two thousand years all the plagues that have appeared in Europe have been transmitted through the communication of the Saracens, Arabs, Moors or Turks with us, and none of our plagues had any other source.' For Europeans concerned with bubonic plague (which was endemic in Europe), the East referred to Muslim lands of the Middle East and North Africa. But in the second half of the nineteenth century, Americans viewed China and the Chinese as a font of disease, especially in California.

This was a function of undisguised racism on the part of European-Americans, who went out of their way to limit Chinese immigrants' access to government, work, and medical facilities. Even after germ theory was widely accepted, the Anti-Chinese Council of the Workingmen's Party of California could write that 'the physician who tries to trace the source of infection is mostly unable to do so, and we believe that the existing evils in Chinatown [in San Francisco] are the proper source.' This applied to virtually all infectious diseases but especially plague, which in 1905 was declared 'an Oriental disease, peculiar to rice eaters', because most of the 118 people who died from it were Chinese. Plague broke out again in the wake of the San Francisco earthquake the next year, when 'very few Orientals were affected', according to an official report, 'almost all of the 160 human cases, of which 77 died, being white persons, many of them in a good condition of life, subsisting on generous diet and dwelling in houses that would commonly be called sanitary.'

Highlighting such details from society's past responses to outbreaks of contagious disease can strengthen the brave, ground the fearful, and give pause to the cocksure. For while we may never forget our collective suffering and worry this year, it's worth noting that the author of *1587, A Year of No Significance* all but ignored the deadly epidemics that afflicted the Chinese in the late 1580s. If the past is a foreign country, though, we must remember that people lived there as vividly as we do now. Those shadows and reflections of the past – they are us.

Edith Schiele, Dying, Egon Schiele, 1918.
Leopold Museum, Vienna.

COUNTING THE COST
OF THE 1918–19 PANDEMIC

Hew Strachan

At 8am on 28 October 1918, Edith Harms, the wife of painter Egon Schiele, died in Vienna of influenza. She was six months pregnant. Schiele had drawn Edith twice the night before in what were to be his last works. He succumbed to the same disease three days later, at 1am on 31 October 1918. He was 28. The link between eroticism and death, latent in so many of Schiele's pictures, seemed to have come full circle. So too did the life of the Habsburg Empire, of which they were both citizens and in whose capital they lived. Five days after Schiele's death Austria accepted defeat in the First World War, signing an armistice with the allies in Italy; its partner in the dual monarchy, Hungary, did so in Belgrade on 13 November. By then Austria was a republic, although the former emperor, Karl, refused to abdicate as king of Hungary. Like the Schieles, Karl and his young family also fell sick; they, however, all survived.

The Habsburg Empire dissolved in a cycle of revolution and civil war, as did the empires of the Romanovs, the Hohenzollerns and the Ottomans. From the Baltic to the Balkans, and from central Europe to central Asia, their peoples sought to redefine multi-national conglomerates as nation states. They did so on the basis of identity, determined by ethnicity, faith, ideology or language, while peacemakers in Paris thought geographically, drawing lines on maps which were overtaken by events on the ground. Nor were the ostensible victors in the First World War in significantly stronger positions. Most faced unemployment, inflation and debt, and they too went in fear of revolution. Britain was under particular pressure, facing conflict across 'the southern arc of empire', from Ireland to India. The First World War did not end in November 1918, but had begun to unravel a year before, with the Bolshevik seizure of power in Russia in November 1917, and its last peace treaty, which created the new republic of Turkey, was not signed until July 1923, in Lausanne.

These major political events which shaped so much of twentieth-century history were accompanied by a steady drumbeat of death, caused not just by violence (although there was plenty of that) but also by disease. The principal cause of morbidity was the influenza pandemic of 1918 and 1919, but it was not the only major killer. Tuberculosis, malaria and hunger also played their parts. And yet neither commentators at the time, nor historians since, have shown much inclination to consider the interconnections in this 'perfect storm'. Did sickness promote or retard revolution? Did it help end the war sooner than the allied powers expected? Did it play a part in the botching of the peace settlements? Did it contribute to the collapse of state authority and so facilitate civil war? Few have even asked the questions, and yet fewer have provided answers. Two recent major studies of the attempts to re-establish order after the Great War, *The Unfinished Peace after World War I* by Patrick Cohrs (2006) and *The Deluge: The Great War and the Remaking of Global Order* by Adam Tooze (2014), have index entries for inflation, but not for influenza.

The influenza pandemic hit in three waves. The first, in the spring of 1918, caused comparatively few fatalities, and given the incidence of deaths from influenza in 1917 might not have aroused particular alarm. The second, which killed the Schieles, began in August and peaked in October and November. It was responsible for 90% of the recorded deaths. The third was less virulent but ran on for most of the first half of 1919. By the time the Second World War broke out it was realised that the initial calculation of total deaths worldwide, 21 million, had failed to take sufficient account of countries for which statistics were less readily available. By 1942, 40 million was being cited, and by the turn of the millennium estimates based on the number of excess deaths ranged higher, some even suggesting a total of 100 million, or 5% of the world's population.

Such losses to natural causes made the impact of the First World War itself no more than a demographic blip. The total number of war-related military deaths has been variously estimated at between 8 and 10 million, with a consensus hovering at around 9.5 million. Although the variation and its attendant uncertainties are much less than those for the deaths from influenza, in some ways they are more remarkable. Armed forces are state institutions, and their members are paid and sometimes pensionable; in the First World War many countries made allowances to their families. In other words, military losses were more amenable to statistical analysis. Some of the variation is due to different methods of counting. The cut-off date for deaths in the forces of the British Empire was 1921, to

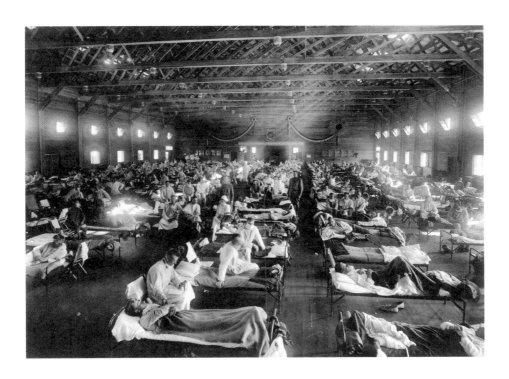

Patients being treated in an army ward in Kansas
during the influenza epidemic, 1918.

allow for losses in the 'wars after the war', in the allied armies of occupation, and from lingering medical conditions incurred between 1914 and
1918 which resulted in death between 1919 and 1921. By the same token,
however, those who died after 1921 from war-related injuries were not
included. For example, gas warfare – for all its horrendous implications
– actually killed few soldiers in the years up to 1918 but inflicted slow
deaths on veterans crippled by lung conditions in the 1930s.

Undoubtedly, a calculation of the deaths caused by the First World
War which counts only those in uniform grossly underestimates its
effects. Some civilians met violent ends caused by enemy action: the
French and Belgians killed by the advancing German armies in 1914
(about 6,500); the Serbs similarly killed by the Austro-Hungarian army
and the East Prussians by the Russians, also in the opening weeks of the
war; and the British killed by the German cruisers in the bombardment
of east coast ports in December 1914 and thereafter in air raids (possibly
as many as 1,500). After the war, Germany would claim that one million
German civilians were starved to death by the allied blockade: this figure was accepted by the British official historian of economic warfare,
although today most historians would cut it by at least half. The total
number of Armenians killed by the Ottomans remains disputed, but a
conservative estimate is one million. We do not know how many
Russians died in the 'great retreat' of 1915, when about three million fled
European Russia in the face of the advancing German and Austro-
Hungarian armies, or how many porters expired carrying the muni-
tions and supplies needed for the troops of the colonial powers on the
long lines of communication in the campaigns of sub-Saharan Africa.

The number of deaths attributed to the Second World War has been
creeping steadily upward from about 55 million to as high as 70 million.
One of the principal causes of this progression has been the inclusion of
civilian losses, and the enormous variation in the final total is an indica-
tor of our lack of certainty as to how to count them. We routinely exclude
civilian losses from the First World War total, but if we do include them
we become vague and uncertain. When in 2012 the British prime minister, David Cameron, announced his government's programme to commemorate the centenary of the First World War, he said the total number of war-related deaths was 16 million. In the same year, Christopher
Clark in *The Sleepwalkers* put it at 20 million. These are simply guesses,
almost devoid of scientific precision, but they remain much lower than

those cited between the wars by scholars keen to warn the world of the cataclysmic effects of modern conflict. In 1920, E L Bogart said that 'the loss of civilian life due directly to war equals, if indeed it does not exceed, that suffered by the armies in the field'. On that basis Hoffman Nickerson, in *Can We Limit War?*, published in 1933, put the civilian dead of the Great War at 13 million. In 1942 Quincy Wright, professor of international law at Chicago, in a weighty, interdisciplinary two-volume study of war, put the total deaths in 1914–18 from military action and war-distributed disease at over 40 million.

There is quite a lot of double counting going on here. One cause is nationality. Were Americans who died before 1917 in the service of France or Britain counted by both the United States and France or Britain? How about Danes who fought for Germany? Another, statistically more significant, cause is disease, and particularly the influenza epidemic. Because Bogart, Nickerson and Wright could not readily differentiate disease attributable to the war from other disease, they were inclined to include it as a cost of war. If we follow that argument to its conclusion, we might arrive today at a total death rate for the First World War not of 40 million (ie roughly 10 million military deaths, 10 million civilian and 20 million from influenza), but of 120 million (the combination of the current maxima of those three categories). Numbers this big comfortably exceed the highest total for the Second World War and dwarf our capacity for comprehension or empathy. They would also be wrong: each of the military and civilian totals already includes deaths from influenza.

The points are easier to grasp when put in individual terms. Because Schiele was a great artist cut down in his prime, we think of his death in terms of the loss to culture, not to the Habsburg Empire. But theoretically he was still a soldier when he died. Although twice exempted on physical grounds from military service in 1914, he was eventually called up in May 1915. As with other artists (the poet Rilke comes to mind), the Austro-Hungarian army managed to find Schiele a berth which did not expose too brutally his almost total unsuitability for a martial career. In 1916 he was put in charge of food supplies at a prisoner of war camp for Russian officers in lower Austria, and in 1917 he returned to Vienna to work for the army's administration in ways which left him free to paint and to plan exhibitions of his own and others' work.

Schiele was not exposed to danger on the battlefield and did not die

HUNGER

For three years America has fought starvation *in* Belgium

Will you *Eat less* — wheat meat — fats *and* sugar that *we* may still send food *in* ship loads?

UNITED   STATES   FOOD   ADMINISTRATION

A United States Food Administration poster, 1918.

as a result of enemy action. Nonetheless, if he had been a soldier of the British, not the Austro-Hungarian, empire, he would today be numbered among the war dead by the Commonwealth (originally Imperial) War Graves Commission. It commemorates the almost one million military dead of the war from across the British Empire, whatever the reasons for their demise. Edith Schiele, although she died from the same illness in the same place three days before her husband, would not be so remembered. The Commission cares for the graves of thousands of service personnel, who died not in battle but of disease, some of which may have been war related, some not. Disease, not fighting, was the big killer in war before 1914, and it still was on fronts outside France and Belgium. Ottoman military deaths from sickness were nearly double those in combat.

In recent years the Commission's criteria for inclusion have been softened, rather than tightened, indirectly adding to the total numbers of British military dead. Private Alexander Ponton of 1st/4th King's Own Scottish Borderers went with his battalion to Gallipoli in 1915 but was discharged on grounds of ill health and died of tuberculosis in October 1916. He was buried in an unmarked pauper's grave in his local churchyard at Hobkirk, near Hawick. In 2017 the Commission commemorated him as a casualty of the war, although there is no evidence that his tuberculosis was a consequence of his military service as opposed to the rural poverty in which he was raised. Ponton was a civilian at the time of his death, but the Commission does not commemorate the civilians who were killed in either war by direct enemy action.

These variations in totals and their categorisation compound the challenge of assessing the impact of the influenza pandemic on the world's emergence from the Great War in 1918–19. After all, the disease did not discriminate between belligerent states and neutrals. Moreover, it did not operate in isolation but in conjunction with other factors which increased its effects. In all the belligerent countries, housing conditions worsened as workers responded to the labour demands of war-related industries by migrating to the towns, while national mobilisation drew labour from the building industries. Rents rose, overcrowding increased, and tuberculosis flourished.

In 1916 the harvest failed across Europe, contributing to the outbreak of revolution in Russia the following March and prompting strikes elsewhere. The globalised food distribution system, on which Britain and

Germany particularly depended, collapsed on the outbreak of war, and the consequences for continental Europe were compounded by the allied blockade of the Central Powers. In April 1917 the world's principal neutral, the United States, entered the war and the blockade was tightened with a ferocity that embraced the neutral states bordering Germany and its allies, as well as the Central Powers themselves. On British insistence the blockade continued after November 1918 until the defeated countries signed the peace treaties, which formally ended the war. The second wave of the influenza pandemic hit peoples whose resistance to disease was already severely compromised.

On 3 October 1918 Germany approached Woodrow Wilson, the American president, to request an armistice. The allies were surprised; they had not expected the war to end until after June 1919, the date by which the American Expeditionary Force in France would reach four million men. Over the following month powerful voices on both sides, including John J Pershing for the Americans and Erich Ludendorff for the Germans, called in vain for the war's continuation. By then, although never mentioned by the generals, influenza was a material factor in the armies' fitness to fight.

In the United States, the second wave of the pandemic had prompted the War Department to cut loading on the troopships by 10%. It could not afford the time to quarantine the soldiers for three weeks before embarkation, and was ready to bear the cost – nearly 1,000 deaths at sea for 130,000 troops delivered to France. The allied commander on the Macedonian front, where the initial allied breakthrough occurred in September, talked about advancing to Vienna and thence to Berlin, so ending the war. But influenza took two entire French divisions out of his order of battle. Between 1 October and 11 November 1918, the French on this front suffered only 264 battle casualties but on 16 October alone had 24,443 from a force of 190,000 hospitalised by disease. The Germans could not reinforce the Macedonian front because they had too few men to do that and hold firm in the west. Their offensives in the first half of 1918 had cost them about 900,000 casualties, while extending the length of front they had to hold. Over the course of July 685,000 German soldiers fell sick, nearly 400,000 of them with influenza.

Douglas Haig, the British commander, argued strongly that the war should be ended while the German offer was on the table. He foresaw the allied advance slowing as the weather worsened and the days shortened, but he must also have been aware of the threat which influenza presented to allied effectiveness. By the war's end nearly 800,000 American soldiers had contracted it and possibly 44,000 had died. The war-winning offensive of 1919 was in jeopardy.

By the time the peacemakers convened in Paris in January 1919, they were men in a hurry and so had insufficient time for the protracted negotiations which the circumstances required. As heads of government they could not afford to be absent from the capitals for too long. Influenza was another pressure to get things done. Its lethality had abated, but, as an American, Hugh Gibson, observed on 25 February, 'everybody has the flu or has just had it or is just going to have it'. Woodrow Wilson himself fell ill in April and seemed shaky thereafter; his disabling stroke followed less than six months later.

Another pressure was widespread hunger. Gibson worked for Herbert Hoover, the food administrator in the United States, who organised famine relief during the war and in its aftermath. Hoover warned that 400 million people faced starvation in enemy countries and elsewhere. The Americans strongly opposed Britain's continuation of the blockade, echoing German complaints that it specifically hit non-combatants. Although Hoover's concerns were humanitarian, those Britons who sided with him were more worried that the Bolsheviks, not the Boche, were now the enemy. They feared that hunger would stoke revolution, which would sweep from Russia across eastern and central Europe, undermining not just Germany and Austria but even Britain and France.

Death in 1918–19 came in many forms. Differentiating between whether people were killed or died for other reasons made little sense after four years of protracted and intense conflict – conflict, moreover, which had not finished. Possibly four million more met violent ends in the fighting that continued until 1923. By the autumn of 1918, war had become institutionalised in the lives of the belligerent nations. It was a part of everyday life, even if one which overturned the normal rhythms of mortality, picking out the young and fit before their time, and leaving parents bereaved and desolate. The influenza epidemic behaved in similar ways, and thus seemed to many to be a by-product of the conflict. The war had promoted the mass movement of peoples, so enabling its transmission, as it had their concentration in factories, transports, barracks and trenches. The war, however, was, like the hunger which accompanied it, a phenomenon over which humanity had some control. That was much less true of the influenza pandemic, whose cause and course were – and in many respects still are – a mystery. Fatalistic acceptance could be easier than energetic resistance.

Portrait of Marcus Tullius Cicero, after Tobias
Stimmer, 1539–1584. Rijksmuseum, Amsterdam.

SURVIVAL LESSONS FROM ANCIENT ROME

Gillian Clark

Humans are social beings. When Aristotle said that they are political animals, he meant that they form communities. Their best way of life is as citizens, members of a *polis*, which is a city and its territory. Stoic philosophers said that humans have a natural sense of 'belonging', of recognising 'one of ours', and should aim to extend that sense in ever-widening circles from immediate family to local community to the world. That, not rootlessness, is what Stoics meant by being a 'cosmopolite', a citizen of the world. Augustine thought that God created people not only as naturally social, but as family, with one common ancestor; that is why God made Eve from Adam, not separately. People like to find connections, and they need to communicate. Humans are alike in nature, but, said Augustine, a man would rather spend time with his own dog than with a foreigner whose language he does not share. 'Social' is the adjective from Latin *socius/a*: associate, partner, ally, companion.

What makes some of these social beings into an identifiable *societas*, a 'society', and what throws a society into crisis?

Cicero's Commonwealth

In the late 50s BC, as Rome lurched from political in-fighting to civil war and dictatorship, Marcus Tullius Cicero composed a philosophical dialogue *De Republica*. This title is best translated as 'on the commonwealth', for *res publica* means literally 'public property' or 'public concern'; it need not mean 'republic' in contrast with 'monarchy'. Cicero had held the consulship, the highest Roman office. He wanted to discuss 'the best condition of the city [*civitas*, the Latin equivalent of *polis*] and the best citizen', and he intended a challenge to Plato's dialogue *Politeia*, which is confusingly known as *Republic* because its title in Latin was *Res Publica*.

Politeia means a community of citizens, and the constitution and form of government by which it is organised. Plato's thought-experiment presents an imagined ideal state, in which justice is maintained because everyone has their due, and everyone does their proper job, not someone else's. Cicero chose to take an actual state, namely Rome almost a century before his own time, as the basis for reflection. His leading character wants to start with a definition, and suggests 'a *res publica* ['public property'] is *res populi* ['property of a people']; and a *populus* is not every assembly of a multitude, but an assembly allied [*sociatus*] by agreement on justice and by community of interest. The first cause of its coming together is not so much weakness as a natural tendency of human beings to congregate.'

Here is a starting-point for thinking about society. The phrase 'not so much weakness' sidelines the argument, made by some Epicurean philosophers, that society begins with safety in numbers, as a defence against predators and rivals; laws follow because the quicker-witted people realise that some rules are needed, for instance forbidding murder.

Instead, Cicero holds that people naturally want to live together, and that a 'commonwealth' is formed when a group is united by agreement on fundamental principles of life, namely what they think is just and what is in their common interest. This 'commonwealth' seems to be what we would now call a society. One obvious difficulty is that its members may change their minds, or may differ, on how to interpret justice and common interest. Aristotle, for example, distinguished 'geometric' and 'arithmetic' equality. In the first, influence is in proportion to status, which may be defined by birth or property or contribution to the community. In the second, one citizen has one vote, regardless of all these factors. Some people thought that 'arithmetic' equality was unjust; surviving law court speeches show that jurors in Athens were swayed by arguments that the accused deserved their favour as a great man and a benefactor of the city. Other people thought that 'geometric' equality was unjust, because wealth and status were inherited rather than earned, and because an ordinary farmer or soldier also contributed to the city.

Cicero's survey of Roman political history showed repeated disputes about justice and equality. People excluded from power fought against their exclusion, and people oppressed by the powerful found ways to resist. Rome was at first a monarchy, but the kings became tyrants and were expelled. Who, then, were the 'people' of Rome, who had the *res publica* as their common property? Patrician families claimed a special inherited status, but were forced to admit others to some of their privileges. Poor people, oppressed and exploited, walked out, and established a rival settlement until they got their own representatives, 'tribunes of the people' who could speak for them and protect them against arbitrary force. Through all these disputes about justice and common interest, Rome survived. What kind of crisis then would bring an end, or a transformation?

A *res publica*, Cicero said, must have a way of making decisions. It can be governed in different ways, as a monarchy or an aristocracy or a democracy. Cicero favoured a 'mixed constitution', and thought that Rome's balance of monarchy (the executive power of the consuls), aristocracy (the advisory role of the senate), and democracy (the people's vote on laws and offices) was about right. But he feared that Rome in his time had inherited a *res publica* like a splendid picture, whose colours were fading with the loss of traditional mores: customs, moral values, the Roman way of life. If monarchy or aristocracy or democracy becomes too powerful, so that injustice prevails, then there is no *populus* united by agreement on justice and community of interest, so there is no *res populi* and no *res publica*. That argument allowed Cicero's definition to survive when other parts of his *Republic* were lost.

Was there Ever a Roman Res Publica?

Almost five centuries later, Augustine quoted it for his own purposes. He did not wish to discuss the best condition of the city and the best citizen: he wished to challenge complaints against Christianity.

Augustine lived through one traumatic event which seemed to some people like the end of the society they knew. In 410 AD barbarians invaded the city of Rome, the capital of the greatest empire (so far as Romans knew) that the world had ever known. Latin-speaking schoolchildren learned from Virgil's *Aeneid* that Jupiter, king of the gods, had given Rome empire without end, without limits of time or extent. To historians in later centuries, and to some people at the time, the sack of Rome signalled the fall of the Roman Empire. How could this happen?

High-status refugees fled to Africa, where Augustine was bishop of the sea-port Hippo Regius. He was asked to respond to complaints that this disaster, like many others, was due to Christianity: the gods of Rome were offended because they no longer received sacrifice. This made no sense, Augustine argued, because the authors whom Romans took as

Illumination with Rome as the City of God, and
St Augustine writing, from *De civitate Dei*, 1459.

authorities showed that Rome had experienced worse disasters in the times before Christianity was known. Rome's classic writers, who were still the core texts of Latin education, revealed a history of moral and physical disasters, defeats and social conflicts, in which the gods of Rome were no help at all. Livy provided narrative, Sallust provided moral and social comment, and according to Cicero's definition, Rome was not merely a *res publica* in very bad condition, as Sallust declared: Rome was never a *res publica* at all.

Augustine would never have finished his work, he wrote, if he tried to discuss all the disasters, moral and physical, recorded by these Roman authorities: harm done by people to each other, especially in war; harm caused by earthquakes and eruptions, wildfires and deluges and floods. Rome's fragile first settlement struggled for independence from its Etruscan neighbours.

War with nearby Veii seemed as epic as the Trojan War, though the territory at stake was no bigger than a tribal hill-town in Augustine's African homeland. (Veii is now a suburb within Rome's inner-city ring road.) Gauls who invaded from North Italy inflicted a bitterly remembered defeat, and had to be bought off with gold; when the Romans protested that the agreed weight had been reached, the Gallic warlord threw his sword into the balance, shouting '*Vae victis!*' ('woe to the defeated').

There was no further invasion until the Goths, more than 800 years later – provided, said Augustine, you discount the times when Rome was invaded by Romans in civil wars. But there were perpetual crises, both immediate and endemic. Rome had citizen soldiers, so when wars dragged on away from home, farmland could not be cultivated. Veterans fell deeper into debt because their pay was always late, and rich people, so far from helping them, took the opportunity to increase their land-holdings. War brought famine and epidemic; frozen winters ended in destructive floods. Wars with the rival great power of Carthage caused more defeats on land and sea, and greater losses of soldiers and civilians, than Augustine could even list, still less describe. Empire was achieved at a horrific cost in blood.

In Sallust's analysis, the destruction of Carthage removed fear of the enemy, so that patriotic self-discipline gave way to unrestrained competition for wealth and power. Augustine summarised the first century BC as 'wars with allies, wars with slaves, civil wars', which ended in dictatorship and the loss of political liberty. Rome reverted to monarchy, at first disguised by republican conventions, then open autocracy.

An 'Afflicted' Empire

Augustine said little about Rome's later history, because he wanted to look at the evidence of the classic authors who wrote before Christianity was known. Would Cicero have recognised Rome in Augustine's time?

Rome survived through crisis after crisis to become a huge city, dependent on imports of grain and olive oil. Farmer-soldiers had long since been replaced by professional armies who were paid for by taxes; few of those soldiers came from Rome or even from Italy. In practice, and increasingly in law, it was not enough to be a freeborn Roman citizen: the 'more respectable' were distinguished from the 'lower orders' who were liable to physical punishments once reserved for slaves. Grants of citizenship became more widespread until, in 212 AD, all freeborn persons within the Roman Empire were Roman citizens. Perhaps that was idealism; perhaps (as one well-connected historian claimed) the point was to make everyone liable for death duties, because there was as usual a crisis in paying the armies. The immense empire was always at war on several fronts, whether fending off 'barbarians' who were themselves displaced by movements of peoples in central Asia, or enmeshed in civil wars which transformed 'usurpers' into legitimate rulers.

There were emperors from Spain and from Africa, from the Balkans and from Syria. Some never visited Rome, because the action was happening elsewhere, or because civil wars removed them too quickly. From the early fourth century there was a New Rome at Constantinople, and more often than not there were two emperors, one in the Greek-speaking east and one in the Latin-speaking west. Some emperors came up through the ranks of the army, which was now full of barbarians; many of the Goths who sacked Rome in 410 AD had recently deserted from the Roman army. Some emperors had powerful barbarian advisers, such as Stilicho, son of a Vandal, who was executed in 408. Some old families and old money survived, but there were many new names. Impressive churches and martyr-shrines joined the ancient monuments and temples.

Christian bishops became new sources of patronage, because they had a duty to intercede for mercy, and to care for the poor with the welfare funds they gathered from legacies and from charitable giving. When

Cicero wrote *De officiis* ('On Duties') he thought carefully about priorities in using the resources of the household, balancing the claims of family members and dependants and fellow citizens, personal friends and political allies. He did not reject common humanity: it would be heartless to refuse a coin or a crust to a beggar. But Cicero did not recognise a general obligation to give in charity to people with whom he had no personal connection. Nor did he see welfare provision as a task of government: its job was to maintain peace and order.

As Augustine said, the empire survived the disasters it experienced: 'The Roman empire was afflicted rather than changed. This happened to it in other times, before Christianity, and it was restored from that affliction. In these times too we should not despair of restoration, for who knows God's will in this matter?'

In 410 AD the Goths left after three days. They were bought off, and seven years on, according to one visitor, the locals said you would not know anything had happened, unless you came upon one of the ruins that had not been rebuilt. Augustine cited another passage of Cicero's *Republic*: 'A city ought to be established so as to be eternal. So there is no natural perishing of a *res publica* as there is of a human being, in whom death is not only necessary, it is often to be wished for. But when a city is removed, destroyed, extinguished, it is in a way (to compare small things with great) as if this whole world perished and collapsed.' Augustine commented that Cicero thought, with the Platonists, that the world would not perish; and that he thought the city would be eternal, although individuals die and are born, in the way that the foliage of an evergreen tree continues though individual leaves appear and fall.

The Vandals Reconsidered

Like an evergreen tree, Roman society survived through crises and disasters, changes of scale and of power-holders. Rome, as Augustine said, was the Romans. But when Augustine died, in 430, his city was under siege by Vandals, a Germanic people who had moved south into Spain, then crossed to Africa. In the next decade they established a kingdom, centred on Carthage, which lasted for a hundred years. They achieved some seapower, they negotiated with the western and eastern Roman emperors, and in 455, when negotiations failed, they in their turn were able to sack Rome. Was that the end of Roman society in Africa? 'Vandalism' became

Following pages: Great Ludovisi, a sarcophagus depicting scenes of battle between Romans and barbarians, third century AD. Palazzo Altemps, National Roman Museum, Rome.

a name for mindless destruction. It took some time for archaeologists to realise that Vandals were responsible not only for burn-layers and for public monuments reused as shops, but also for building grand African churches. Vandals were Arian Christians, who sometimes (according to some sources) persecuted Christians who held other views; theological writing flourished, and one Vandal king himself engaged in theological debate. Vandals commissioned (or so the poets claimed) elaborate Latin verse, which combined praise of Vandal rulers with allusions to classical literature. Vandals appreciated silk, and gardens, and theatres, and Roman baths; this, said the Greek historian Procopius, weakened their moral and physical fibre, so that it was easy for the emperor Justinian to defeat them.

Roman culture and education continued, but Vandalic culture and values are almost unknown. Their language is lost, there is no Vandalic literature, and (as is usual for 'barbarian' kingdoms) the written sources are Latin and Greek. Those sources, together with inscriptions, provide evidence that Roman civic culture also survived. A cache of wooden tablets, dated by the regnal year of a Vandal king, documents property transactions made in accordance with Roman law; Fulgentius the theologian, according to his biographer, began his career as a tax-collector for the Vandal rulers. Roman imperial administrators, in Egypt and elsewhere, allowed local custom to continue. If Vandal rulers did the same, it may have made little difference to farmers and traders when Vandal warlords displaced Roman proprietors.

Economy, tradition, cultural memory, expectations and acknowledgement of duties, all contribute to the sense of belonging to a society. Did the Vandal conquest, after the initial trauma, do more than place different people in power at the top of a familiar system? Did parents begin to decide that their sons should learn Latin and Vandal not Latin and Greek, and practise fighting skills not writing and speaking skills? Perhaps the conquered population began to feel like Vandals, loyal subjects of Thrasamund or Geiseric, taking pride in a history of conquest. Or perhaps they simply acquiesced in Vandal rule, because it was not more oppressive than they could bear, and because it was better than the alternative of continued war. That too is a kind of society, allied by community of interest in peace and by agreement in observing the rules.

Augustine held that all human beings want peace, in their own bodies, in their households, and in their cities. Peace can be achieved only by agreement, at all levels of society, on who gives the orders and who takes them. Without that agreement, there will be perpetual conflict, because all human beings inherit from their common ancestor the desire to have their own way. In his view, it does not matter who conquers and who is conquered, because all that matters is the relationship of individual human beings to God; good rulers are a blessing, bad rulers are spiritual training.

According to Cicero's definition, Rome never was a *res publica*, allied by agreement on justice and on community of interest, but, Augustine said, there are other ways of defining a *populus*. He suggested 'a *populus* is a gathering of a rational multitude allied by sharing with concord in the objects of its love'. ('Rational' means only that non-human animals are excluded, not that people think clearly.) What it loves may be better or worse, as in the case of Rome, but that does not mean that the Roman *populus* is not a *populus* and that it has no *res publica*. The same applies to Athens or Egypt or Babylon or any other people. 'So long as there is some kind of gathering of a rational multitude, allied [*sociatus*] by common agreement in concord about the things they love', there is a *res publica*. There is also a starting-point for thinking about society surviving through crisis.

MEDICINE AND MORALITY

The Uprising (*L'Emeute*), Honoré Daumier, c. 1848.
The Phillips Collection, Washington, D.C.

CHALLENGING THE 'GREAT RESET' THEORY OF PANDEMICS

Mark Honigsbaum

Few events are as compelling as an epidemic. When sufficiently severe, an epidemic evokes responses from every sector of society, laying bare social and economic fault lines and presenting politicians with fraught medical and moral choices. In the most extreme cases, an epidemic can foment a full-blown political crisis. Thus, Thucydides describes how the repeated visitations of plague to Athens in 430–426 BC provoked widespread social disorder and the breakdown of civic norms.

'Men, not knowing what was to become of them, became utterly careless of everything, whether sacred or profane,' writes Thucydides. 'All the burial rites before in use were entirely upset and...many had recourse to the most shameless sepulchres.'

As the plague progresses, Thucydides describes how Athenians were swept up in a wave of hedonism and lawlessness, threatening the foundations of Athenian democracy: 'Men now coolly ventured on what they had formerly done in a corner... fear of gods or law of man there was none to restrain them.'

The resulting crisis, Thucydides claimed, undermined Athenians' faith in the rule of law and the democratic principles that underpinned the Greek city state, paving the way for the installation of a Spartan oligarchy known as the Thirty Tyrants. Even though the Spartans were later ejected, Athens never regained its confidence.

Covid-19 appears to have engendered a similar crisis in the modern world, the main difference being in scale. Whereas the crisis Thucydides describes was confined to Athens, the coronavirus pandemic has destabilised governments from Brazil to Belarus. The political reckoning has been particularly rapid in the United States, where Donald Trump's inability or unwillingness to check the spread of the coronavirus was a key factor in his recent election defeat. Now, the lockdowns and social distancing measures look set to plunge the world into the worst economic depression since the 1930s, raising the spectre of further political instability.

Given the wide-ranging social, economic and political impacts of Covid-19, it is natural to assume that the same must have been true of past epidemics and pandemics. But is this the case? Do pandemics really have the historical impacts that are often claimed for them or are these claims simply the product of particular narratives and readings of history?

For instance, in numerical terms, the most devastating pandemic of all time was the 1918–19 'Spanish influenza'. Coinciding with the end of the First World War, the Spanish flu is estimated to have killed between 17 to 100 million people worldwide. However, while 1919 was the first year since records began that the death rate exceeded the birth rate, those that survived generally enjoyed longer and healthier lifespans and, in many instances, benefited from higher wages too. Moreover, while the global death toll was immense, in developed industrial countries the mortality rate averaged 2%, meaning the Spanish flu left most of society unaffected. Indeed, the Spanish flu appears to have made little impression on public memory and social institutions, hence its historiographical characterisation as the 'forgotten pandemic'.

Narrating Epidemic Crises

A crisis is normally conceived of as an isolated moment in time in which our lives are shattered and plunged into disorder – what the cultural anthropologist Henrik Vigh has called 'a momentary malformation in the flow of things'. Vigh observes that for many people crises are 'endemic rather than episodic' and cannot be delineated as an aberrant moment of chaos or a period of decisive change. This is particularly the case for those living at the margins of society, for whom crises are ever present. Indeed, social critics such as Naomi Klein argue that instability is baked into the capitalist system, hence the way that in the last few decades neoliberal societies have lurched from one financial crisis to another.

Nevertheless, crises have long been regarded as a way of accessing deeper historical truths. As Janet Roitman has argued, in *Anti-Crisis* (2013), a crisis 'marks and generates history'. This is particularly the case for epidemics and pandemics which, unlike other natural disasters such as famines, are not limited to a particular region or moment in time but may come to encompass the whole globe. As the medical anthropologist

Christos Lynteris puts it, disease outbreaks involve a 'radically different ontological order', a mode of being that is simultaneously 'pathological and infectious'. Or to put it another way, one could conceivably outrun a famine but those who try to flee a plague may become unwitting carriers, contaminating new communities and introducing the pathogen to new places.

What is also not widely appreciated is that the roots of the term 'crisis' lie in the Ancient Greek word *krinô* (meaning to separate, choose, cut, decide, judge) and can be traced back to Hippocrates, whose scientific method influenced Thucydides' approach to history. For the Hippocratic school of medicine, prognosis took precedence over diagnosis, the point being to identify the turning point of a disease in order to intervene and bring about a satisfactory resolution to the illness. Similarly, Thucydides hoped that by tracking the social and moral dissolution that envelops Athens under the strain of the plague, his history could serve as a 'great case-book of social pathology', enabling readers to recognise similar historical patterns in future and intervene so as to restore order and stability. In this way, it has been argued, Thucydides applied a medical template to epidemic crises that has coloured our interpretation of them ever since.

The Black Death and Demographic Change

Perhaps the standout example of the transformative power of disease is the fourteenth century Black Death. Caused by the plague bacillus, *Yersinia pestis*, the pandemic coincided with the transition from medieval to early modern European society and was greatly enhanced by new shipping networks linking Venice and Genoa with Constantinople, Tunis, London and Bruges. The larger broad-bellied ships required for these long voyages provided perfect conveyances for plague-carrying rats and were soon sparking outbreaks across Europe.

Some scholars claim the pandemic killed a third of Europe's population between 1347 and 1353; others say up to one half. Whatever the true mortality, there is little doubt the Black Death represented a massive external shock to medieval society and, together with the famines that preceded it, contributed to a declining or stagnant population in Europe for almost 150 years afterwards. The result was a demographic, economic and political crisis.

E fut vne mer
ueilleuse kepous
de petite condui
te et fondacion
sont si grande et si perilleuse
pestilence sourdi en angleter
re Et pour donner exemple
a touttes maneres de gens
jen parleray et monstreray
selon ce que du fait et de
la maniere jen fuz adont
informe   Vntt vsaute
est en angleterre et aussi
est il en plusieurs pays que
les nobles ont grant fran
chises sur leurs hommes et
les tiennent en seruaite ·
c est a entendre quilz soi
uent de droit et par coustu

me labourer les terres des
gentilz hommes cueillir les
grains et amener a lostel
et mettre a la grange la
tre et banner et les fons
fenner et amener a lostel
la busche copper et amener a
lostel et touttes telles cou
urees · Et souent seulx
hommes par seruaute tout
ce faire aux seigneurs Et
trop plus a de telz gens en
angleterre que ailleurs et
en sont les gentilz hommes
et les prelatz seruiz Et par
especial en la conte de kent
dexxesses de soukesses et de
betfort et y en a plus que
on demourant de toutte

The Peasants' Revolt in 1381 was a demographic,
economic and political crisis that followed the
Black Death in the mid-fourteenth century.
A scene from the revolt where leader
Wat Tyler and John Ball meet is depicted in
Jean Froissart's *Chronicles*, c. 1480.

A smaller population meant less demand for grain putting downward pressure on the price of basic foodstuffs. At the same time, a diminished population fuelled competition, exerting upward pressure on wages and challenging the villeinage system of forced labour that underpinned the feudal system. The result was a wave of popular uprisings across Europe, including the Jacquerie in France in 1358, the revolt of the Florentine *Ciompi* or wool carders in 1378–82, and the 1381 Peasants' Revolt in England.

The demands of English peasants included the abolition of an inequitable poll tax and the removal of a statute, passed in the wake of the Black Death, that sought to restrict wages to pre-pandemic levels. The Florentine carders meanwhile demanded a more equitable fiscal policy and the right to establish guilds, the forerunners of trade unions. Today, we take collective wage bargaining and trade unions for granted, but in the fourteenth century these demands threatened the basis of the feudal system, hence the observation of the French chronicler Jean Froissart that: 'Never was any land or realm in such great danger as England at that time.'

This economic levelling also spurred a series of social and cultural changes, including the right of everyone except the lowliest manual worker to wear furs – a privilege that previously had been the preserve of nobles and clerics. In most cases the political reforms were short-lived. For instance, Wat Tyler, the leader of the English rebels, marched to London to petition King Richard II with 60,000 peasants at his back. Demanding that 'all men should be free and of one condition', the rebels occupied the Tower of London, ransacked the palaces and mansions of wealthy Londoners, and executed the Archbishop of Canterbury and the Lord Chief Justice, as well as other hated representatives of the nobility. Within a few weeks Wat Tyler and other leaders of the revolt had been arrested and executed and the crisis was over. Nonetheless, the movement resulted in concessions to peasants: the poll tax was abandoned, and wage bargaining expanded over time, leading to the emergence of a new yeoman class.

The Collapse of the Aztec and Incan Empires
Similar claims have been made about the crisis that enveloped the Aztec and Incan empires following the Spanish Conquest of Central and South America in the early sixteenth century. In *Plagues and Peoples*, William H

McNeill argued that 'disaster is to be expected whenever some previously remote and isolated tribe comes into contact with the outside world and there encounters a series of destructive and demoralising epidemics.'

In the case of the Aztecs and Inca, the root cause of crisis and societal collapse was the introduction by Columbus and, later, the conquistador Hernan Cortes, of smallpox, measles and other Old World diseases to which Amerindian populations of modern-day Mexico, Guatemala and Peru had little or no immunity. The result was that within a century of Cortes's arrival in the Gulf of Mexico in 1518, the population of Central Mexico had been reduced, according to some estimates, from 25 million to 1.5 million. A similar demographic catastrophe occurred in the Andes, wiping out perhaps as many as six million Quechua and Aymara Indians and bringing the Incan empire to its knees.

But is this the whole story? In recent decades, Nahuatl scholars have questioned the role of disease in clearing the way for the Spanish, arguing that the size of pre-conquest populations has been consistently exaggerated, as has the extent to which smallpox and measles were responsible for dramatic population declines in the Americas. These pathogens may have contributed to the die-offs in Central and South America in the sixteenth century, but just as important was the exploitation by the Spanish of pre-existing political tensions and rivalries between the Aztecs and other indigenous groups, such as the Tlaxcaltecas, and the *encomienda* system which saw the extraction by the Spanish of indigenous property and the enslavement of Indians in gold and silver mines. By this reading, had the indigenous peoples of Central and South America simply experienced the new pathogens, their populations would have declined and recovered, as happened in Athens in the fifth century. In other words, the collapse of the Aztec and Inca empires was a process that had as much to do with the appalling violence inflicted on them by the conquistadors and the turbulence of colonisation as to the immediate crisis engendered by Indians' susceptibility to imported European pathogens.

Cholera and Revolution

With the possible exception of yellow fever, no disease is more closely associated with revolutions and political crises than cholera. Beginning in 1830, recurrent epidemics of cholera sparked widespread rioting and protests in Paris, London and other European capitals. Similar protests

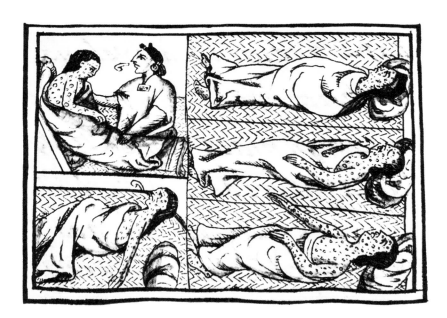

Tenochtitlan people sick with smallpox illustrated
in *The Florentine Codex* (originally *The Universal
History of the Things of New Spain*), by Fray
Bernardino de Sahagún, 1577.

occurred in Asiatic Russia and New York City, where in 1832 cholera was
carried to the Lower East Side of Manhattan by the newly opened Erie
Canal, sparking outbreaks in the Five Corners district and killing nearly
3,000 people. These were decades marked by revolutions, wars and social
and political reforms. For example, the 1831–32 cholera epidemic reached
Britain during the profound political crisis over the Great Reform Bill of
1832, a year which some historians have argued saw the only real possibility of a political revolution in modern British history. Cholera next swept
across Europe in the revolutionary year of 1848. Further cholera epidemics coincided with the overthrow of the Second Empire in France in 1871
and with pogroms against Jews in Russian Poland in 1892.

On that occasion, thousands of Jews fled across the border to Hamburg
by train. As Richard Evans recounts in *Death in Hamburg*, the sudden
influx of Jewish immigrants prompted demands for quarantines and dis-
infection measures to prevent cholera spreading to the local population.
The wealthy Hamburg merchants who dominated the city's administration refused to believe that cholera could be carried in water and rejected
initiatives for the construction of a sand-filtered water supply that might
have prevented discharges from cheap lodging houses and insanitary
barracks where the migrants were housed from entering the River Elbe.
The result was that cholera-laden discharges soon reached Hamburg's
water intake point, sparking a major outbreak. In the space of six weeks
10,000 people died and 40,000 fled Hamburg.

As with cholera outbreaks in other cities in Europe and North America,
the disease hit the poorest hardest since they tended to live in overcrowded, unhygienic dwellings where they shared toilet facilities and
were unable to take simple precautions such as boiling water. The episode
incensed working class voters and supporters of the Social Democratic
Party who used the outbreak to castigate the state administration for
serving the interests of a rich minority and neglecting the health of the
mass of ordinary people. The result was that in the 1893 national elections, all the city's Reichstag seats fell to the Social Democrats.

Cholera epidemics also sparked widespread conspiracy theories. For
instance, during the 1832 Parisian cholera epidemic, the German poet
Heinrich Heine reported that the Parisian sanitary commission ordered
mounds of rubbish that could be a source of contamination to be hauled
beyond the city limits. In response, ragmen who made their living sorting
through the debris spread rumours that those who had died of cholera

had been poisoned by the health authorities and took to the streets in protest. 'The more extraordinary these reports were, the more eagerly they were received by the multitude,' noted Heine in an echo of today's coronavirus conspiracy theories.

To many observers, the protests recalled the mass uprisings that had marked the French Revolution and seemed of a part with the political turmoil of the 1830 July revolution. 'For fifty years Paris has been the scene of distressing events,' the official medical report for the 1832 cholera outbreak noted. 'The violence of the [political] parties has armed citizens against one another; their blood has flowed in the streets, and horrible battles have created a spectacle.' Unlike the Black Death, there was no demographic deficit after cholera. Nor, according to Evans, is there evidence that cholera provoked permanent political change or significant social movements. '[Cholera] epidemics', he concludes, 'were less causes than consequences of revolutionary upheavals, and the government reactions associated with them.'

There is little doubt that fear of revolutionary upheaval combined with concern about urban overcrowding spurred major sanitary reforms in Paris, London and other newly industrialised European cities. The result was a gradual amelioration of living conditions and improvements to the health of the urban poor that drew the sting out of mass protests. With the expansion of the hospital system and the advent of new medical technologies, such as vaccines, in the twentieth century it was now possible to regulate the health of populations, thereby avoiding the recurrent cycle of epidemics and crises that had accompanied cholera outbreaks in the nineteenth century.

Covid-19 and the Politics of Life

The question raised now is whether we have reached the limits of these medical responses, or if the crises that have followed Covid-19 are a temporary blip that will disappear once new coronavirus vaccines become widely available and governments begin to reopen their societies. According to the French sociologist Michel Foucault, the central question facing modern liberal states is how to balance the health of populations with the need to keep economic goods and services circulating. Foucault termed this logic, which takes the administration of life and populations as its subject, biopolitics and biopower. During the plague epidemics of the seventeenth and eighteenth centuries, states had little choice but to resort to blunt instruments such as *cordons sanitaires* and quarantines to prevent pathogens crossing borders. The result was widespread disruption to trade. But with the arrival of more sophisticated medical systems and modern forms of biopolitical management in the nineteenth century, it became possible to persuade individuals to regulate their health for the common good, making all of us complicit in the central calculus of biopower: namely, as Foucault put it, who to make live and who to let die.

Covid-19 has thrown these political choices into sharp relief. Should governments impose strict lockdowns in order to protect lives and prevent health systems being overwhelmed, or should they allow some economic activities to continue knowing that it could result in higher deaths for the elderly and other at-risk groups?

Both choices have consequences for political stability: lock down too hard and for too long and you risk mass protests by people whose businesses have been shuttered or who resent the curtailment of their civil liberties. Relax the restrictions too early or fail to offer adequate protection to hospitals and care homes, and you risk the ire of health workers and the elderly. Given the way that the coronavirus has exposed glaring inequalities in access to health care and the role that income, occupation, and race play in adverse health outcomes, particularly for blacks and other ethnic minorities, it is little wonder that these frustrations have spilled into the open – hence the Black Lives Matter protests that swept the United States and Europe following the death in police custody of an unarmed black man, George Floyd, in Minneapolis in May 2020.

Belarus, Brazil, Angola and Thailand have seen similar mass protests, albeit sparked by a different combination of factors. It is too early to say whether Black Lives Matter and other pandemic-inspired protests will result in significant political reforms. Perhaps the reason we are inclined to view pandemics and other crises as moral and political turning points is that we have been conditioned to view them through a medical-historical lens. History suggests it might be better to regard pandemics less as crises than as occasions for political 'reckoning' that may – or may not – see the resolution of long-standing social and economic grievances.

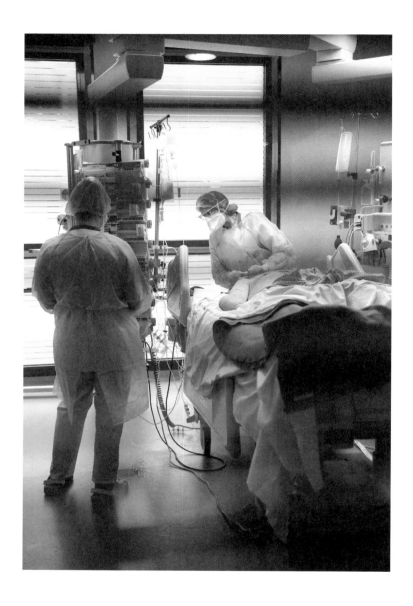

Medical staff treat Covid-19 patients in a hospital
in France, 2020.

COVID-19 AND THE MORAL CASE FOR PERSONAL JUDGEMENT

David Seedhouse

The tension between independence and compliance is omnipresent. It begins at a birth, as the baby asserts its interests over its mother's, and she responds with benign control. From nursery to school to the workplace to end-of-life care, we are pulled in opposite directions. We accept systems managed by other people so long as they deliver results, but at the same time we want to make our own decisions.

We live on a shifting spectrum – obedience to rules at one end, faith in ourselves at the other. At the extremes of obedience, consistency is the gold standard. To achieve it we must have rules for best practice. If the rules are followed the outcomes will be the same whichever professional is helping whichever client; for the sake of reliability and to minimise risk, we should observe standards and protocols.

The opposite view, which prioritises individual difference over conformity, is that however much humans impose rules, sooner or later they lose their relevance. Human life is too rich to be governed by technical solutions. Life is not standardised. Intelligent healthcare, for example, requires personal reflection and intuition. Where there are rules it is necessary to decide which, if any, to apply. There is no alternative but to trust ourselves.

Algorithms versus Heuristics

Different perspectives on this tension abound in psychology and the social sciences. The most general distinction is between algorithms and heuristics, in which an algorithm is a set of well-defined instructions for carrying out a particular task and a heuristic is a short-cut technique that helps you look for an answer without going through every step.

A very simple illustration of the difference is in searching for lost car keys you know are in your kitchen: an algorithmic approach would systematically search every inch of the room until the keys are found, guaranteeing success. A heuristic approach would use experiences of similar situations to look first in the most obvious places. There is no guarantee of success, but it is likely to be a quicker search.

Nobel prize winner Daniel Kahneman states that decisions based on algorithms are more reliable than human judgements. He claims that countless psychological experiments show that we overrate our decision-making powers. Our thoughts are distorted by psychological biases, so we make worse decisions than we would were we to use scientifically tested formulae. For Kahneman, our reverence for 'intuition' is a delusion. He observes that when you compare clinical predictions based on subjective impressions of trained professionals with statistical predictions made by combining even a handful of ratings, the algorithms are more accurate 60% of the time.

Kahneman gives many examples: longevity of cancer patients, length of hospital stays, prospects of success for new businesses, evaluation of credit risks for banks, winners of football games – even future prices of Bordeaux wine. He cites bookmakers as the perfect example of the supremacy of algorithms over human guesswork – the wisest and most informed punter may win sometimes, but with simple rules on their side the bookies will always triumph in the end.

Kahneman's long-standing colleague, Gary Klein, favours the more natural approach. Klein rejects Kahneman's conclusion because it is mostly drawn, he argues, from 'artificial tasks assigned in laboratory settings'. He focuses instead on 'naturalistic decision-making'. Klein spent years watching fire commanders, fighter pilots, paramedics and others making 'split-second decisions on the job', which led him to conclude that 'the expert decision-maker who behaves according to rational models' is more of a myth than a reality. Klein found that expert decision-makers do not go through a mechanical process of 'comparative evaluation' – there is just no time to do this. Rather their experience allows them to identify the most reasonable reaction as the first they consider, so they do not bother with any others.

The Tension in Healthcare
In healthcare the tension between obedience and independence is manifested in a conflict between practical wisdom and bureaucracy. Using practical wisdom, clinical care is an interpretive art in which health

professionals apply 'tacit knowledge' or 'unconscious knowing' gained through experience to diagnose and care. As Klein discovered, seasoned health professionals grasp patients' situations intuitively through unconscious pattern recognition, often more quickly and reliably than following step-by-step diagnostic algorithms.

At the bureaucratic end, echoing Kahneman, while we all experience tacit knowledge in our daily lives (cooking automatically, riding bikes without thinking, absorbing text on billboards unconsciously), in complex, organised systems it is necessary to have uniform procedures rather than leave things to chance. The managerial mind does not trust personal judgement – it is simply too risky, too maverick, too inconsistent. And there is a significant probability it will come to the wrong conclusions.

The 'Mid-Staffs Scandal'

The 'Mid-Staffs Scandal' is a largescale example of this tension in a clinical setting. The scandal took place between January 2005 and March 2009, when hundreds of hospital patients at two hospitals in Mid-Staffordshire in England died because of substandard care and staff failings. Some patients received the wrong medication or no medication; receptionists rather than doctors decided which patients to treat; nurses switched off equipment because they did not know how to use it; and there was pressure to meet arbitrary targets set by NHS managers, including a four-hour limit to treat people in accident and emergency.

According to the *Daily Telegraph*, the scandal is thought to have occurred because managers attempted to cut costs and meet targets for caring for patients within certain time limits, in order to achieve a coveted 'foundation status' for the Trust.

These targets apparently ruled supreme, overriding any other considerations – including personal judgement. NHS managers staffed the hospital so thinly that there were never enough consultants to supervise junior doctors adequately, so the juniors took their instructions from senior nurses and matrons, who religiously enforced the arbitrary targets. Health workers who failed to meet them were threatened with the sack. Junior nurses and doctors were repeatedly forced to abandon seriously ill patients to treat minor cases who were in danger of breaching the four-hour accident and emergency waiting time limit.

An extensive inquiry chaired by Robert Francis QC recommended reforms designed to embed personal judgement in the system as a humanising element. Francis identified an 'unhealthy and dangerous culture', highlighting a failure to 'put the patient first', and pinpointing characteristics which contributed to this failure including a lack of candour; low staff morale; disengagement by medical leaders; and secretive, defensive cultures.

Francis made an astonishing 290 recommendations, chief of which was that the NHS should operate according to a common set of values and standards. He also proposed a process called 'values-based recruitment' – a mechanism to appoint people with 'the right values' by using psychological tests and asking them what they would do in situations which require a 'caring approach'.

Francis wanted to move NHS culture toward 'practical wisdom'. He was alarmed by how easily orders to follow insensitive instructions outweighed personal judgement in staff, none of whom were unusually cruel in everyday life. His recommendations might have been expected to lead to more autonomy for staff – and indeed they were encouraged to 'whistle blow' and be 'candid' about uncaring practice.

Yet Francis's reforms brought about a significant increase in Codes of Practice and checkbox protocols. Despite his emphasis on the importance of value judgements, the stronger impulse was to try to ensure that every patient would receive the same standard of care and be 'safeguarded' above all else. Values are notoriously open to interpretation and cannot be relied upon to produce consistent practice, so the bureaucratic urge won out and a deluge of reforms followed. Thanks to the prime minister, David Cameron, it also led to a practice called 'intentional rounding', which requires nurses to see patients every hour to ask them set questions about their needs, whether or not it makes clinical sense to do so. Naturally enough, such regimentation has driven many experienced health professionals away, so alienating them that many feel they may as well be replaced by robots.

Are Rules Inevitably Dominant?
Examples of the apparent dominance of rules occurs in all spheres of society. Schools assert independence, individuality and creativity yet, the world over, they teach and examine the same, limited number of subjects,

set in stone in a hierarchy with maths and languages at the top and dance and drama at the foot.

In the early 1970s, presaging the contemporary preoccupation with health and safety, Lord Robens was asked to investigate factory safety in the UK. He concluded there was too much prescriptive law, which expanded every time a new hazard arose. Instead Robens recommended a new form of legislation which laid down principles rather than precise instructions. His concept eventually took shape as the curiously named Health and Safety at Work etc. Act of 1974, which required those in charge of safety to do everything 'reasonably practicable' to reduce risk, in a bid to emphasise the salience of personal judgement over a blanket application of concrete rules. To Robens' dismay, however, this merely prompted a flood of further guidance from various quarters, each offering different interpretations of 'reasonably practicable'.

Children's play is a pointed example of distrust in personal judgement. The provision of stimulating play space provides the young with opportunities to develop and gain experience in experimenting with risk. Yet for the last 30 years this aim has been increasingly impeded because of fear of injury and – perhaps more importantly – of litigation, even leading to traditional swings (and roundabouts) being banned in some areas. Managed play has become progressively safer, and ever more unsatisfying.

Which brings us to today's predicament. In 2020, to control the spread of a virus, citizens around the world have been subject to restrictions on civil liberties undreamt of a few months earlier. Governments have relished their power, rushing to control citizens without involvement or consent. The authorities have swiftly copied each other, as if in competition to see who can get away with the harshest policies.

Despite the severity of the measures, and in the face of clear evidence they are causing more damage to health and the economy than the virus itself, the great majority of citizens have conformed. When governments tell people to stay at home they mostly do; when they shut hospitality outlets people shrug and accept it; when they are told to wear masks, they wear masks; and when government measures contradict themselves – even when the latest law is the exact opposite of the previous one – most go along with them. A few people protest, in writing and through civil disobedience, but the majority either believe what they are told or find it safer to toe the line than rock the boat.

Restricting children's play shows distrust in
personal judgement across all ages.

Personal Judgement is Intrinsic to Human Existence

Over the last few months opinion polls have repeatedly shown that people want greater restrictions on their freedom. People value safety, certainty, predictability, and assurances about the future. We are condemned to be free and we resolutely resist our freedoms.

There are countless examples of the human willingness to conform, even in the most extreme circumstances: junior pilots choosing not to challenge their superiors even to avoid their own deaths; prisoners preferring prison to freedom; experiments in psychology in which subjects will inflict painful punishment on strangers when instructed to by an authority figure they have never met; soldiers committing barbaric acts in their thousands – mass mutilations, torture and rape – because their unthinking acceptance of the assumed morality of their group overruled any individual sense of right and wrong. It can seem that obedience is the strongest force.

Yet, the need to be free is more deep-seated than the apparent haven of conformity. Ultimately it is what it means to be a human being. As disruptive and unwelcome as it may be, we cannot *be* without personal judgement. We have no choice but to make choices. If we are unable to choose then there is no reason for us to exist.

Personal Judgement is Everywhere

Arguing for the importance of personal judgement requires an understanding of what it is to be a person. Though we tend to think of ourselves as being consistent in our judgements, reflection on life's experience shows that we are changeable creatures, made up of all sorts of influences, most of which we are usually not aware of.

Each of these influences, and many more, continually combine to create us. Some of the influences are relatively static (our personalities for example), some are volatile. Just as our moods fluctuate, so our stresses, health status, pain levels, relationships, knowledge, and emotions change us incessantly. The John Smith who woke feeling calm and beneficent is different from the John Smith who ten minutes ago opened an email from human resources summoning him to an urgent performance review.

We see circumstances differently dependent on our personal makeup at the time. We perpetually combine ourselves with external conditions, creating endless, unique situations. Personal judgement varies as we vary. In every meaningful context it is both necessary and unpredictable, placing the responsibility to choose on individuals, whatever the rules.

Personal judgement is the daily reality of coalface healthcare. Consider some examples: you find your colleague in the staff room eating food from the patients' trolley. The food is left over and will be thrown away, but it is against the rules for staff to eat it. Your judgement of the circumstances is a personal matter. Others will judge differently from you. Maybe you see theft, maybe you see need. Maybe you are irritated, maybe you are empathetic. Which would it be?

Or perhaps you are a doctor in a pain clinic. Your client wants more pain relief, but you worry he is becoming addicted. How do you balance these considerations? There are rules and scales you can use, but ultimately pain is subjective, and interpretation is necessary. How would the situation seem to you?

Or maybe you're a third-year student nurse working on a busy care of the elderly unit. It's your first day. The senior nurse is showing you around. You're stopped by an 82-year-old woman, who's sitting beside her bed. She grabs hold of your trousers, asking, 'What's the time?' 'What's for lunch?' She is obviously in need of comfort. Before you can help, the senior nurse states loudly and impatiently, 'Mrs Smith's demented. She forgets everything. Come on dear, she'll have you there all day.' Would you stay?

Towards Collective Personal Judgement
Margaret Thatcher famously declared that society is a myth. Specifically, she said:

> There are individual men and women, and there are families, and no government can do anything except through people and people look to themselves first…There is no such thing as society. There is living tapestry of men and women and people and the beauty of that tapestry and the quality of our lives will depend upon how much each of us is prepared to take responsibility for ourselves and each of us prepared to turn round and help by our own efforts those who are unfortunate.

Citizen's assemblies invite open dialogue and
careful deliberation providing an alternative
to top-down decision making.

One reading of this is fiercely individualist: people are naturally separate and responsible for themselves. An ardent admirer of the philosophy of Friedrich Hayek, Thatcher believed there was no sensible alternative to free market libertarianism. It was the collective outcome of personal judgements, rather than central planning and control, that made nations prosperous.

Arguments for the primacy of personal judgement are often used in support of this outlook, but this is not the only interpretation available. The idea that 'there is no such thing as society' can also be understood as an apolitical expression of a fundamental philosophical truth, namely that personal judgement is the quintessence of meaningful life and precedes politics.

A belief in the power of collective planning and trust in personal judgement are not necessarily at odds. Encouraging personal judgement does not imply a narrow political view of individuals as distinct entities in perpetual competition. Since people are fascinatingly complex, with varied knowledge and life experience, praising personal judgement not only celebrates difference, but can also support a case for implementing decision-making methods which tap into our rich subjective wisdoms.

An obvious alternative to top-down decree is to broaden decision-making processes to include diverse voices, knowledge, values, experiences, and cultures – as an effective way to arrive at well-informed consensus. This could be achieved by properly organised and funded citizens' assemblies, with decision-making powers, where policies like lockdown could be properly explored and debated, and different personal judgements could be heard. Our current leaders would be invited to present their viewpoints, which would then be subject to scrutiny from assembly members from many walks of life. In these assemblies our leaders would have to defend and justify their opinions and would, in the process, learn about and be able to reflect on intelligent and compassionate alternatives, improving their own capacity for personal judgement in the process.

This is not a new idea. There are many successful examples of collective decision-making including a wide-ranging project in the USA – Citizen Voices on Pandemic Flu Choices – which explored what should be done in an influenza pandemic. The idea was to enable policymakers to understand the range of society's values via public engagement which involved both experts and hundreds of citizens with diverse backgrounds and perspectives. It was an inclusive public process which provided an opportunity for frank, open dialogue and careful deliberation. It is worth noting that despite the different backgrounds of their members, the groups involved reached a 'very high level of agreement': namely that the first immunisation goal should be to assure the functioning of society, followed by the goal of reducing individual deaths and hospitalisations due to influenza – the very opposite conclusion to the current consensus among a bunkered group of scientists and politicians.

The pandemic has revealed a decision-making crisis rooted in the preference of ill-equipped officials to command rather than to listen. If society is no more than a 'tapestry of individuals', as Margaret Thatcher controversially asserted, then we are all equally entitled to decide what happens to us.

Lord, have mercy on London, unknown artist,
seventeenth century (colouring later).

REMEMBERING LONDON'S LAST
GREAT PLAGUE

Vanessa Harding

Should epidemic diseases be considered as natural disasters, or as events brought about by human actions or inactions? Are they so exceptional that they offer no insights into other situations, or do they shed useful light on social tensions, the robustness of governmental structures, embedded assumptions and beliefs? The plague of 1665–66 was not the worst to strike Britain, but it has a prominent place in the cultural imaginary because it was the last plague, and because in London it was so swiftly followed by another cataclysm, the fire of 1666. The plague epidemic of May to December 1665 killed at least 70,000 Londoners; the fire of 2–6 September 1666 destroyed four fifths of the city centre, incinerated hundreds of thousands of pounds' worth of real estate and material goods, and made some 60,000 people homeless. The temporal coincidence is, strictly speaking, just that; but they had a profound effect on each other, and were linked in the minds of contemporaries and interpreted as part of a wider pattern.

1665 is also the best-recorded epidemic before the nineteenth century, thanks to accounts from eyewitnesses such as Samuel Pepys in London, and still more to the documentation generated by activity at all levels of government, from the parish to the Privy Council. However, the fire somewhat obscures our understanding of the plague: it is impossible to know how swiftly the city would have recovered socially or demographically from the trauma and losses of the epidemic, given the dispersal of its population and the disruption to economic activity in 1666, not to mention the loss of some relevant records.

When considering responses to the London plague of 1665, three themes stand out: the conflict between principle and pragmatism in the governmental response; the role played by communications; and the confusion of medical and providential views swirling among the population. A fourth important point, however, is the historical moment. 1665 was the mid-point of a half-century or more of extreme political instability, and the country was still marked by the divisions of the recent civil war, religious ferment, and ongoing political dissension; tensions over the respective roles and authority of Parliament and the executive remained. From March 1665 England was at war with its commercial rival and neighbour, the Dutch Republic. These circumstances shaped the policies and actions of national government and influenced perceptions of the epidemic and its causes.

Plague was familiar, and evoked well-tried practical responses. It had been a feature of London life for so long that it had its own playbook and cast of players. The three principals were the Privy Council, the mayor and aldermen of the City of London at Guildhall (together with the justices of the peace for the large areas of the metropolis outside the Lord Mayor's jurisdiction), and, collectively, the vestrymen and officers of London's 130 parishes. The script was the Plague Orders, a list of regulations originating with the Privy Council, with input from physicians and more than a nod to continental practice, and evolved over time. They were issued by the mayor and aldermen, printed by the City's printer, and by and large implemented by parish and other local officers. They had last been issued in 1646, when plague cases surged in a minor local epidemic, and were re-issued, with some additions, in June or July 1665.

The Plague Orders of 1665 had four main heads: the appointment of special officers including surgeons; 'orders concerning infected Houses, and Persons sick of the Plague', which covered quarantine of infected houses, burial of the dead, and the decontamination of materials; environmental and public hygiene measures; and public order. Essentially they provided an agenda for local and civic governments, to be implemented either by newly-appointed officers or the existing agencies of local government.

In London, the network of wards and parishes provided personnel with the local knowledge and experience to put the orders into practice. Every parish met the challenge in its own way, but the case of St Bride Fleet Street, a large inner-city parish, offers an example. The vestry met on 16 June, 'to consider of several things necessary in this time of visitation'. At this meeting they organised searchers of the dead to inspect every dead body and report the cause of death. They appointed bearers for the plague dead, fixed their wages, and established accommodation for them in the churchyard where they would not mix with other people. On 3 July they decided to give extra remuneration to the gravedigger to encourage him to dig graves deep 'as it is ordered and as the time requires'. In August, they ordered burial in large pits in the parish churchyard rather than individual graves. Over the course of the epidemic, they appointed new officers to replace those who had died, including the senior churchwarden and his successor in late September and early October. At the local level, the records seem to show St Bride's parish as an administrative unit and as a community struggling under the pressure of events but not overwhelmed; other parishes likewise weathered the storm.

One vital area not covered by the Plague Orders was the organisation of relief for the infected and quarantined. It was recognised at the beginning of the epidemic that people might suppress evidence of infection for fear of the practical and financial consequences, and suggested that 'if it were published that every infected person shall have medical attendance, &c., and payment for loss of time, persons would not conceal their misfortune'. Shutting up 40 houses in good time might prevent the infection of 10,000. This proposal was probably both too costly and too radical to be adopted, and parishes, the normal distributors of poor relief, certainly faced huge demands on their funds. St Bride's spent £494 4s between 19 June and 8 October on 'poore visited persons and families', 'for their nurses, and for coffins and bearers for the burial of many such that died and other incident charges concerning their keeping and burials'. The ordinary poor rate was insufficient to cover this, and one of Guildhall's most important roles was to collect and redistribute money for these purposes. Private benevolence went some way, but across London, the flight of the wealthy and well-to-do hampered fundraising.

In many respects national, civic, and parish governments worked effectively together. The City appointed and remunerated physicians and surgeons, as required by the Orders. The Crown and City shared fears of the poor and their potential for disorder, and came down hard on possible occasions of it. The Plague Orders banned 'Playes, Bear-baitings, Games, Singing of Ballads, Buckler-play, or such like causes of Assemblies of people'; the mayor and aldermen in addition closed grammar and other schools, especially dancing and fencing schools. The Plague Orders prohibited dinners at taverns, alehouses, 'and other places of common entertainment'; the mayor and aldermen instructed innholders not to feed strangers within doors but permitted them to sell food and drink at the door.

Following pages: Nine illustrations from a 1665 plague broadsheet depicting scenes such as the sick at home; the wealthy (including the king) fleeing the city; a funeral procession and the return to London. Museum of London.

FACSIMILE REPRODUCTION FROM A PICTORIAI

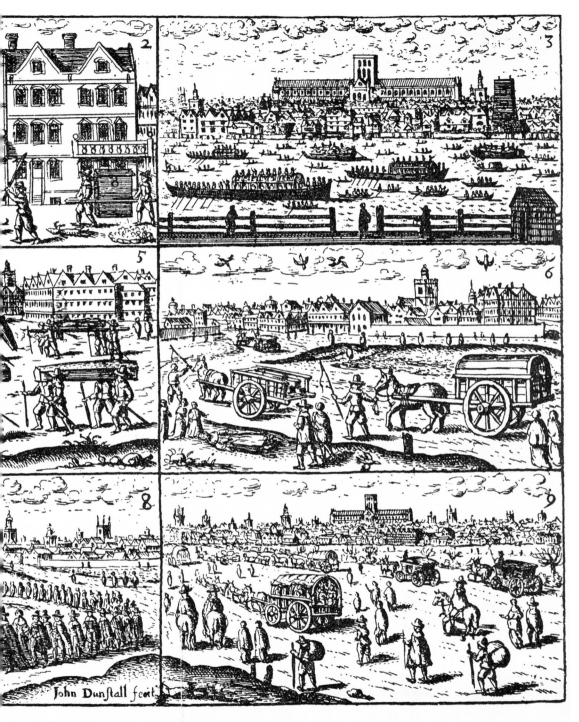

John Dunstall fecit

However, the apparent unity of approach concealed a history of dis-agreement over policies, especially the practice of household isolation versus the institution of pesthouses. Recommendations earlier in the cen-tury to establish a medical magistracy or board of health for the whole of London had foundered, and though the City maintained and expanded its pesthouse, this was clearly inadequate for the scale of the epidemic: only 156 plague deaths were reported there, out of some 30–35,000 in the area within the City's jurisdiction. It seems clear that the City authorities considered some of the Privy Council's orders unworkable or even counter-productive, and the fact that so many social and political leaders and government officers left London, while the mayor, aldermen and civic bureaucracy remained at their posts, did not go unnoticed.

Information was key both to government's programme of action and to the individual response. Since the sixteenth century civic and national government had collected data on London mortality; from the early seventeenth this had been released to the public in the form of weekly handbills listing numbers of deaths, and plague deaths, by parish: the Bills of Mortality. By 1665 the procedures were finely honed: parish clerks returned their weekly figures to Parish Clerks' Hall, where they were collated into a single document, communicated first to the lord mayor and Privy Council, and printed for public dissemination on the Thursday. Though some questioned their accuracy – almost everyone knew of cases of plague unreported or misdiagnosed, and the unexplained rise in deaths attributed to 'spotted fever' was also noted – on the whole they were felt to provide a reliable guide to a rapidly-changing situation.

The weekly bills could alert authorities to an incipient epidemic, if plague deaths ceased to be random and rose steadily week on week or spread across the capital. In 1665, official concern about plague may have been sparked by the weekly bill for 2–9 May, in which nine plague deaths in four parishes were reported; a committee of the Privy Council 'for prevention of the spreading of the Infection of the Plague' met on 13 May.

The weekly bills were available to the public both for an annual sub-scription, and for individual sale. Though comparatively few originals have survived, contemporary letters and diaries demonstrate their readership and use. Outside epidemics, the reports of 'casualties' – mostly accidental deaths – provided a regular topic of conversation; during epidemics the weekly bill communicated vital information on which to base decisions about personal safety and business strategy, as well as

Parish	Bur.	Plag.	Parish	Bur.	Plag.	Parish	Bur.	Plag.
St Alban Woodstreet	11	8	St George Botolphlane			St Martin Ludgate	4	4
Alhallows Barking	13	11	St Gregory by St Pauls	9	5	St Martin Orgars	8	6
Alhallows Breadstreet	1	1	St Hellen	11	11	St Martin Outwitch	1	
Alhallows Great	6	5	St James Dukes place	7	5	St Martin Vintrey	17	17
Alhallows Honylane			St James Garlickhithe	3	1	St Matthew Fridaystreet	1	
Alhallows Lesse	3	2	St John Baptist	7	4	St Maudlin Milkstreet	2	2
Alhallows Lumbardstreet	6	4	St John Evangelist			St Maudlin Oldfishstreet	8	4
Alhallows Staining	7	5	St John Zachary	1	1	St Michael Bassishaw	12	11
Alhallows the Wall	23	11	St Katharine Coleman	5	1	St Michael Cornhil	3	1
St Alphage	18	10	St Katharine Crechurch	7	4	St Michael Crookedlane	7	4
St Andrew Hubbard	1		St Lawrence Jewry	2	1	St Michael Queenhithe	7	6
St Andrew Undershaft	14	9	St Lawrence Pountney	6	5	St Michael Quern	1	
St Andrew Wardrobe	21	16	St Leonard Eastcheap	1	1	St Michael Royal	2	1
St Ann Aldersgate	18	11	St Leonard Fosterlane	17	13	St Michael Woodstreet	2	1
St Ann Blackfryers	22	17	St Magnus Parish	2	2	St Mildred Breadstreet	2	1
St Antholins Parish			St Margaret Lothbury	2	1	St Mildred Poultrey	4	3
St Austins Parish			St Margaret Moses	1		St Nicholas Acons		
St Bartholomew Exchange	2	2	St Margaret Newfishstreet	1		St Nicholas Coleabby	1	
St Bennet Fynck	2	2	St Margaret Pattons	1		St Nicholas Olaves	3	1
St Bennet Gracechurch			St Mary Abchurch	1		St Olave Hartstreet	7	4
St Bennet Paulswharf	16	8	St Mary Aldermanbury	11	5	St Olave Jewry	1	1
St Bennet Sherehog			St Mary Aldermary	2	1	St Olave Silverstreet	23	15
St Botolph Billingsgate	2		St Mary le Bow	6	6	St Pancras Soperlane		
Chrifts Church	27	22	St Mary Bothaw	1	1	St Peter Cheap	1	1
St Christophers	1		St Mary Colechurch			St Peter Cornhil	7	6
St Clement Eastcheap	2	2	St Mary Hill	2	1	St Peter Paulswharf	5	2
St Dionis Backchurch	2	1	St Mary Mounthaw	1		St Peter Poor	3	2
St Dunstan East	7	2	St Mary Sommerset	6	5	St Steven Colemanstreet	15	11
St Edmund Lumbardstr.	2	2	St Mary Stayning	1		St Steven Walbrook		
St Ethelborough	13	7	St Mary Woolchurch	1		St Swithin	2	2
St Faith	6	6	St Mary Woolnoth	1	1	St Thomas Apostle	8	7
St Foster	13	11	St Martin Iremongerlane			Trinity Parish	5	3
St Gabriel Fenchurch	1							

Christned in the 97 Parishes within the Walls——— 34   Buried——— 538   Plague——— 366

Parish	Bur.	Plag.	Parish	Bur.	Plag.	Parish	Bur.	Plag.
St Andrew Holborn	252	220	St Botolph Aldgate	238	212	Saviours Southwark	160	120
St Bartholomew Great	58	50	St Botolph Bishopsgate	288	236	S. Sepulchres Parish	403	274
St Bartholomew Lesse	19	15	St Dunstan West	36	29	St Thomas Southwark	24	21
St Bridget	147	119	St George Southwark	80	60	Trinity Minories	8	5
Bridewel Precinct	7	5	St Giles Cripplegate	847	572	At the Pesthouse	9	9
St Botolph Aldersgate	70	61	St Olave Southwark	235	131			

Christned in the 16 Parishes without the Walls——— 61   Buried, and at the Pesthouse——— 2861   Plague——— 2139

Parish	Bur.	Plag.	Parish	Bur.	Plag.	Parish	Bur.	Plag.
St Giles in the fields	204	175	Lambeth Parish	13	9	St Mary Islington	50	45
Hackney Parish	12	8	St Leonard Shoreditch	252	168	St Mary Whitechappel	319	270
St James Clerkenwel	172	172	St Magdalen Bermondsey	57	36	Rotherith Parish	7	2
St Kath. near the Tower	40	34	St Mary Newington	74	52	Stepney Parish	371	273

Christned in the 12 out Parishes in Middlesex and Surry——— 49   Buried——— 1571   Plague——— 1244

Parish	Bur.	Plag.	Parish	Bur.	Plag.	Parish	Bur.	Plag.
St Clement Danes	94	78	St Martin in the fields	255	193	St Margaret Westminster	220	191
St Paul Covent Garden	18	16	St Mary Savoy	11	10	whereof at the Pesthouse		13

Christned in the 5 Parishes in the City and Liberties of Westminster——— 27   Buried——— 598   Plague——— 488

K. 3

A page from the 15–22 August Bill of Mortality, 1665. From 'London's Dreadfull Visitation: or, a collection of all the Bills of Mortality for this present year: beginning the 27th of December 1664 and ending the 19th of December following: as also the general or whole years bill. According to the report made to the King's most excellent Majesty / by the Company of Parish-Clerks of London, 1665'.

contributing to a sense of the situation as a collective trial. Private individuals as well as government officials forwarded the London figures to correspondents elsewhere.

Samuel Pepys's diary, written almost continuously, records his reactions and responses. He first mentions reports and rumours of plague at the end of April, and noted seeing houses shut up in Drury Lane in June. As the epidemic progressed he clearly kept informed by reading the weekly bills, and often notes the figures, using them to draw conclusions about the progress of the disease. He sent his wife to Woolwich in early July, but himself remained based in London for several more weeks. On 26 July he noted that 'the sicknesse is got into our parish this week', information that he almost certainly took from the bill published that day.

The height of the epidemic came in September. On the 7th of that month, Pepys 'sent for the Weekly Bill and [found] 8252 dead in all, and of them, 6978 of the plague – which is a most dreadfull Number'. On 20 September he had advance notice, from the Duke of Albemarle – 'brought in the last night from the Lord Mayor' – that the weekly total had increased by over 600, 'which is very grievous to us all'. However, a week later, he was able to record: 'Here I saw this week's Bill of Mortality, wherein, blessed be God, there is above 1,800 decrease, this being the first considerable decrease we have had.'

Pepys's practice is paralleled by that of William Allin, an Anglican minister resident in Southwark. Like Pepys, Allin first heard of plague in April. He monitored the rise in the weekly bills and reported the figures to his correspondents in Rye, commenting through August and September 'the sickness increaseth', 'the sicknes yet increaseth', 'the sicknesse encreased very much last bill'. With relief, he noted on 27 September: 'The Lord hath decreased this weekes bill 1839.' And on 19 October: 'A very mercifull abatement of the bill of mortality, viz. 1849 decreased this weeke.'

The weekly bills were an official publication, issued by the parish clerks, but other printers flooded London with broadsides, handbills, leaflets and other printed ephemera. Notable among these were the composite or commemorative bills that offered food for thought in the form of mortality figures from previous epidemics. 'The Four Great years of the Plague' presented (somewhat questionable) weekly mortality figures for 1593, 1603, 1625, and 1636. A broadsheet printed on or after 27 June 1665 was entitled 'General bills of mortality for seventy-three years last past'.

Another broadsheet, 'The Mourning-Cross', printed on or after 29 August, offered figures for the major plague years alongside information on historical plagues and 'A necessary prayer for this present time'. The last two both left gaps for the reader to fill in figures for future weeks, an invitation that was taken up in the two surviving examples. More substantial publications included John Bell's London's Remembrancer, discussing mortality for eighteen 'years of pestilence', first published at the beginning of September 1665, and, after the end of the year, London's Dreadfull Visitation (a collection of all the weekly Bills for 1665), and Reflections on the Weekly Bills of Mortality.

The appetite for information on the progress of the disease, and reflection on historic parallels, was matched by one for medical advice and remedies. Some of the composite bills included remedies; other handbills offered advice that sometimes turned out to be a puff for some patent medicine. 'The Observations of Mr LILLIE', probably published in early July, discusses the origins and cause of plague, and offers both 'a prayer to be used in all families', and 'several excellent receipts & approved medicines'. 'Remedies against the Infection of the Plague, Composed by John Belson esquire', gave explicit directions about the fumigation of rooms and textiles together with the description of a perfumed bag, 'Celestial water', and a cordial tincture, and notes of where to buy them.

More reputable medical practitioners, such as Gideon Harvey, a naturalised Dutchman, trained at Leiden and claiming the degree of MD, also stepped in. He published his Discourse of the Plague in July or early August 1665, explaining that the disease was bred in the earth and exhaled into the air as 'flaming Arsenical corpuscles'. Londoners could choose between a range of different medical approaches, from traditional humoural or Galenic theory to modern 'chemical' practice. The broadsheet remedies are largely Galenic, relying on sweats, bleeding, and purges to expel the poison, following the line of the College of Physicians. Harvey combined both humoural analysis and treatment with more chemical remedies, including sulphur and metals. George Thomson's Loimologia, also published during 1665 ('these contagious times'), was for the most part a sustained critique of Galenic theory, practice, and practitioners, especially blood-letting and purging, and also the notion of astrological influence.

But what many of these publications explicitly acknowledged was that medical science by itself was not enough; the prime cause of the plague was divine intervention, and the remedy must include prayer, fasting and repentance. As seen above, many broadsheets included prayers. The Christians Refuge, published in July 1665, was a hybrid of medical and spiritual instruction. The printer Cotes stated that her motive for collecting all the 1665 bills and reprinting them as London's Dreadfull Visitation was so that the information they contained might prompt Londoners to repentance.

The pulpits were another obvious medium for communication. Official responses included the order in July to keep a general fast day once a month, 'for stay of the plague now visiting London and Westminster', and publishing prayers to be read on those days. Ministers added their own interpretations in sermons, including 'the author's opinion and judgment, for which and why it is, that this unparallel'd visitation is now laid upon us', which seemed to lie in 'a catalogue and collection of all the particular capital sins mentioned in Scriptures'. London's 'pestilential visitation' was evidence of God's 'more than ordinary' judicial dispensation, and the city's failure to be reformed, even after twenty years of trials an ongoing affront. However, if the plague was some kind of divine judgement, for what, and on whom? Was it retribution for republicanism and the killing of the king, or for the restoration of the monarchy? Was it a divine judgement for past iniquities, or a call for timely amendment – or even an indication of God's special favour and his desire to reform the not-yet-incorrigible city? Likewise, if it was a judgement, was it right to seek self-preservation, or should one resign oneself to likely death?

There are obvious parallels between the experience of one epidemic and another. There will always be conflicts between theory and practice, hard-headed pragmatism and compassion, the best interests of the many and the liberties of the few. As well as stories of suffering and loss, there will always be heroic sacrifice, diligent fulfilment of duty, and self-interested evasion. However, if some commonalities with the experience of 2020 can be found, the differences remain profound. The Londoners of 1665 confronted menacing dangers and existential questions, finding answers in their own world-view.

SOCIETY AND LEADERSHIP IN CRISIS

John Lennon, 1968.

HISTORY SHOWS REVOLUTIONS
ARE A DISASTER

Richard Whatmore

John Lennon's 1968 song 'Revolution' gave The Beatles' verdict on contemporary demands for the transformation of the world by revolutionary action. Lennon described many of his lyrics as political broadsheets and 'Revolution' was especially pointed in its message, taking on agitprop revolutionaries and Maoists.

Revolutionaries, Lennon said, talk about destruction. He responded, 'you can count me out'. During the recording process in mid-1968, Lennon's views vacillated. On the slower, acoustic version of the song he sang that when it came to insurrection 'you can count me out, in'. In the faster, electric version used as the B-side to 'Hey Jude' he switched to 'count me out', sparking criticism from the 'new left'.

Two years later Lennon reversed his position. 'Power to the People' was penned after a meeting in 1971 with Tariq Ali and Robin Blackburn from the *New Left Review*. Now with the Plastic Ono Band, Lennon supported immediate revolutionary action: 'We better get on right away.' In one of his last interviews before his assassination, Lennon stated that the views expressed in the single 'Revolution' had been authentic and that he wished he had stuck to his anti-revolutionary stance.

Lennon's views matter because they captured a general ambivalence about revolution evident by the late 1960s. By this time the event that was at the time seen on the left to be the greatest revolution of the twentieth century, that of the Russian Bolsheviks, had turned sour. Victory in the Great Patriotic War and the establishment of the Union of Soviet Socialist Republics did not translate into happy lives characterised by liberty or wealth. Rather, it was increasingly said that the USSR was a totalitarian empire that crushed dissent, where there was no rule of law and where the deaths of millions of citizens was deemed acceptable as necessary to the socialist cause. In 1956 thousands died during the crushing of the Hungarian Uprising by the invading Russian military. The Prague Spring of 1968 met a similar fate. Aleksandr Solzhenitsyn's *One Day in the*

Life of Ivan Denisovich (1962) had been published with official sanction during a short period of the relative thawing of state control after Stalin's
death. Revelations about the existence of brutal labour camps for the
re-education of dissidents caused shock waves within and beyond the
USSR. After 1964 the oppression of literature critical of the regime was
resumed and intensified. At the same time *samizdat* literature began to
circulate revealing the truth behind the Soviet veil. Solzhenitsyn's brilliantly titled *Gulag Archipelago* provided a first-hand indictment of the
Russian communist system when it appeared 1973. However justified the
revolution of 1917 against Czarism might have been and however many
people had welcomed it, the creation of a socialist society in Russia had
resulted in decades of war, famine, terror, censorship, oppression and
death. The lives of those who refused to toe the party line, and many who
were dedicated party members, were often miserable. State oppression
was both a fact of life and recognised as being frequently arbitrary in
nature.

As Lennon's 1968 lyrics indicated, if the reputation of Soviet Russia
had been tarnished by events, the left continued to express faith in the
Maoist alternative. As in the Soviet case, there was a general lack of information about what was happening in such a closed society.

Revolution in China was often presented as a variant on the Marxist
model. There were parallels. China had undergone, between the late
1950s and early 1960s, the forced transition from an agrarian to an industrial society. As in Russia, famine had resulted. In the Chinese case as
many as 30 million people had died. Mao's response to the Great Leap
Forward, as the economic 'progress' had been termed, was to purge
society of what were described as being the residual capitalist and bour-
geois elements at the ideological level. In other words, people had to be
trained to think like Maoists so that their socialist behaviour would
become habitual. The decision was taken, however, that many people
could not be trained and ought instead to be killed, all in the name of
social progress towards a better society. Some of the massacres justified
during the Great Proletarian Cultural Revolution made the evils of
Stalinism look like Marxism with a human face. The Maoists in the West
in the early 1970s who tried to persuade Lennon of its benefits were not
aware that up to another 20 million people were being sacrificed at the
altar of Chinese communism. The abandonment of the Cultural
Revolution by Deng Xiaoping only occurred between 1978 and 1981.

That revolution would become the archetypal political tactic of left reformers in the twentieth century had everything to do with the authority of Karl Marx and Marxism. Sometimes the pull of Marxism is difficult to appreciate these days. It has to be acknowledged that the ideology that has done more than any other to shape our world is Marxism, either directly through revolution or as the bugbear to justify measures to prevent the Marxist virus from spreading; remember that this was Hitler's aim in promoting Nazi National Socialism in the 1930s just as it was Truman's in justifying the Cold War in 1947.

Marxism as a philosophy was powerful because it promised to heal the ills of society and predict the future, being the supposedly inevitable transition from the unjust capitalist system to one based on the labour of all (socialism) and then to a society where the needs of every person would be satisfied (communism). Historical analysis and societal improvement could be combined in a straightforward fashion, yielding real dividends in the form of indisputably 'true' policy, being in accordance with the 'science' of historical materialism and the public good defined on a world scale.

Marxism was attractive to high-minded moralists and cosmopolitans, enemies of national borders, inequality, war or division. The battle against the ruling capitalist bourgeoisie might be bloody but history was moving in a single direction. A better world was inevitable and death in the struggle might well be the most laudable of sacrifices. Today it is often said that we are the first generations to live in a global world. This is nonsense. Marx self-consciously advocated global revolution from the 1840s with the aim of the entire planet enjoying a single system that he was certain was in accordance with the true interests of every person on earth. Revolution was the necessary means to this end.

If there are in the present few advocates of Stalinism or Maoism, Lenin often gets a good press along with Trotsky, Castro or Chávez. It is frequently said that what we all need is the right kind of revolution. What this means is a revolution without the murder and shattering of countless lives that have accompanied all of the revolutions of modern history. Marx's model was of course the French Revolution that commenced in 1789 with declarations that the rights of man and the citizen were being realised on earth, that a paradise of liberty, equality and fraternity was on the horizon. The French Revolution then descended into 'The Terror'. Factions took control of the government more interested in destroying

Following pages: Marx viewed the French Revolution as a model, believing revolution must involve violence. *An Execution, Place de la Revolution*, Pierre Antoine Demachy, c. 1793. Musée Carnavalet, Paris.

those held to be deviationists (ie the people who disagreed with those in power) than with adhering to a moral system asserting the virtues of compromise or non-violence. Terror worked not only because it removed from the stage revolutionaries suddenly perceived to be enemies of the 'true' revolution, but also because there is nothing like state-sponsored massacre to unite a population in need of a bogeyman to define itself against.

Commentators upon the French Revolution in the following two generations frantically attempted to find means of having the benefits associated with the revolution, an egalitarian republic without monarchy or aristocracy, without the element of terror. Marx's own response was characteristically brutal. In his view the French Revolution had necessarily to be terroristic because it could only succeed by destroying the existing ruling class. Those who tried to promote non-violent revolution were naïve utopian fools. Marx was certain that the tactics he was advocating were proven by history. The shedding of blood would be worth it. Marx especially warned against those who argued that changing the government of a society mattered. The whole point of revolution was social transformation or nothing. This is why Marx would have considered events such as the largely non-violent Velvet Revolution that Czechoslovakia experienced in October to December 1989 or the subsequent 'colour revolutions' of the early twenty-first century not to have been worth the name. If you don't break the old society you are not really creating a new one. Revolutions only work if you have a class war. Wars are only wars if they are violent.

Revolutionary tactics and the language of revolution still permeate radical discourse. John Lennon was uncomfortable with the idea of revolution but he did not really come up with an alternative beyond 'Give Peace a Chance' and, in the lyric of 'Imagine': 'There's no countries/It isn't hard to do/Nothing to kill or die for/And no religion, too.' A different way of approaching the question is to ask whether genuine radicals have to be revolutionaries? Marxist historians have often answered the question in the affirmative. Looking back, history is scrutinised for revolutions from the Roman revolution that put an end to the rule of Lucius Tarquinius Superbus, the Athenian revolution that cast out the tyrant Hippias, the removal of the Umayyad Caliphate or the Puritan,industrial and digital revolutions that are said to mark substantial social change past or present. It is unlikely that Marx would have considered all of these events to have been worthy of the epithet 'revolution'; the point is that even if few of us consider ourselves to be Marxists, when discussing change we remain addicted to Marxist perceptions and tactics.

One way of generating an alternative is to recover lost traditions of radicalism. This is one of the things intellectual historians can do. From a Marxist perspective there is a single radical tradition through history which can evaluate individual historical actors as good (proto-Marxist) or bad (not revolutionary in a Marxist way). Many radicals who sought change, especially in early modern Europe, worried about revolution as a political tactic. The reason was that revolution tended to lead to the rise of Caesar figures. In January 49 BC Julius Caesar had been fighting Rome's enemies in Gaul for ten long years. He was about to be replaced as a general by the Senate. Just south of Ravenna, Caesar addressed his troops. He asked them to march on Rome to allow him to take control of the empire. The reasons given were selfish. The troops were not being paid and would not be given land for their victories. The soldiers, however, were patriots. They believed in the Roman Republic. A veteran sergeant named Aurelius stepped forward. He was, he reported, reluctant to fight and kill members of his own family. That was what Caesar was asking of them. But his loyalties, Aurelius decided, lay with the general rather than the state. The soldiers followed Caesar across the river to establish a military dictatorship by means of civil war. Caesar was initially victorious. Despite his assassination on the Ides of March, liberty died at Rome.

If a revolution is to be successful it needs a leader. All leaders in conditions of political crisis and revolution turn themselves into Caesars and tyrants. They become more important than the cause. They initiate violence and turn the world upside down. Leaders who do this have always been men. They tend to have acute rhetorical or demagogic skills, what Max Weber called charisma. They are able to weave a web which makes it appear to the would-be cadre that there is no other option available, that apocalypse is the alternative to bowing down to the revolutionary/tyrant and carrying out his bidding. Even republicans who believed that God sat on their shoulder and was judging every action they took, such as Oliver Cromwell, ended up justifying terror. Even republicans who saw themselves and were seen by others as the most virtuous in a society, such as the 'incorruptible' Maximilien Robespierre, ended up justifying massacre.

It is possible to draw a parallel between John Lennon and his eighteenth-century equivalent Jean-Jacques Rousseau. Rousseau, like

Frontispiece of *Emile*, 1782 edition.

Lennon, wanted to change the nature of popular music, in Rousseau's case by creating a new musical notation and writing opera. Rousseau, unlike Lennon, had an acute sense of political tactics. In his sensationally popular novel *Emile* of 1762 – so influential that it was credited with persuading mothers to start breastfeeding their own children rather than relying upon wet nurses – Rousseau warned that the great monarchies of Europe would not last. The continent was 'approaching conditions of crisis and a century of revolutions.' Rousseau was throughout his life an arch-critic of existing society. The assaults he launched against fake forms of living, false happiness/politeness in commercial societies during the Enlightenment era were at least as brutal as those of Marx upon capitalism a century later.

Yet for Rousseau the idea of revolution was disastrous, amounting to the abandonment of political control and the handing of power to Caesars/generals. Revolutions, he argued, were always ultimately led by Caesars. Their followers, the people who advocated revolution and took to the streets, needed to be identified as soldiers. Soldiers followed their generals, fomented civil war and died for dictators. People recruited from the mass population ended up killing their own kind. Rousseau held that armies throughout history have been recruited from rural populations. Facing economic crisis, people came to the towns from the countryside to get work. Whenever an urban economy went downhill they joined the army in order to survive, angry at the lack of opportunities offered by their government. When the revolutionary/tyrant called on them they saw new opportunities, willing to take the step into the unknown as they felt that they had nothing to lose.

Rousseau is regularly associated with the French Revolution. Indeed, he is often seen as its author. This is entirely false. Rousseau detested violence and predicted long before 1789 that revolution would lead to the rise of strong men. The outcome of the French Revolution in the imperial rule of Napoleon Bonaparte – of course a republican general who presented himself as the saviour of the people before turning himself into an emperor– was entirely predictable. If Rousseau had been able to read the Marxist version of the old revolutionary story he would have considered it to have been equally predictable in terms of its outcome. For Marx revolution was supposed to begin with the spontaneous rising of the reserve army of the unemployed. At this point Rousseau would have tried to identify the one Caesar figure making promises to the reserve army and making sure they put the 'right' persons into power as soon as 'the people' took control of the institutions of the state. When the revolutionary leader could be seen to have become a monster, history would be seen to be repeating itself.

There are older and far more realistic radical traditions that we ought to return to in order to develop better political tactics than those with which Marx has swamped the globe. In Rousseau's case the key argument was drawn from Machiavelli – there was no point in changing a society until the populace was ready for it. Education had to precede change. Otherwise, whatever new laws or institutions were introduced would fail because the people would not be ready for them. Abrupt change or revolutionary politics amounted to introducing a throw of the dice or random element into everyday life because if the people were not predisposed they could go in any direction. More than likely they would unite around violence towards others. In politics we should talk more about transition mechanisms from where we are to where we might inadvertently end up. So often a new and better world is imagined or described but not how to get there, especially at the level of the state. For authors such as Machiavelli or Rousseau – and all of the contributors to the Commonwealth tradition of political radicalism including Catherine Macaulay or Mary Wollstonecraft – education had to come before action. This was why education and educators were valued. This was why education had to be about politics. This was why the subtitle of Rousseau's *Emile* was 'On Education'.

At present, change is in the air and discussions widespread about doing things differently. There is little evidence that productive change in politics will come about as a result. Rather, economic crisis is likely to increase the number of would-be revolutionaries and Rubicon crossers across the political spectrum. Revolutionary leaders are especially dangerous when economies are depressed and other states are portrayed as enemies. We become more sympathetic to the rhetoric of grand unsubstantiated promises. Tyrants also thrive in a public culture characterised by the demonisation of those we disagree with or the blaming of those we identify as contributing to our woes. When international rivals see such a situation in a country, it can be tempting to give the process a push and intervene to stoke the Caesarist fire. In a febrile atmosphere of identifiable political chaos, it becomes easier for the Rubicon to be crossed, by calling the military onto the streets, cancelling elections or refusing to abide by their outcomes. The institutions protective of liberty can quickly crumble. From an eighteenth-century perspective, nothing is new except that we still have an impoverished sense both of the problems we face and how to address them.

Adam and Eve, Lucas Cranach the Elder, c. 1529.
Koninklijk Museum voor Schone Kunsten,
Antwerp.

A GOVERNMENT OF LAWS

Philip Bobbitt

W e live in a culture that prizes individual access to choice, and in an era that has provided greater opportunity for choice than has ever occurred in our history, perhaps in all history. The constitutional order within which we have lived since the 1870s – the industrial nation state – has been a resounding success by almost any measure. Our people are healthier, better educated and freer to choose where they live, what vocation to pursue, whom to love and marry, what cultural institutions can be accessed. Yet at the moment of its greatest triumph, this constitutional order is losing its legitimacy, largely because of its success.

Having tasted the fruits of the tree of knowledge, the American people are now growing alienated from the present constitutional order, an order not designed to cope – perhaps not even capable of coping – with demands for even greater individuation of opportunity and greater devolution of national identity. Nor are Americans unique in this alienation, which is evident in many countries (I leave for another day the international and national security challenges facing the industrial nation state).

This alienation is reflected in the character of our politics. The role of polling as a factor in the Clinton impeachment in 1999; the Republican drive to postpone hearings for the Supreme Court nomination of Merrick Garland until the presidential election in 2016 (and, for that matter, the push from Democrats to put off confirmation hearings for Amy Coney Barrett until after the election in November, 2020); the Republican refusal to consider evidence in the Senate trial of Donald Trump in 2019; and the offering of lists of potential nominees to the Supreme Court as part of Trump's election manifestos in 2016 and 2020: all are symptoms of a larger shift in political culture. This shift can be characterised as an effort to bypass the constitutional norms of the American industrial nation state in order to give the public a greater say in government decision-making. Powered by the habits of new generations that will grow up online, it is hard to see how this movement to bypass representative institutions can be slowed down. Indeed, it is further evidence of the march toward a new constitutional order – the informational market state.

If the Emancipation Proclamation was the opening constitutional fanfare of the new, industrial nation state – a constitutional order that promised to override the market and secure greater material well-being and equality for all Americans – then perhaps the all-volunteer army that replaced the draft was the opening trumpet call of a new constitutional order that promised to use the market to achieve greater access to choice for individuals and for those cultural, ethnic, linguistic, historical and sexual groups that are submerged in the industrial nation state, one that characteristically promotes a single dominant national group.

The industrial nation state exalted the rule of law: it was law that tamed and regulated and even replaced markets. The informational market state – as I call the new, emerging constitutional order – tries to manage or even supplant the rule of law by superimposing the will of consumers. Whether the subject is conscription, marriage, women's reproduction, or the deregulation of industrial practices, the United States is changing its basic orientation between the law and the market. And that is precisely what is happening with respect to unwritten constitutional norms.

A carefully crafted system of legal rules is being subordinated to polling, to pressure groups, to campaigns on Twitter and Facebook. Impeachment, for example, is becoming a vehicle for recall movements, as characteristic of the informational market state as voter initiatives and referenda. Just as these have gained momentum in the last few decades, we can see the time between impeachments shortening and their number increasing. For the first 200 years we had two presidential impeachments; now we have had three more in just twenty years.

Although the substance of the charges against President Clinton – perjury and obstruction of justice arising from his attempt to cover up an affair with a White House intern – were a far cry from the 'high crimes and misdemeanors' contemplated by the drafters of Article II of the US Constitution, the party line vote in the Senate acquitting the president suggests that that judgment was in any case not made by strictly adhering to a legal rationale. On the contrary, the president's approval ratings during the impeachment proceedings appear to have been his salvation. Polling immediately after twelve hours of debate showed that the

In 1868 Andrew Johnson was the first president
to be impeached in the US. Photograph from
1866. Library of Congress, Washington D.C.

hearings had no impact on the public's opinion of the impeachment case or indeed of Clinton himself. Indeed, 'Clinton's popularity was as high as it had been at any point during his presidency, and 9 out of 10 respondents said that nothing during the [impeachment] hearings had shifted their view of the case,' reported the *New York Times* in an article that year. Shortly after President Clinton became the second US president to be impeached, 72% of respondents voiced their approval of his job performance while 60% of respondents said that the Republicans were seeking the removal of the president for solely partisan reasons, as observed recently by Mary Jean Whitsell.

Laurence Tribe and Joshua Matz, in *To End a Presidency: the power of impeachment* (2018), record that after conceding that he believed Clinton to have committed an impeachable offence, former Democratic Majority Leader Robert Byrd said that he would 'reluctantly vote to acquit [because] the people's perception of this entire matter...tip[s] the scales for allowing this president to serve out the remaining 22 months of his term.' Impeachment was itself becoming plebiscitary as part of the movement toward market states.

So, too, can the manoeuvre by Senator McConnell be understood when the majority leader denied Judge Merrick Garland even a hearing on his nomination to be an associate justice of the US Supreme Court. There is nothing in the constitutional text of Article II about confirmation of Supreme Court nominees being a voting matter for the public, any more than there is about impeachment in the same article. Nevertheless, the Republican leadership insisted in 2016 that voters should decide who would succeed the late Justice Scalia.

Similarly, during the first trial of President Trump, Senator Lamar Alexander was keen to explain his vote to deny the Senate crucial witnesses by saying that the election was soon enough to resolve the matter whether the president's acts, which Alexander accepted as proved, were impeachable high crimes. In other words, he wished to replace the legal indictment and trial mechanisms of impeachment with an election.

Also in 2016, the Republican candidate for the presidency went beyond the pledges of his predecessors to appoint conservative justices and became the first presidential candidate to release a list of names of those lower court judges he would nominate for the Supreme Court. Then in 2020, Trump did it again, naming twenty conservatives he would choose among for any future nominations to the court. 'Candidates for president owe the American people a specific list of individuals,' he said, so people can 'properly make a decision as to how they will vote' for the presidency.

That is where we are heading, as plebiscites repeal legal procedures specified in the Constitution. This is because, contrary to the expectations of the direct democracy lobby, referenda are creatures of the market and erode when they don't destroy the legal mechanisms of representative government, checks and balances, and the rest of the complicated structure of American governance. In an information era, in contrast to the industrial era of group politics, 'direct democracy' has more in common with targeted advertising than it does with New England town halls or even the party conventions of the last 150 years.

If I am right about the future of the constitutional order, it does not however follow that the fundamental modalities of constitutional argument are doomed, along with the edifice of law that they support. On the contrary, they offer one essential means by which we can move to a new constitutional order without sacrificing the humane values these forms of argument have preserved. If our present constitutional order is freighted, if its legitimacy is rapidly and irreversibly decaying, this need not mean that the liberal values that have been supported by the rule of law must be abandoned. It means rather that we are in need, as we have not been for a century and a half, of some creativity on the part of our constitutional thinkers.

Indeed, the Americans, those restless innovators and sometimes reckless pioneers, may be the best people to make this transition because they have done it before. I call your attention to six words uttered by President Lincoln on the field of a decisive battle of the worst war humanity had experienced up to his time. These words were: 'Four score and seven years ago our fathers brought forth upon this continent a new nation...' With those words, Lincoln announced that he was no longer seeking the war aim of preserving the Constitution. Had he been, the words would have read, 'three score and fourteen years ago', marking the date of the ratification of the Constitution. Instead, his war aim had changed. Now he sought a new constitutional order, to support other values of the Declaration of Independence oriented around the value of human equality. These were values that the old constitutional order – the order of the imperial-state nation, the order of racism, patriarchy and imperialism – could not deliver and sustain.

Following pages: President Lincoln, writing the Proclamation of Freedom, January 1st, 1863.
Ehrgott, Forbriger & Co., after David Gilmour Blythe.

WITHOUT SLAVERY THE WAR WOULD NOT EXIST
AND WITHOUT SLAVERY
IT WOULD NOT BE CONTINUED.

MAP
of
EUROPE

WASHINGTON

CALL

PETITION

PROTEST

PETITION
CHICAGO

FROM J.B. FLOYD
Asking to be EXCHANGED

MEMORIAL
from the
U.P.
CHURCH.

PROTECTION
from
RAIDS

MEMORIAL
from the
QUAKERS

DEMOCRATIC
RESOLUTIONS

SUPPORT
TO ALTER
CONSTITUTION

HELPER
UNCLE TOM

U.S.
COURT

THE ARMY
of THE
UNITED
STATES

PROTEST
FROM ARMY of
POTOMAC
AGAINST
GUARDING
PROPERTY
of
TRAITORS

ABE LINCOLN

It will be the challenge of the new generation to return again to the Declaration of Independence – specifically to its values of inalienable rights, rights that the industrial nation state can no longer deliver and sustain. The right to a healthy natural environment, to freedom from terror, to access to knowledge and information, and the right to private lives – all these require more individuation and stronger international security than industrial nation states can provide. Some day a new armed conflict or perhaps an environmental catastrophe or deadly pandemic will sweep away the old order. When that comes, we must take care that our habits of law – our constitutional ethos, the one thing that truly makes the US exceptional – are not also swept away.

Perhaps there are not many alive now who remember Barbara Jordan's electrifying remarks before the House Judiciary Committee at the inception of the Nixon impeachment hearings. I was a law student at the time, and have never been able to forget them: 'My faith in the Constitution is whole, it is complete, it is total. I am not going to sit here and be an idle spectator to the diminution, the subversion, the destruction of the Constitution.'

When Barbara Jordan died, her long-time companion Nancy Earl called me up and asked to come see me. She said that Barbara had told her that if something happened to her – she suffered from multiple sclerosis and had had a couple of life-threatening episodes – she wanted me to have the little pocket constitution she always carried in her purse. When Nancy left, I was thumbing through the small edition, the pages of which were well-worn, when a strip of paper fluttered out. I picked it up and unfolded it. On it was typed this message, a translation from a letter of Einstein's to Max Born: 'All one can do is try to set a fine example and stand up for ethical values in the company of cynics.'

Effects of the pandemic. A single taxi waits at
Sydney Airport in April 2020.

THE CONSEQUENCES OF THE COVID CRISIS

Peter Burke

One of the best arguments that I know for the importance of the study of history is that it challenges us – and encourages those of us who respond to the challenge – to view the problems of the present time in what is called 'historical perspective', in other words the perspective of changes over the long term, over the centuries. Today, everyone is talking about the crisis of Covid-19 and its aftermath. Employing the emotive term 'crisis' may inhibit our thought but it may also provoke it.

Historians, like their colleagues the journalists, love the term 'crisis' – crisis in the government, crisis in the economy, crisis in the humanities and so on. The word has been employed so frequently, whether in the titles of books or in the headlines of newspapers, and also in contexts so various, that one is tempted to say that the concept is worn out, that it has lost much of its value owing to excessive use. What was once a vivid metaphor has become a dead one, a word that is used almost without thinking. For that very reason, it now discourages thinking rather than, as concepts should, provoking it. In this case, conceptual inflation has devalued the linguistic currency. To avoid further devaluation, anyone who employs the term today should be required to contrast 'their' crisis with periods of non-crisis, as well as offering their readers, listeners or viewers a fairly precise definition.

For such a definition we might be well advised to return to the origins of the concept in ancient Greece. At that time, it was used to refer to a relatively brief moment of decision. In a medical context, the word *krisis* referred to what doctors still describe as a 'critical condition', the moment when a patient was poised between recovery or death (as in week two in the case of the Covid-19 virus). Some 2,000 years later, in the seventeenth century, when it was commonplace to view the state and other institutions as analogous to the human body, the term came into use to refer to political illnesses. A few years before the Civil War, an English member of parliament, Sir Benjamin Rudyerd, famously claimed that the conflict with King Charles I had produced what he called a 'crisis of Parliaments', since 'we shall know by this if parliaments live or die'.

Generalising from these examples, we might use the term 'crisis' in a precise sense to refer to a relatively short period of turbulence that is followed by a change in structure that remains in place for a much longer time. In the case of France in 1789 or Russia in 1917, historians call the turbulence a 'revolution', but agree that those revolutions followed a 'crisis' of the old regime. In similar fashion, economic historians speak of 'subsistence crises', leading to famine in the short term and a change in the structure of agriculture in the long term. A classic study of the history of ideas, Paul Hazard's *La Crise de la conscience européenne* (1935), focused on the 1680s as the turbulent moment in which an old regime of thought was replaced by a new one, calling itself the age of 'enlightenment'.

'Crisis' is not the only name for the short period of turbulence. Historians have often spoken of 'turning points', of a 'watershed' between two periods, or, more recently, of 'tipping points', or, in the case of the German historian Reinhart Koselleck (1923–2006) of the 'saddle period' (*Sattelzeit*) around the year 1800, separating an old regime from the modern world marked by industry, capitalism and class conflict. Whether the term chosen is 'crisis' or 'tipping point' is not important. What matters is awareness that some major changes in structure do not creep up on us gradually, but happen fast, too fast for us to take them in. In the case of the *Sattelzeit*, for instance, contemporaries such as René Chateaubriand complained about the acceleration of history, with events happening faster than he could write about them. We might say the same today.

The Covid-19 Pandemic

Are we now experiencing such a crisis? To believe the news that we read, hear or see in the media, the pandemic that began in early 2020 certainly qualifies. But if the definition of crisis that I placed on the table is accepted, it follows that we can only recognise a crisis after it is over. The turbulence is obvious enough: the real problem is to know whether or not structural changes will follow. A prudent answer to the question would be 'ask me again in 30 years', but we cannot afford to wait so long for an answer.

What we can do now is to speculate, with more or less plausibility.

What follows is my own speculation, which is not based on any kind of expertise and is intended, like the term 'crisis' itself, to provoke thought. It is confined to what social scientists call the 'foreseeable future', although the experience of 2020 is a reminder, like that of the banking sector in 2008 and the collapse of communist regimes in Central and Eastern Europe in 1989–90, that unforeseen events not infrequently happen in the economic, social and political worlds. We need to expect the unexpected.

With those caveats, to study the situation in which the world is in at the moment it may be illuminating to follow the example of individuals or groups whose job it is to take decisions – whether in business, politics or war – in conditions of uncertainty about the future, and to identify different possible scenarios in order to see which of them appear to be the most plausible. Even though precise predictions are impossible, an awareness of possible alternative outcomes opens the mind and liberates the imagination.

As a first step, three different scenarios obviously come to mind. In the first scenario, the current crisis might be followed by a return to 'normal', in other words to what was viewed as normal before the outbreak. Some businesses will have gone bankrupt, but others will take their place whenever the demand for particular goods or services continues. Many of us will have acquired new habits, in the domain of hygiene, for instance, but a change of habits does not count as a change in structure.

In the second, converse scenario, the crisis might lead to a 'new normal'. Peter Hennessy, a leading historian of twentieth century Britain, recently remarked that the present moment is a watershed and that a future history of the country will be divided between BC, 'Before Corona', and AC, after it. As for the third scenario, it is a hybrid mixed one in which continuities in some domains of our lives will coexist with major changes or even revolutions in others.

I admire Peter Hennessy's work and recognise that he knows much more than I do about the recent history of Britain. All the same, I remain unconvinced by his chosen scenario, whether for Britain or the world. I remain unconvinced largely because so many watersheds identified by historians have turned out to have divided the waters much less than was originally suspected. Returning to the first scenario, I do not find the idea of a simple return to normal convincing either, although I am sure that

The new normal after the pandemic? Commuters
in London wear masks as they pass through
Vauxhall underground station in June 2020.

many people, perhaps a majority of the world's population, are hoping for it. The economic and the political fallout from this pandemic bomb is surely too great for that.

In short, I find the third, hybrid scenario the most plausible, not least because it is more complex. It offers an invitation to disaggregate the data that have been collected so far and to consider different domains of existence one by one, as well as to distinguish consequences in the short, middle and long terms.

The Corona Virus in Historical Perspective
In carrying out this programme of disaggregation, a comparative historical approach may be useful. After all, this is not the first health crisis to have happened in history, even if it is very probably more global than any of its competitors. It is actually far from the biggest crisis of this kind in terms of the number of deaths, even if we place mortalities in the next few months into the balance. To place our own problems in perspective, it is worth recalling to mind that the bubonic plague that infected Europe and the Middle East around the year 1348, the so-called 'Black Death', is believed to have killed 60% of the European population, or 50 million people. The Spanish flu epidemic of 1918–20 also killed about 50 million people worldwide.

Turning to the economic consequences, historians of the Middle Ages have pointed out that by 1348, the population of Europe was pressing on the means of subsistence, so that one disaster, the plague, actually saved people from another imminent one, famine. Survivors were often better off because they had inherited property from dead relatives, while wages increased because the supply of workers had diminished, putting them in a better bargaining position than before. The historian John Hatcher has written that 'the later fourteenth and fifteenth centuries saw the real wage rates of craftsmen and labourers apparently reach levels not be exceeded until the second half of the nineteenth century'. Risking a grand generalisation, I should like to suggest that there are always both winners and losers in all crises or revolutions. For example, craftsmen and labourers were collective winners in what now appears to have been a 'bad' crisis in 1348. Conversely, in the years after 1989, in what had been East Germany, a number of social groups, ranging from university teachers to factory workers, were losers in what seemed at the time to be a 'good' crisis.

In the case of the Spanish flu, a recent case-study of the United States in 1918 estimates that in industry, production fell by 18%. Demand also decreased, but not enough to avoid a labour shortage that was followed, as in the fourteenth and fifteenth centuries, by wage increases. However, comparisons between the flu and the plague are difficult for two reasons. The first is the difference in levels of mortality (60% in Europe in 1348, but less than 1% in the USA in 1918). The second reason is the concentration on the short term in analyses by economists of the effects of Spanish flu, contrasting with the interest in the long term shown by medieval historians, who think in centuries rather than in years or decades. Another point worth bearing in mind is the difference in the impact of these destructive events on different generations, or to be more precise, different cohorts. Sociologists have shown that members of the cohort born in 1918 remained lower in income and status and also in worse health than the cohorts who were born immediately before and after them.

Turning to the longer-term consequences of our own pandemic, we might think about the situation of the cohort born in and around the year 2000. The education of those at university has been disrupted, while their prospects for employment after they graduate look dimmer than they did only a few months ago. Unlike millennials, who are poised to enjoy an 'inheritance boom', the generation of 2020 has little to look forward to.

Looking at the economy as a whole, it may be suggested that thanks to their resources, big firms such as chain stores and multinationals have a better chance of riding out the pandemic than smaller ones. Hence a change in the balance between the two forms of economic organisation is only to be expected, a 'survival of the biggest' that will speed up a trend that had already existed years before the outbreak.

In similar fashion, the decline in the sale of printed newspapers has accelerated since the pandemic began, but it had actually been going on for years, if not for decades. As a British newspaper commented, with pardonable exaggeration, it is extremely ironic to discover that 'the biggest news story in a lifetime is killing off the very industry that exists to report it'.

In the field of education, another acceleration is taking place. The gradual movement from face-to-face teaching to online teaching (especially the 'massive, open, online courses' known as MOOCs), has suddenly put on a spurt since schools and traditional universities based on 'live' lectures and classes had to close in so many countries. What will happen when these schools and universities re-open properly? In the near future, there will surely be a return to the traditional face-to-face regime. In a few more years, however, when the time comes to replace members of staff who are retiring, rectors of universities and headmasters of schools may prefer to go for online teaching in order to save money.

In the world of entertainment, cinemas are most obviously at risk in the post-virus environment, since there has been a long-term decline in their numbers, lamented by critics and members of the public, as I well remember, since the 1960s. British pubs are in a similar situation: in 2018, over 900 of them closed for good. Similar trends can be documented in other countries. Pessimists must already be asking: Will live concerts and exhibitions now temporarily cancelled in so many places, join the list of permanently endangered events in the foreseeable future?

In politics, prediction is surely more difficult than it is in the case of the economy. It is too early even to guess whether a major change will occur in the global balance of power. All I can say is that I have been much impressed, in the course of corresponding by email in the last year with friends and colleagues in different parts of the world, by the kind of global solidarity that I once thought to be impossible – except in the case of an invasion from another planet. Before this temporary solidarity dissipates, it could surely be used to encourage and to institutionalise new forms of international cooperation, beginning in the field of health but, one may be allowed to hope, extending far beyond it.

Many of the guesses made in the previous paragraphs have been gloomy ones. In the case of the environment, so often a topic for gloomy reports, we may for a change look at the bright side. There have been many recent comments from individuals living in different countries on the positive effects for the environment of the diminution of traffic, whether by car or plane: the reduction of air pollution and the return of animals, birds and insects to places from which pollution had driven them. When the crisis is over, will there be a return to the old normal? Travel by plane may go into a downspin, but many people are sure to get back in their cars, all the more readily because of the risk of infection now associated with public transport.

However, 2020 also followed the year of the 'Thunberg phenomenon', while her dramatic appeal formed part of a longer trend. It was in October 2018 that the United Nations Intergovernmental Panel on Climate Change warned that – to avoid a 'crisis' in the strong and precise sense

Following pages: Lockdown in Kathmandu. A Nepalese woman works beneath a clear sky in the city which normally ranks as one of the most polluted in the world.

– the world had only twelve years to keep global warming to a maximum of 1.5C. By now, this warning has had time to sink in, creating a favourable moment that governments could, should and might seize in order to organise collective and collaborative responses to this warning. If 2020 really turns out to have been a tipping point in this respect, future generations may even feel grateful to the virus.

Margaret Thatcher at 10 Downing Street, 1990.

CONTINUITY THATCHER – RESCUING A COMPLEX LEADER FROM HISTORICAL CLICHÉ

Graham Stewart

H istory has no full-stops, but every history book has to start and end somewhere. For those works that take as their theme post-war Britain, the obvious entry point is either the election victory of Clement Attlee's Labour government in 1945, or the wartime planning that it enacted.

This is followed by an outlining of a broad political consensus: a verte-brae of public sector continuity that is buffeted by events and frayed by maverick critics on the left and right, but which evolves and endures until the victories of Margaret Thatcher. That is where it ends. 'Mrs T' blows the roof off the house that John Maynard Keynes and William Beveridge (and Herbert Morrison, Nye Bevan, Rab Butler and Harold Macmillan) built.

This, of course, is the long view of post-war Britain for the historian – and reader – with stamina. A shorter narrative, particularly if focusing on social and cultural life, withdraws the 'post-war' tag from Britain some-time between the end of rationing in 1954 and 'the satire boom' of the early sixties.

But for the politically-minded, the long view seems logical. It is a post-war period that might just as rightly be termed the Cold War period: the disintegration of the Soviet Union and its Warsaw Pact – conclusive events that neatly coincided with Thatcher's fall from power in November 1990 – ended a period of continuity in British foreign policy (and, with it, the country's strategic importance in world affairs) that had been con-stant since an iron curtain descended from Stettin to Trieste, and which had guided the actions of every foreign secretary from Labour's Ernest Bevin to the Conservatives' Douglas Hurd.

A further contention is the theme of this essay – that during the course of her three terms of office between 1979 and 1990, Margaret Thatcher ended a post-war consensus on what Britons should expect from the state. It is a claim which often fosters agreement between her most vehement admirers and detractors. For they both take her at her word, agreeing that 'The Iron Lady' (aka 'That Bloody Woman') was a consensus-breaker who brought a full-stop to the old certainties that were, according to outlook, bonding society together or holding Britain back.

'This is My Faith and My Vision'

Anticipating the 1979 general election campaign that was about to commence, the prime minister, James Callaghan, made a television broadcast in which he argued that Labour stood for continuity, the Conservatives for an end to it. Given the industrial chaos that had so recently marked the 'winter of discontent', these were definitions that his Tory opponent gleefully embraced when she addressed the first major party rally of the campaign.

'There used to be in this country, a socialism which valued people,' Thatcher suggested to the packed hall in Cardiff. 'Its methods were those of the collective, of putting all decisions to the centre, which was why it was not our creed,' she continued, conceding that its aims were noble, unlike the 'ugly apparatus' of intimidation, enforced trade union membership and 'flying pickets' that were 'turning worker against worker, and society against itself.' These wreckers now held such sway, she suggested, because the corporatist state put them at the heart of the decision-making process. 'The Old Testament prophets didn't go out into the highways saying, "Brothers, I want consensus",' Thatcher perorated, 'They said, "This is my faith and my vision! This is what I passionately believe!"'

Widely reported, it was a vivid articulation of her uncompromising attitude as a 'conviction politician'. It set the tone for how she would be viewed – and caricatured. But which period of misrule had she in mind when she sneered at consensus: the recent past of Harold Wilson, James Callaghan (and her one-time boss, Edward Heath) or that of the Beveridge/Attlee post-war settlement and the political culture that endured through the 1950s?

Thatcherism in action did not emerge fully-formed when the MP for Finchley challenged and defeated Heath for the Conservative Party leadership in 1975. Indeed, it was still evolving in 1990 when her grip on power was wrenched from her. What can be said of her first term in Downing Street from 1979 until 1983 is that it neither achieved, nor set out to undertake, the unpicking of the post-war settlement. Its targets were far more immediate – the reversing of policies that were not the work of the leading Attlee-to-Macmillan consensus builders.

During her first term, hardly any of the big nationalisations achieved by Herbert Morrison between 1945 and 1951 were reversed or were even scheduled for privatisation. That the NHS should be free at the point of use was not even up for debate in Downing Street – and nor was it at any time in her tenure there. As for removing redistributive social justice from fiscal policy, only the recent stratospheric levels of tax were chipped away at: top rate tax was reduced from the self-defeating 83% to 60% and standard rate from 33% to 30%; higher rate corporation tax remained at 52% and inheritance tax at 60%; indirect taxes like VAT soared. Her government was in its ninth year before these rates fell significantly. Any administration that these days perpetuated such high tax rates might be regarded as to the left of Jeremy Corbyn.

Margaret Thatcher's primary objectives in office were bringing to heel the twin enemies of inflation and trade union power. Given recent experience this was not surprising. But they were linked because government strategy for the past decade had strengthened the connection by seeking to curb inflation through a corporatist pay-bargaining policy involving senior management, trade unions and Whitehall. Although the Treasury under the Labour chancellor, Denis Healey, had begun to study the money supply, it was still the primary assumption that inflation was caused by big pay rises. Moderate them, and inflation would be tamed.

It was an approach that owed little to the post-war consensus. Until the late 1960s, both Labour and Conservative governments had been reluctant to tread into this area of industrial relations, preferring to leave collective bargaining to the employers and unions it concerned. But with Harold Wilson, incomes policy became central to the management of the economy. This tightened further under Edward Heath in the early 1970s, who made his incomes policy statutory. Upon returning to power in 1974, Labour believed it could work with the unions more fraternally to achieve the same results. This miscalculation ultimately resulted in the 'winter of discontent'.

At that time, the majority of the country's employees counted amongst their personal effects a trade union membership card – far more than had a credit card. Of the 30% of the national workforce that were state employees (by 2019 the proportion was down to 16.5%), four out of five were union members. So, union-government pay bargaining had considerable leverage. What is more, having agreed a pay deal, enforcement came through a statutory Price Code which meant that any significant employer that paid for wages above the agreed 'norm' through higher prices was breaking the law. Different categories of major businesses had to report intentions to increase their prices to the Price Commission, a bureaucracy that adjudicated on the fairness of the price increase. The market was not the mechanism.

To this cats' cradle, the doctrine of monetarism offered escape. Semi-scientific disputations about which measure of the money supply was best became a near theological obsession in the early years of the Thatcher government, but at least the theory offered a neat alternative to making the fragile goodwill of trade union leaders the lynchpin upon which controlling inflation rested.

But breaking this link came with a vicious economic cost. The counter-inflationary strategy of the chancellor, Sir Geoffrey Howe, depended upon high interest rates at a time of global downturn, and when North Sea oil pushed the price of sterling up further, Britain's exporters were handicapped. Thatcherism's belief in 'Tina' ('There Is No Alternative') was hammered on the anvil that the alternative had already failed. But she was at least three years into her first term before she could point to evidence for success.

The same results might have been achieved much less painfully if the supply-side reforms that could have lubricated such a transformation had already been in place at the start of the 1980s, as they were by the end of it. But that is to inhabit an alternate universe. Doubtless, the policy's hardest blows would have been lighter if the globally low inflation of the twenty-first 'Great Moderation' had prevailed in 1980. Again, Thatcherism did not enjoy that luxury.

But the central point is that the replacement of incomes policy and price codes with tight monetary policy unpicked ideas from the 1970s, not the 1940s. Many of the accompanying legislative measures and strategies that disabled the ability of the trade unions to determine industrial relations were promoted out of revulsion for recent provocations, and drew wide popular support from that experience.

Privatisation Postponed
To the modern reader, what stands out from re-examining the Labour

Party's 1945 general election manifesto is how briefly it deals with what are now seen as the main achievements of the Attlee government. Combined, the NHS and the implementation of William Beveridge's version of the welfare state were the stuff of six very short and vaguely-phrased paragraphs. Instead, the manifesto's emphasis was overwhelmingly on the benefits that industrial planning and nationalisation would bring.

Of all Margaret Thatcher's consequences for the post-war consensus, one that is almost universally attributed to her is the comprehensive dismantlement of the state's ownership and control of large parts of the British economy. The reality is more nuanced.

Before winning the 1979 general election, the Conservatives had made only limited plans for privatisation because of what Nigel Lawson described in his memoirs as 'Margaret's understandable fear of frightening the floating voter'. The first phase focused not on the post-war nationalised industries upon which some degree of consensus had taken hold in the 1950s (from that period, only Cable & Wireless and Amersham International were privatised). Rather, the goal was to reverse the highly contentious recent nationalisations undertaken by the Wilson and Callaghan governments between 1975 and 1977: the state-owned British Leyland taking over the country's consolidated car industry; the bringing of almost all shipyards under state control as British Shipbuilders; the nationalisation of the aerospace industry and the creation of the British National Oil Corporation (subsequently Britoil) to extract oil and act as a middleman in the North Sea. With varying levels of success, the state's shares in these industries were duly sold.

Only in Thatcher's second and third terms were the major stock market flotations attempted. It was the privatisation in 1984 of British Telecom – the largest privatisation the world had at that point seen – that really made popular capitalism a central tenet of Thatcherism. But the state-ownership consensus to which BT belonged was an Edwardian one, it having become a department of the Post Office (which monopolised telecoms) in 1912. Two other major privatisations that followed were also of businesses that were government concerns before 1945, namely BP (the state's controlling share dated from 1914) and British Airways (nationalised in its previous guises by Neville Chamberlain in 1939).

Of the major nationalisations of the post-war Labour government, only two were privatised by Margaret Thatcher. These were the road

Following pages: A scene from the 'Winter of Discontent'.
Broadwick Street in central London during the dustmen's strike, 1979.

haulage industry through the National Freight Corporation – sold to its employees in 1982 and floated on the stock exchange seven years later – and British Gas. The latter was created in 1973 but descended from Herbert Morrison's nationalisation of the regional gas boards in 1949. British Steel, privatised in 1988, had never been part of any sort of post-war 'consensus' – having been controversially nationalised in 1951, de-nationalised by Winston Churchill in 1952 and re-nationalised by Harold Wilson in 1967.

The state owned 44% of the UK's capital stock in 1979. Thatcher's privatisations reduced that to 30%. She did not reverse the other key nationalisations of post-war Britain: the Bank of England (given operational independence by Gordon Brown in 1997) or the NHS (for which an internal market was created but no effort to de-nationalise was entertained). Following her victory in the 1984 miners' strike, Thatcher reorganised the National Coal Board into a nationalised corporation, British Coal. It was John Major who privatised it, four years after he replaced Thatcher.

It therefore fell to the market to shut an industry central to Labour's heritage that, had it remained alive and heavily subsidised in state hands, would have been administered the kiss of death by Tony Blair and Gordon Brown to cut carbon emissions. Thatcher also kept under state control another 1940s nationalisation, British Rail. In privatising it in 1994, Major travelled a track Thatcher had helped engineer, but it was not towards an ideological terminus. The privatisation of the network infrastructure was reversed by the creation of Network Rail in 2002, and emergency Covid-19 measures *de facto* nationalised the whole system in 2020.

Thatcher – Beveridge's Most Faithful Disciple?

What of the welfare state? When Thatcher referred to the Beveridge Report it was usually favourably. It had, as she was wont to point out, been commissioned by 'Winston'. Having been a parliamentary secretary at the ministry of pensions and national insurance in Harold Macmillan's government, she boasted that 'one got right to the heart of it'. Her criticism was not with Beveridge, but with how successive governments had undermined his insurance principles and compromised his advocacy for additional private provision. In that sense, she was a closer disciple of Beveridge than any of the post-war prime ministers who more readily took the credit for implementing his vision.

Addressing her party's Central Committee in 1983, she proclaimed that 'our party has no more intention of dismantling the welfare state than we have of dismantling the Albert Hall'. What she wanted was a 'partnership between the individual and the state' because 'we can't snatch for ourselves what we want and have no concern for its cost or who pays for it. It is that sense of obligation and of duty which ought to mark our attitude towards the welfare state.'

She enthusiastically quoted Beveridge's instruction that the state 'in organising social security should not stifle incentive, opportunity, responsibility; in establishing a national minimum it should leave room and encouragement for voluntary action by each individual to provide more than that minimum for himself and his family.' And she reminded City dignitaries later in 1983 that, 'even those who planned the reconstruction of our society in the last days of the war did not have a vision of an all-providing government. It was Lord Beveridge himself who wrote: "The underlying principle of the report is to propose for the state only those things which the state alone can do, or which it can do better than any local authority or than private citizens."'

Prompted in 1986 by a friendly interviewer for the *Sunday Telegraph* who suggested that 'the welfare state mentality' was making Britain lethargic, Thatcher was more nuanced, saying: 'The welfare state is intended to help people who come across hard times through no fault of their own.' She supported the Beveridge concept that 'you insure, while you are working, against being unable to work because you cannot get a job, because you are ill, because you are too old to work.' She distinguished Beveridge's national insurance from the non-contributory supplementary benefit system. In order to reduce the potential for the latter providing almost as much income as paid employment, she supported incentivising work with family income support for those on low wages 'so that their children will get as much as those children on supplementary benefit'.

Conservatism's Old Direction

When Margaret Thatcher first entered 10 Downing Street as its tenant, the social security budget was 26% of total government spending. Eleven years later, when she faced eviction, the social security budget exceeded 30%. 'I came to office with one deliberate intent,' she had explained in

1984, 'to change Britain from a dependent to a self-reliant society – from a give-it-to-me, to a do-it-yourself nation.' Many impediments to doing business and keeping more of its proceeds were lifted, but enduring unemployment alongside shifting social attitudes and changing family structures had sapped the ability of millions to stand on their own feet, unaided.

Nor was the social security budget the only area in which Thatcherism perpetuated rather than curtailed the welfare state. Throughout her time in office, she faced repeated accusations of under-funding the NHS. The reality was mixed: on her watch, spending on the NHS increased by a third (in real terms, ie above inflation), but the rising costs of, and expectations for, the healthcare sector meant that was never sufficient. The NHS might not have been in her heart in the way that it set the pulse of Labour opponents, but the raw statistics do not show Thatcher as kicking against the grain of long-term health funding priorities. Government spending on the NHS ranged between 4 and 4.5% of GDP during the Thatcher years whereas throughout the 1950s it had hovered above and below 3%. In this respect, it is the last twenty-year period, not that between 1945 and 1990, that has broken with a long-term trajectory (NHS spending as a share of GDP soared in the first decade of the twenty-first century and, prior to the 2020 coronavirus outbreak, was plateauing above 7%).

'I don't think I have changed the direction of Conservatism from that of the 1950s,' she assured the journalist Hugo Young, pointing out to him that as chancellor and prime minister, Harold Macmillan's priorities had been to restrain inflation below 3%. Five years into her tenure, the state was spending 42% of GDP and it was not until the end of her time in Downing Street that government spending was heading down towards the 33% of GDP typical of Harold Macmillan's years as prime minister.

Restoring the Post-War Consensus
Margaret Thatcher had an unshakable belief in some pillars of the post-war consensus, the Atlantic alliance and NATO being among the handiwork of Churchill, Clement Attlee and Ernest Bevin she treated most reverentially. Other props of that consensus had collapsed long before she came to power. The grammar schools set up by Rab Butler's 1944 Education Act had exemplified the efforts to create a post-war meritocracy, but they fell foul of 1960s progressivism to such an extent that as

education secretary in Heath's cabinet she was prevented by her own party's commitments from saving the grammars. In 1988, city technology colleges were one imitation of Butler's Act that had not developed as envisaged the first time around, and they failed to take off at the second attempt too.

The Thatcher governments' record in education was not one of dismantling the post-war consensus but of failing to restore it. In no decade was the comprehensivisaton of Britain's secondary schools more complete than during the eighties.

That decade has been cast as the period where government gave up on the attempt to secure the post-war goal of full employment. It was an ambition that had already ceased to be realisable in the 1970s and whilst there was a marked shift from Keynesian demand management to supply-side reforms during the Thatcher years, she always maintained that John Maynard Keynes had been ill-served by successors who affected to be his disciples. Certainly, looking from the perspective of 2020, it does not appear that the Treasury has given-up on the idea of stimulating economic demand in tough times. Of more lasting significance was the removal of exchange controls (a measure introduced in 1939 to limit capital flight but which had never been revoked): one of the first and most vital of Thatcherite reforms. Do we really miss a government department telling us how much money we can carry out of the country for our summer holiday or to buy a property abroad?

Some other forms of economic management had been jettisoned before she took office. For instance, the Bretton Woods system of fixed exchange rates had ended in 1971. Perhaps it may be said that a floating currency was one of the few developments of that decade that she came to appreciate. Indeed, the manoeuvres of the Tory pro-Europeans amongst her cabinet colleagues to reintroduce constraints on the pound's movement through the Exchange Rate Mechanism was the prologue to her downfall. In her final, belated, repudiation of British immersion in Europe's ever closer union she drifted far away from the establishment consensus thinking of the 1960s and 1970s and back to the outlook of Attlee and Bevin.

For the reality is that Margaret Thatcher was a politician who had spent her first ten to fifteen years in parliament articulating relatively mainstream Conservative views only to realise in the 1970s that, as she put it, 'things started to go wrong in the late sixties,' and were getting worse as

Margaret Thatcher and Ronald Reagan pose for photos together with other NATO Summit Meeting participants in Bonn, 1982.

the seventies progressed. Her priority upon entering Downing Street was to attack this 'management of decline'.

Some causes of that decline she traced to the post-war period, and these she sought to address. But there was much that she valued in that inheritance. To portray her as the alarm clock that ended the post-war dream is a convenient way to punctuate a long narrative. But to do so is to caricature, not illuminate, Margaret Thatcher's importance to British history.

Plato conversing with his pupils, from the House
of T. Siminius, Pompeii, first century BC.
Museo Archeologico Nazionale, Naples.

LEADERSHIP IN CRISIS – WHY THE WEST NEEDS PLATO MORE THAN EVER

Adrian Wooldridge

Benjamin Disraeli, speaking in the House of Commons in 1872, said of then Prime Minister William Gladstone's cabinet: 'Behold, a range of extinct volcanoes; not a flame flickers upon a single pallid crest.' 'Extinct volcanoes' would be far too generous a phrase to describe the current crop of Western leaders – if political regimes could be said to decay from the head downwards, then we are in some trouble. The political scientist Vilfredo Pareto said that leaders can be divided into two types – lions who are distinguished by their machismo and foxes who are distinguished by their intelligence. In world politics, the lions are on the rampage because the foxes have abandoned the public weal.

In America, the proportion of people who say that they trust government has fallen from about three-quarters in the early 1960s to less than a third today. Across the rest of the West, opinion is moving in the same direction if not quite as sharply. Governance has emerged as a central feature of the Covid-19 crisis: we have learnt that good government can make all the difference between living and dying. One problem with poor government is that it is self-sustaining. The lower government falls in public esteem the more likely it is that able people will shun it. And the more able people shun it the more government becomes a butt of jokes, even the object of outright contempt.

The problem of good government and leadership is nothing new. In the eighteenth and early nineteenth centuries, England's political system was known as 'Old Corruption' because it was so self-serving. An entrenched elite treated the state as a source of jobs and benefits. The state was so disconnected from the forces of industry and commerce that were transforming society that many liberals wanted to reduce government to a night-watchman. These tensions are never far away from the contemporary scene. Modern politicians routinely take up lucrative jobs in the private sector when they leave office – often working for the industries that they once regulated. Indeed, 'reciprocal nepotism' is now so commonplace on Capitol Hill, with members of Congress giving jobs to the children of friends in return for their friends giving jobs to their children, that Melanie Sloan, of Citizens for Responsibility and Ethics in Washington, comments: 'Members of Congress basically are profit centres for their entire families.'

How did the Victorians shake themselves out of this cycle of decline? A cohort of reforming politicians and educators realised that a successful commercial society required a successful modern state. They suggested a solution: a collective immersion in the wisdom of Plato. They set about revitalising the patronage-ridden civil service and educational world by opening opportunities and jobs to competition. They treated Plato's *Republic* as a near deified talisman against the twin evils of self-indulgence and short-termism. In the present day, this spirit requires us to set down self-help guides and leadership manuals in favour of the same text that inspired the Victorians. Not only does Plato provide a comprehensive explanation of why a republic needs a leadership class, he also provides a guide to producing one.

The great philosopher's starting point is that government matters. A republic is rather like a ship at sea, he says. Whether the ship can survive the ever-changing hazards that confront us – storms, pirates, jagged rocks – depends on the quality of the ship's leadership. If the ship is well run, then at least it has a chance; if it is badly run, then it will flounder and everybody aboard will drown. What does being 'well-run' mean? Plato asks a simple question: should we give the job of steering the ship safely to the members of the crew at large, when they can't agree on where they're headed and most of them don't know the rudiments of navigation? Or should we give it to a captain who has spent his entire life studying 'the seasons of the year, the sky, the stars, the winds and other professional subjects'?

The metaphor of the ship is a way of driving home Plato's wider point about the importance of 'guardians'. Plato argues that a successful republic is run by a class of people whose job it is to think about the long-term success of the polis. What threats are there on the horizon? What trade-offs do we need to make in order to ensure success? How might we be scuppered by known unknowns and unknown unknowns? Despite being an aristocrat, Plato argued that potential guardians – or men of gold as he described them – might occur in every class of society, and indeed might be women as well as men. If they are to escape decay, successful societies have to re-allocate leadership positions in each generation. The second job is to train the guardians through a prolonged education that involves not just academic education but also character-training designed to ensure that guardians put the public good above private interests. Morality is arguably even more important than intellect because the leaders possess so much power over everybody's lives: if they are corrupt they will not only lead the country in the wrong direction – from the light to the darkness in Plato's view – but will also set a model of corruption that the rest of society will only too happily follow.

If a society run by educated guardians is the best sort of society, in Plato's view, a society run by the masses is the worst. Plato conceded that democracy is in many ways the most attractive form of society, because it combines the maximum of opportunity for the regular citizen with the maximum of freedom. But these attractions are purely superficial – democracy is like a 'coat of many colours', he says, that looks good when you see it in the market but turns out to be threadbare after you've worn it a couple of times. Voters invariably favour the short-term over the long-term and the exciting over the wise. And they are usually drawn towards bad leaders – demagogues who can weave wonderful fantasies about the state's future but are really nothing more than charlatans, lying their way to power or buying votes with other people's money. Plato was particularly scathing about aristocrat-demagogues who enjoy the advantage of the best education that money can buy but nevertheless prefer to pander to the mob rather than to guide it to the light.

Democracy's fetishisation of freedom inevitably gives way to anarchy. Fathers pander to their sons, teachers to their pupils, humans to animals, and 'the minds of the citizens become so sensitive that the least vestige of restraint is resented as intolerable'. Anarchy produces class struggle, as the poor attack the rich and the rich retaliate; class struggle produces war and disorder. When all this becomes intolerable the masses will turn to a dictator who can restore order.

If tyrants are the unavoidable consequence of democracy, they are also the antithesis of philosopher kings. They regard power as an end in itself rather than a means to an end, and they are governed by their passions rather than their reason. Thus the paradox at the heart of tyranny: even though tyrants have absolute power over other people, they have no power over themselves. Slaves to their own passions – 'ill-governed' in their own souls as Plato puts it – they use their positions to inflict those passions on the entire population. A tyranny is a psycho-drama in which everyone is caught up in the tyrant's raging ego.

Many of Plato's suggestions for producing successful guardians strike us today as, at the minimum, bizarre. He believed that the guardians should be banned from getting married or owning private property in order to focus their minds on the common good. He was so keen on producing the best guardians that he advocated eugenic breeding programmes (guardians would be compensated for not getting married by being allowed to participate in regular orgies with women selected for their brains and beauty). But even if he was far-fetched in his solutions, he was right in the problems that he identified. Guardians will cease to be guardians if they put themselves and their families among the public good, degrading public offices and turning the people against them.

William Gladstone, the greatest liberal reformer of the nineteenth century, believed that, if the seventeenth century was the age of the rule of prerogative, and the eighteenth one of rule by patronage, the nineteenth century should be ruled by virtue, and Plato was to be the new age's guiding force.

Gladstone was so fluent in Ancient Greek that, in 1858, he gave a speech to the inhabitants of the Ionian Islands (a British protectorate) in the language. Thomas Arnold, the headmaster of Rugby and the greatest school reformer of his age, adopted many of Plato's signature ideas: that education was as much about shaping character as shaping intellect; that group loyalty should trump individual self-expression; and that physical education was as important as book learning. The two most influential civil servants of the age, Charles Trevelyan and Cyril Northcote, abolished patronage in the civil service and introduced open competition in order specifically to promote the rule of a Platonic 'natural aristocracy'.

Benjamin Jowett, the master of Balliol from 1870 until his death in 1893, devoted his life to two great projects: producing a definitive edition of Plato and turning his college into a production line for Platonic guardians. Though he failed at his first task – his edition of the *Republic* was only completed after his death by his friend and biographer Lewis Campbell – he succeeded spectacularly at the second. Balliol became the leading educational institution in the empire. Jowett's pupils included Lord Curzon, a future viceroy of India, Lord Grey, a future foreign secretary, Herbert Asquith, a future prime minister, Cosmo Gordon Lang, a future archbishop of Canterbury and Charles Gore, a future bishop, many of

Professor [Benjamin] Jowett, 1864.
Photograph by Julia Margaret Cameron in
Freshwater, Isle of Wight.

whom remained loyal to the cult of Plato for their whole lives. Florence Nightingale, who was one of Jowett's closest friends, wrote to ask him if a young soldier she had met in the Crimea was one of his pupils: 'He talks to his men about Plato and tells them they don't do what Plato would have them do, and don't realise Plato's ideal of what soldiers ought to be.'

The Plato cult intensified as the franchise was extended in the late nineteenth and early twentieth centuries, sweeping up socialists as well as conservatives and working-class autodidacts as well as public school products. H G Wells wrote several novels about utopias run by Platonic guardians. A D Lindsay, master of Balliol from 1924–1949 and a staunch supporter of the Labour Party, preserved some of Jowett's spirit, producing a popular Everyman edition of the *Republic* and lecturing to the Workers' Education Association classes on the philosopher.

America's East Coast establishment also followed Britain's lead. Educational institutions such as Groton and Yale put both Plato and Christianity at the heart of their syllabus. Members of the elite trained to take over from Britain as the world's leading power by studying the philosopher. McGeorge Bundy, who was appointed dean of Harvard at 34 and went on to be national security advisor to both Kennedy and Johnson, chose the *Republic* as his subject of study when he was elected to a junior fellowship by the Harvard Society of Fellows. According to a friend, he 'saw himself as one of the guardians, the chosen elite'.

There was a certain amount of priggishness in the cult of Plato. But it nevertheless produced an elite that was remarkably public-spirited by today's standards: too dignified to put its fingers in the cookie jar and too well-educated to be blown hither and thither by the latest intellectual fads. The old elite didn't hog publicity for the sake of publicity – most of them were happy to work in the background without any public credit – and they wouldn't dream of piling up vast private fortunes. This was a world of modest but tasteful cottages in the country, not swanky apartments in Belgravia or Manhattan. Dignified public service was its own reward.

The Plato cult eventually ran out of momentum when critics such as Richard Crossman, in *Plato Today* (1937), and Karl Popper, in *The Open Society and its Enemies* (1945), the entire first volume of which was devoted to Plato, argued that Plato was an antiquated and dangerous figure. Plato, of course, viewed democracy with outright hostility (though it must be remembered that in Plato's Athens 'democracy' didn't mean representative democracy but direct democracy in which an assembly of all the citizens made decisions and important jobs were allocated by lot). Yet in the nineteenth century, proper use of the *Republic* was viewed as a reinforcement to modern democracy rather than a guide to its replacement.

Improving the intellectual and moral quality of people going into government strengthens modern electorates' faith in its leaders, and handing some power from electorates to experts can also strengthen the core of democracy – or as an American academic, Gareth Jones, has put it, 10% less democracy can be better democracy. Giving independence to central banks has kept inflation under control; Sweden's decision to ask specialists to review the pension system to prevent it from going bankrupt has put the public finances on a sound foundation (not something that can be said of the United States which contemplated a Swedish-style solution but backed out at the last moment). Plato's most important insights hold true regardless of his strictures about democracy: that government matters immensely – and can make all the difference between a society thriving or going into decline.

The Covid-19 crisis has shocked us by revealing the weakness of Western government, particularly in the United States and Britain, and the strength of the Chinese government. The Chinese may have unleashed Covid-19 on the world but they eventually got to grips with the disease far more effectively than the Anglo-Saxon world. This not only revealed superior ruthlessness but also the fact that the Chinese have been quietly improving their state machinery while Western governments left theirs to atrophy. We are poised between two futures – one in which the West succeeds in reviving itself and another in which it continues to decline and hands global leadership to China, a regime that has no time for freedom or democracy. If we continue to neglect government, then we are doomed to see global leadership passing to the East, but if we re-energise our government, mixing a bit more wise leadership into our liberal formula, we may be able to resume our successful voyage. The philosopher and the cult of Plato provide us with both a model and an inspiration for how to fix the ship of state. Like our predecessors, it's up to us to heed his words.

Following pages: Chinese epidemic control workers wait to perform nucleic acid swab tests for Covid-19 in June 2020.

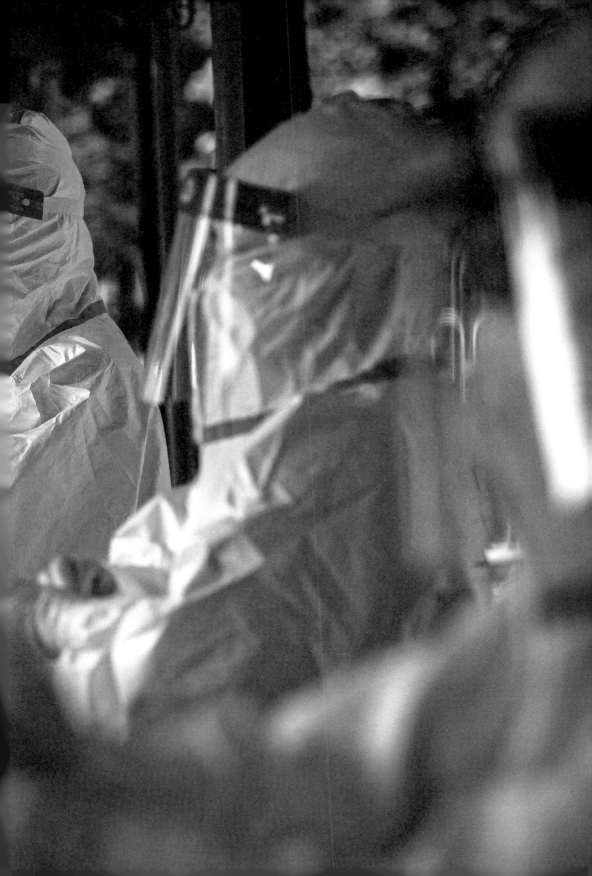

CONTRIBUTORS

CLIVE ASLET is an award-winning architectural historian and journalist, and was for many years the editor of *Country Life* magazine. His many books include *Landmarks of Britain: the five hundred places that made our history*, *The English House*, *An Exuberant Catalogue of Dreams*, *The Americans Who Revived the Country House in Britain*, *The Real Crown Jewels of England* and *Old Homes, New Life: the resurgence of the British country house*.

PHILIP C BOBBITT is a leading constitutional scholar and historian. He is Herbert Wechsler Professor of Federal Jurisprudence at Columbia Law School, and a Fellow of the American Academy of Arts and Sciences and the Royal Historical Society. He has served in the US government during seven administrations. His books include *The Shield of Achilles*, *The Garments of Court and Palace: Machiavelli and the world that he made*, and *Terror and Consent: the wars for the twenty-first century*.

PETER BURKE is Professor Emeritus of Cultural History at Cambridge University and a Life Fellow of Emmanuel College. A Fellow of the British Academy, he has published more than 30 books, from *Culture and Society in Renaissance Italy* to *Exiles and Expatriates in the History of Knowledge*. His most recent publication is *The Polymath: a cultural history from Leonardo da Vinci to Susan Sontag*.

GILLIAN CLARK is Professor Emerita and Senior Research Fellow of Ancient History at the University of Bristol. Her research field is known to classicists as late antiquity and to theologians as early Christian studies. Her continuing project is a commentary on Augustine's *City of God*. She co-edits, with Andrew Louth, the monograph series *Oxford Early Christian Texts/Studies* (OUP), and her books include *Body and Gender, Soul and Reason in Late Antiquity*, and *Monica: an ordinary saint*.

JONATHAN FENBY is a British writer, journalist and analyst. A former editor of the *Observer* and the *South China Morning Post*, he was appointed a CBE for services to journalism and has also been made a Knight of the French Legion of Honour. An associate at the London School of Economics and London University's School of Oriental and African Studies, he is the author of many books including *Tiger Head, Snake Tails: China today*, *Will China Dominate the 21st Century?* and *Crucible: the year that shaped our world*.

PETER FRANKOPAN is Professor of Global History at Oxford University, Director of the Oxford Centre for Byzantine Research and Senior Research Fellow at Worcester College. He specialises in the history of exchange, and in the history of Russia, the Middle East, Central and South Asia, and China. His books include *The Silk Roads: a new history of the world* and *The New Silk Roads: the present and future of the world*.

JESSICA FRAZIER is Lecturer in Theology and Religion at Trinity College, Oxford, and a Fellow of the Oxford Centre for Hindu studies. She is the managing editor of the *Journal of Hindu Studies*. Her publications include *Reality, Religion and Passion: Indian and Western approaches*, *Categorisation in Indian Philosophy: thinking inside the box*, and *Hindu Worldviews: theories of self, ritual and divinity*.

LAWRENCE FREEDMAN is Emeritus Professor of War Studies at King's College London. He was the official historian of the Falklands War and a member of the UK's Inquiry into the Iraq War. A Fellow of the British Academy and appointed a CBE, he was knighted in 2003. His publications include *Strategy: a history*, *Nuclear Deterrence*, and *The Future of War: a history*.

MATTHEW GOODWIN is Professor of Politics at the University of Kent, and Associate Fellow at Chatham House. He is the co-editor of *The New Extremism in 21st Century Britain* and co-author of *National Populism: the revolt against liberal democracy*, and *Brexit: why Britain voted to leave the European Union*. His latest book, *This England: nation, identity and belonging* is due to be published in the autumn of 2021.

ANDREW GRAHAM-DIXON is an art historian, critic and broadcaster. He is the author of numerous books on subjects ranging from the art of the Middle Ages and the Renaissance to the present day, including *A History of British Art*, *Renaissance*, *Michelangelo and the Sistine Chapel*, and *Caravaggio: a life sacred and profane*, which was shortlisted for the UK's most prestigious non-fiction book award, the Samuel Johnson Prize.

JOHAN HAKELIUS is the political editor-in-chief of *Fokus*, Sweden's leading current events weekly. He has written several books on English eccentrics and British social history. He should currently be working on his next book – tentatively on the social scene in Manhattan from the end of the Civil War to Trump – but the garden, a puppy and his first grandchild always seem to get in the way.

VANESSA HARDING is Professor of London History at Birkbeck, University of London. Her research and writing focus on the social history of early modern London, circa 1500–1700, and especially on family and household, environment, health and disease, death and burial. She is the author of *The Dead and the Living in Paris and London, 1500–1670* and is currently working on a book-length study of seventeenth-century London, and developing a project to map London on the eve of the Great Fire.

TOM HOLLAND is an author, broadcaster and historian of antiquity and the early Middle Ages. A Fellow of the Royal Society of Literature, his books include *Rubicon: the triumph and tragedy of the Roman republic*, *In the Shadow of the Sword: the battle for global empire and the end of the ancient world*, *Æthelstan: the making of England*, and *Dominion: the making of the Western mind*.

MARK HONIGSBAUM is a writer specialising in the history and science of infectious disease, and a Senior Lecturer in Journalism at City University of London. A regular contributor to the *Observer* and *The Lancet*, his books include *The Pandemic Century: one hundred years of panic, hysteria and hubris*, *The Fever Trail: in search of the cure for malaria*, and *Living with Enza: the forgotten story of Britain and the Great Flu Pandemic of 1918*.

ALEXANDER LEE is a research fellow at the University of Warwick and a specialist in the cultural and political history of the Renaissance in Italy. He has previously held posts at the universities of Oxford, Luxembourg and Bergamo, and writes a regular column for *History Today*. His publications include *The Ugly Renaissance, Humanism and Empire: the imperial ideal in fourteenth-century Italy*, and *Machiavelli: his life and times*.

TIM MARSHALL is a journalist, broadcaster and author. A former diplomatic and foreign affairs editor for Sky News, he is the founder and editor of news web platform thewhatandthewhy.com. His books include *Prisoners of Geography, Divided: why we're living in an age of walls*, and *Worth Dying For: the power and politics of flags*.

LINCOLN PAINE is a maritime historian, speaker, teacher and author. As well as producing more than 100 articles, reviews, and lectures on maritime history, he has written five books which include the award-winning *The Sea and Civilization: a maritime history of the world, Down East: an illustrated history of maritime Maine*, and *Ships of the World: an historical encyclopedia*.

ISKANDER REHMAN is the Senior Fellow for Strategic Studies at the American Foreign Policy Council, in Washington DC, where he leads a research effort on applied history and grand strategy. He is currently writing a book entitled *The Forgotten Virtue: prudence, grand strategy and the history of statecraft*.

DONALD SASSOON is Emeritus Professor of Comparative European History at Queen Mary, University of London. His publications include *Mona Lisa, One Hundred Years of Socialism, The Culture of the Europeans* and *The Anxious Triumph: a history of global capitalism 1860–1914*. His most recent book is *Morbid Symptoms: an anatomy of a world in crisis*.

DAVID SEEDHOUSE is Professor of Deliberative Practice at Aston University, Birmingham and a widely read author in health philosophy, ethics and decision-making. He is also owner and creator of the Values Exchange, an online tool for reflection and debate on healthcare. He has recently published *Using Personal Judgement in Nursing and Healthcare* with Vanessa Peutherer, and *The Case for Democracy in the Covid-19 Pandemic*.

GRAHAM STEWART is a Senior Research Fellow in 20th Century British History at the University of Buckingham, the political editor of *The Critic*, and is the official historian of *The Times* newspaper. He is the author of six books including *Burying Caesar: Churchill, Chamberlain and the battle for the Tory party*, and *Bang! A History of Britain in the 1980s*.

HEW STRACHAN has been Wardlaw Professor of International Relations at the University of St Andrews since 2015. He is a Life Fellow of Corpus Christi College, Cambridge, and an Emeritus Fellow of All Souls College, Oxford. A Fellow of the British Academy, his publications include *The First World War: to arms*, *The First World War: a new illustrated history* (based on his ten-part series for Channel 4), and *The Direction of War*.

HELEN THOMPSON is Professor of Political Economy at Cambridge University, where she is a Fellow of Clare College and Deputy Head of The School of the Humanities and the Social Sciences. She contributes a fortnightly column to the *New Statesman* and is a regular contributor to the Talking Politics podcast. Her publications include *Oil and the Western Economic Crisis*.

RICHARD WHATMORE is Professor of Modern History at the University of St Andrews and Director of the Institute of Intellectual History. His books include *Republicanism and the French Revolution, Against War and Empire: Geneva, Britain and France in the eighteenth century, What is Intellectual History?* and *Terrorists, Anarchists, and Republicans: the Genevans and the Irish in time of revolution*.

ADRIAN WOOLDRIDGE is the *Economist's* political editor and author of the Bagehot column. His books include *The Great Disruption: how business is coping with turbulent times* and *Masters of Management,* and he is co-author, with John Micklethwait, of *The Wake-Up Call: why the pandemic has exposed the weakness of the West – and how to fix it*.

Image rights©

SOCIETY IN CRISIS
Our Capacity for Adaptation and Reorientation

Published by Bokförlaget Stolpe, Stockholm, Sweden, 2021

© The authors and Bokförlaget Stolpe 2021,
in association with Axel and Margaret Ax:son Johnson Foundation for Public Benefit

The essays were originally published on the website Engelsberg Ideas during 2020.

Edited by
Kurt Almqvist, President, Axel and Margaret Ax:son Johnson Foundation
Mattias Hessérus, project manager, Axel and Margaret Ax:son Johnson Foundation
Iain Martin, journalist and editor, Engelsberg Ideas

Translation of Kurt Almqvist's introduction: Ruth Urbom
Text editor: Andrew Mackenzie
Design: Patric Leo
Layout: Petra Ahston Inkapööl
Cover image: Thomas Cole, *The Course of Empire: Destruction*, 1836.
VCG Wilson/Corbis via Getty Images
Prepress and print coordinator: Italgraf Media AB, Sweden
Print: Printon, Estonia, via Italgraf Media, 2021
First edition, first printing

ISBN: 978-91-89069-93-0

BOKFÖRLAGET STOLPE

AXEL AND MARGARET AX:SON JOHNSON FOUNDATION
FOR PUBLIC BENEFIT